Location Lighting for Television

Dedicated to the memory of my grandson, Adam

Location Lighting for Television

Alan Bermingham

AMSTERDAM • BOSTON • HEIDELBERG • LONDON • NEW YORK • OXFORD
PARIS • SAN DIEGO • SAN FRANCISCO • SINGAPORE • SYDNEY • TOKYO

Focal Press is an imprint of Elsevier

Focal Press
An imprint of Elsevier
Linacre House, Jordan Hill, Oxford OX2 8DP
200 Wheeler Road, Burlington MA 01803

First published 2003

British Library Cataloguing in Publication Data
Bermingham, Alan
    Location lighting for television.
    1. Television – Lighting – Handbooks, manuals, etc. 2. Video
    recording – Lighting – Handbooks, manuals, etc.
    I. Title
    778.5′343

Library of Congress Cataloguing in Publication Data
Bermingham, Alan.
    Location lighting for television / Alan Bermingham.
    p. cm.
    Includes bibliographical references and index.
    ISBN 0 240 51937 X (alk. paper)
    1. Cinematography – Lighting. 2. Television – Lighting. I. Title.

    TR891.B47 2003
    778.59′2–dc21   2003048750

ISBN 0 240 51937 X

For information on all Focal Press publications visit our website at:
www.focalpress.com

Typeset by Integra Software Services Pvt. Ltd, Pondicherry, India
www.integra-india.com
Printed and bound in Great Britain by Biddles Ltd *www.biddles.co.uk*

Contents

Acknowledgements

My thanks to Peter Ward, Chris Watts, Ian Perry, John O'Donnell, John Rossetti and Tony Grant for reading the manuscript and making helpful and constructive suggestions.

My thanks also to ADB UK Theatre & Studio Lighting Division, Airstar (UK) Ltd., ARRI(GB) Ltd, CCT Lighting, Cirro-Lite (Europe) Ltd, DeSisti Lighting (UK) Ltd, ETC Europe Ltd, Lee Filters, Lightfactor Ltd, Manfrotto, Martin, Matthews, Minolta, Optex, Philips Lighting, Power Gems Ltd, Roscolab Ltd, Sony Corporation, Strand Lighting, Videssence, Dedo Weigert, and the Society of TV Lighting Directors for permission to reproduce drawings and to Andy Collier, Martin Christidis, Adrian Ewen, Mike Gorman, Eddie Dias, Brian Fitt, Peter Wing, Nick Villiesid, Gareth Jones and my many former colleagues at the BBC, TV-am, and Television South West for helping to make 'the pennies drop!'

Also special thanks to Peter Hodges for permission to reproduce the photograph from *An Introduction to Video Measurement*, and to Craig Hardy and David Howarth for taking the photographs, and Debbie Lathey for the front cover design.

1
Introduction

Lighting on location is a mixture of technology and technique. It is a skill required by cameramen, and in the world of freelance cameraman where 'you are only as good as your last programme', it is essential that all cameramen have a good grasp of the principles and practice of lighting on location, in order to ensure continuity of work. Many video cameramen operate without the luxury of large budgets supporting ideal resources. Consequently, there is often a need to work with minimum crewing levels, requiring multi-skilling abilities. Hence, this book explores the areas of skill and knowledge needed to cope with this situation.

The objective of any location shoot obviously is to get a good result. However, safety of personnel, equipment and the location should also be a high priority. Invariably most lighting problems, however complex, can be solved by returning to basic principles – the material of this book.

Location lighting is, like most jobs, all about solving problems. An awareness of potential problems is a definite plus when venturing away from the more controlled environment of a television studio. The aim of the book is to introduce some of the problems and solutions and shorten the learning time-frame. Learning the 'hard' way is generally a drawn-out process, requiring many years of practice before 'all the pennies have dropped'.

Video cameraman have to be able to cope with a wide range of lighting problems, often short-handed, requiring a knowledge of many impinging areas of concern. This book is structured to lead the reader through the 'facts of light' and the technology associated with lighting, before looking at lighting technique.

After over thirty years of being involved with lighting I have to confess that 'the pennies still drop' – I hope the readers will find the text useful and informative.

Hunter and Fuqua in their book *Light – Science and Magic* explain the key to success in lighting, namely, understand light and the technology – the magic will follow! How very true. . .

Alan Bermingham

Note: All measurements are quoted in metric unless custom and practice dictates imperial. A basic conversion table is included on page 278. Male gender is used throughout the book to avoid having to use 'he or she', but common gender is understood in all cases.

1.1   Overview

Lighting is an important part of the television production process. Good lighting is essential if the viewer is to believe the reality of the pictures being presented. Bad lighting may distract the viewer or prevent the 'illusion of reality' being created. Lighting for television on location may be for single-camera or multi-camera shooting, by a director of photography (DoP)/lighting cameraman/lighting director to ensure continuity of lighting style.

The overall aim of the director of photography/lighting cameraman/lighting director is to produce pictures, which are artistically and technically 'pleasing', i.e. the pictures look right!

So how can this aim be achieved? Making a television programme is very much a team activity, as part of the production team the first requirement is to **know what is required of lighting for the particular production**.

This illustrates the need for good communication and planning if the lighting person is to understand fully the director's requirements, e.g. the correct interpretation of a drama script, or to be able to make a creative input to the programme 'look'.

A director will expect his lighting person to have well-defined responsibilities, knowledge and skills. These are listed below.

(a) Lighting responsibilities include:

- identifying the lighting needs of a production, including budget restraints
- planning the lighting treatment for a production, within the given budget
- setting the appropriate lighting equipment, safely and within the given time scale
- using the rehearsal to obtain a satisfactory lighting balance
- carrying out remedial lighting adjustments as needed
- reproducing rehearsed conditions for recording.

(b) Interested in lighting career then:

- learn about the job of lighting – know what is required of you
- learn to see what you are looking at – become more observant
- observe nature and how people are lit in different environments
- observe artificially lit environments and how people are lit
- observe creative lighting personnel at work
- sharpen your powers of observation, by taking up watercolour painting in a 'serious' way
- build up a library of information on the hardware of lighting
- learn about the technology of lighting
- learn about lighting techniques by watching others and reading as many different viewpoints as possible to get a 'well-rounded' knowledge
- develop a critical attitude to picture quality
- analyse your own qualities, be aware of any shortcomings you feel you may have and try to improve your performance, e.g. be more flexible, improve your communication skills etc.

(c) Required essential knowledge of:

- production techniques (know what is required!)
- human perception, behaviour of the eye/brain
- lighting techniques
- associated techniques, i.e. camera, sound, chroma key etc.
- lighting hardware, e.g. luminaires, control systems, rigging systems, special effects
- lighting costs
- the basic television system as it applies to lighting
- safety
- standards, i.e. good lighting/bad lighting
- role of responsibilities of other team members especially Gaffer/Best Boy.

(d) Desirable qualities for a DoP, lighting director/lighting cameraman:

- enthusiasm towards programme making
- enthusiasm towards team colleagues – a team person
- willingness to compromise
- planning skills and communication skills
- good imagination and aptitude for lighting
- good powers of observation
- man-management skills
- ability to cope with the unexpected, i.e. last-minute changes
- ability to recognise lighting/vision faults and be able to fix them
- ability to apply lighting techniques effectively within the given time-scale and budget
- ability to work under pressure
- should be decisive, ability to decide quickly what is needed
- good sense of humour.

How can one become a director of photography/lighting cameraman/lighting director?

Lighting is a coveted job in television, providing enormous job satisfaction. Consequently, anyone wishing to progress in lighting must be able to demonstrate flair, interest and knowledge better than the competition. Some recommendations are listed above.

The aim of this book is to introduce the reader to the basic principles and practice of lighting on location for television cameras. Lighting is a mixture of art and craft. One has first to visualise the final result and then realise it by using the appropriate hardware.

The lighting process is dictated by **time, technology and technique**, and the technique used will be influenced by the time and technology (hardware) available. Very few lighting problems have unique solutions; what works one day may not be as effective on another day for a variety of reasons. There is a need to have a flexible approach to lighting problems, constantly looking for new solutions to old problems.

Often some of the best results are obtained by 'breaking the rules'. However, the 'rules' need to be known before they can be broken, deliberately!

The techniques offered in this book should form a good basis on which to build and develop your own particular style of lighting.

1.2   The need for lighting on location

With the excellent sensitivity of modern CCD cameras there is often a misconception about lighting on location, namely 'why do we need extra light when the cameras are so sensitive?' Another comment, very valid of course, is 'you cannot improve on Nature!'.

Natural lighting

Unfortunately, Nature may produce lighting which is unsuitable for direct shooting. It may:

● contain too much contrast between the highlights and the dark tones
● contain shadows which are too dark, resulting in no shadow detail seen on camera
● be contrary to the lighting in previous shots, i.e. lack of continuity of light direction, colour of light or quality of light (direct sun – overcast)
● be unflattering due to the harshness or the direct sunlight and/or the steepness of the sunlight, e.g. mid-day sun at summertime
● be totally overcast, resulting in pictures with little contrast and little separation of planes within the picture
● be insufficient for cameras if supplementary lighting is required, e.g.

    – moonlit scenes
    – scenes lit by street lighting
    – candlelit scenes
    – scenes with no natural lighting.

Working with natural lighting

It is necessary to consider each scenario and decide if supplementary lighting is needed to maintain or create the illusion of reality (not necessarily absolute reality). Depending on the circumstances, it may be necessary simply to **modify** the natural lighting to achieve the criterion of 'the picture looking right'! That is,

● reflect the sunlight or skylight with suitable reflectors
● diffuse the sunlight with diffusion media on frames
● reduce the sunlight/skylight with veils/nets/neutral density material
● block the sunlight/skylight with appropriately sized black flags.

Unfortunately, Nature can be unpredictable, and there is a need to be aware of the wide range of possibilities of lighting condition which can exist. For example, in the United Kingdom there can be over a hundred times the incident lighting level on a bright sunny

Table 1.1 Lighting problems of location shooting

Weather is uncontrollable
Weather is unpredictable
   – except on a short timescale
   – unless global position is favoured with a stable weather pattern of fine weather
Wide range of lighting levels
Wide range of colour temperature
Continuously changing position of the sun
Variation in quality of natural lighting
   – hard light/soft light
   – high contrast/low contrast
Need for suitable mains supply
Need for suitable luminaire suspension
Need for absolute safety with any lighting operations
Motto – **be prepared!**

day compared to that on a dull overcast day. Clouds passing in front of the sun can reduce the lighting level by as much as 3–4 f-stops (a factor of 8–16)!

Continuity of lighting condition is often a major problem with large variations during the day of:

● incident lighting level – illuminance
● colour of the light – colour temperature
● quality of the light – hard/soft light
● scene contrast – shadow density
● vertical and horizontal lighting angle.

There is a need to anticipate these effects and provide some means of coping! It is very important that on-site recce meetings are done at times which have a direct bearing on the shooting time-scale so that potential problems may be identified (see Table 1.1).

Clearly, situations with no natural lighting will require to be appropriately lit. Where natural lighting exists, one should make judgements on what is required to make it 'look right', i.e. assess what Nature has provided (or may provide) before wheeling in an array of lighting equipment. The adage 'keep it simple' applies to lighting as well as to many other areas of television production.

2
Lighting basics

2.1 Psychology of perception

How we see changes in scene brightness should be appreciated when lighting for television, film and theatre, namely the logarithmic nature of the eye/brain.

Logarithmic perception

Most human perception operates in a logarithmic manner, e.g. changes in pitch, changes in loudness and also our perception of changes in brightness. What is meant by a logarithmic law? A logarithmic change, or progression, is when each succeeding term of a series of numbers is a common **multiple** of the previous one, for example:

Number	1	2	4	8	16	32	64	(i.e. ×2)
Logarithm of number	0.0	0.3	0.6	0.9	1.2	1.5	1.8	(i.e. +0.3)

The logarithmic scale of the changes produces a **fixed** increment scale, i.e. **equal** changes.
   Another example is:

Number	1	10	100	1000	(i.e. ×10)
Logarithm of number	0.0	1.0	2.0	3.0	(i.e. +1)

The basic logarithmic law is shown in Figure 2.1.
   Returning to human perception, it is important to be aware that the eye/brain is more sensitive to changes in stimulus (areas of different luminance) in a dimly lit scene than in a brightly lit one. Another way of looking at this is to think in television terms. The setting of the camera black level control is extremely critical, and a small percentage error will result in black crushed pictures or 'thin' pictures, desaturated and with no black level. At the peak white end of the television dynamic range a small percentage variation in signal level will not have such a marked effect.

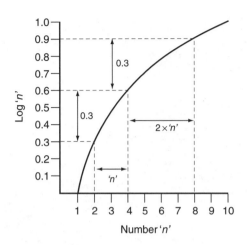

Note: Linear change by a factor of ×2 results in the
same change in logarithmic values

Figure 2.1 Basic logarithmic law

Whenever trying to judge evenness of lighting, it is easier to use a 'pan' glass – a 1% neutral density viewing filter or simply 'screw-up' the eyes so that you are viewing the scene dimly. Any differences in brightness will show more readily.

One of the most common logarithmic scales is, of course, the lens aperture f-number or f-no. or f-stop scale, i.e.:

f1.4 f2.0 f2.8 f4.0 f5.6 f8.0   etc.

The common multiplying factor is 1.4 or $\sqrt{2}$, resulting in the area of the aperture doubling or halving between f-stops, i.e. doubling or halving of exposure.

The significance of the logarithmic exposure control is that as the lens aperture is opened the image brightness will **appear to change equally** between f-stops, i.e. it will appear to give a **linear** change in the perceived effect.

The need for luminance changes to be logarithmic is reflected in the design of grey scale charts. For the eye/brain to see the changes in grey scale step brightness in equal amounts, the reflectances of the different steps need to follow a logarithmic law. For example, starting at 100% and decreasing by $1/\sqrt{2}$ or 0.7 (half of one f-stop) we get a grey scale similar to the one shown in Figure 2.2.

100.0% White
 70.0%
 50.0%
 35.0%
 25.0%
 17.5% Mid-grey (average scene luminance)
 12.5%
  9.0%

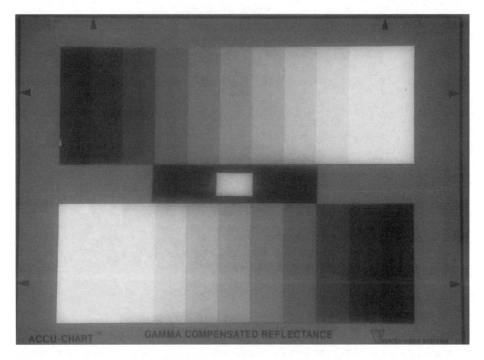

Figure 2.2 Changes in grey scale step brightness

6.0%
4.5%
3.5% Black

Note that the mid-grey step of 17.5% is the average reflectance of nature. This is normally rounded off to 18% and this is the figure used in exposure meter calculations and with camera auto-iris systems

It is essential to be aware of the following:

- colour adaption
- brightness adaption
- revelation of shape, form and texture
- psychological power of colour, light and darkness
- perception of depth.

Colour adaption

The eye and the brain are continually adapting to make 'sense' of what we see. In many cases, we see things as a certain colour because the eye/brain know the colour an object should be. White is a particularly good example. We accept as white many colours which are in fact very different, for example tungsten light, daylight, fluorescent lighting etc. Colour vision theory is based on the concept of the eye having three basic types of receptor, which respond to red, green, and blue light. When the eye is exposed, for example, to a scene lit with a warm light (amber), the eye/brain removes the warm bias to some extent so that if we replace the warm scene with one of no colour bias it will look '**cold**', i.e. a complementary colour to the warm amber. This is called **local colour adaption** where we get a complementary colour image in areas of strong colour.

Lateral colour adaption

This occurs when a strong colour area induces a complementary hue in the background colour. This is most noticeable when strong colours are used on backgrounds to present-ers. The colour perception of the presenter's face will be affected by the use of strong background colour, e.g. a strong magenta background will induce green into the fore-ground – the presenter's face!

Brightness adaption

In a similar way, we judge the brightness of an object relative to the brightness of the object's surrounding (Figure 2.3). For example, when seen against a daytime window the face will look dark. With the same illumination on the face against a night-time window, the face will look very bright. So remember:

- colours appear lighter against a dark background
- colours appear darker against a light background.

Grey squares are identical

Figure 2.3 Simultaneous contrast – brightness adaptation

Revelation of form and texture

The eye/brain interprets the shape of objects by the shadows they cast and the patterns of light and shade introduced by the source of illumination (Figure 2.4). The degree of modelling produced is basically determined by the angle between the keylight and camera, and the type of light source used, i.e. hard or soft.

In a similar way the nature of a surface, its texture, whether rough or smooth, is revealed to a maximum when the angle between the keylight and camera is large and when a hard

(a)

(b)

Figure 2.4 Modelling and texture. (a) Large angle between camera and light source; (b) small angle between camera and light source

light is used. Conversely, to avoid revealing texture (i.e. ageing lines, eyebags) use a soft source with little angle between keylight and camera.

Psychological power of colour etc.

This concerns the effect that light and colour have for us. Basically, we can use light, colour and shade to help to create a particular mood. Generally, lightness is associated with good, darkness and heavy shadows are associated with bad.

- Red/orange colours are associated with warmth.
- Blue colours are associated with cold and night-time.
- Green is a colour when used in pastel shades suggests cool/calm. Strong green hues, in moderation, are used to suggest evil.

The term '**key**' is often used to describe the mood of a picture, i.e.

The **distribution** of tones and tonal **contrast**

High key picture – one which has a predominance of light tones and '**thin**' shadows, an almost two-dimensional lightweight picture (Figure 2.5(a))
Low key picture – one which has a predominance of dark tones and heavy shadows, resulting in a very solid dramatic-looking picture (Figure 2.5(b))
Medium key picture – one which has a '**normal**' distribution of tones (Figure 2.5(c)).

Perception of depth

Generally, the eye is drawn towards the areas containing highlights or the areas which contain the greatest contrast. This, in fact, is one of the principles of theatre lighting where lighting emphasis is used to direct the audience's attention to the appropriate part of the stage. In Nature, saturation of colours decreases with distance so that a distant horizon appears lightest and most desaturated. Immediate foreground areas are most saturated. In addition, blue colours enhance depth, i.e. appear further away, while red colours reduce the illusion of depth.

So, to create depth, consider the lighting of the foreground, midground and background planes. Avoid overlighting the foreground; adding highlights to the background will help to create depth; deeply saturated red cycloramas will lack depth.

For good depth and good separation of planes put light tones against dark tones and dark tones against light tones (Figure 2.5(d)).

2.2   Light units

Light is part of the electromagnetic spectrum of radio waves, which over a limited range of wavelengths is visible. Figure 2.6 illustrates the position of the visible spectrum within the electromagnetic spectrum, and the colours perceived for the different wavelengths of radiation.

Light is usually referred to in terms of its wavelength (not frequency) expressed in nanometres (nm) where one nanometre is 10^{-9} m. Visible light extends from approximately 400 nm (blue) through to approximately 700 nm (red). The human eye/brain response is not uniform, falling to either side of a peak-sensitivity of 555 nm. The average response of the eye/brain is known as the **photopic curve** (Figure 2.7). It is important that any light measurement relates to how we see, i.e. all lighting measuring instruments should have a **photopic response**.

Light units are based on comparison with a visual standard. Figure 2.8 illustrates the different lighting parameters that we need to be able to measure.

Figure 2.5 (a) High key; (b) low key; (c) medium key; (d) light/dark example

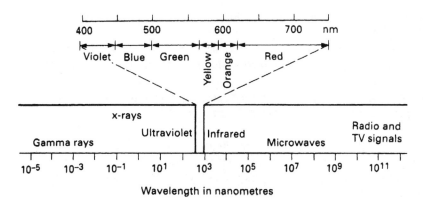

Figure 2.6 The position of the visible spectrum

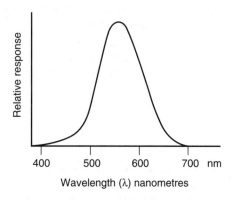

Figure 2.7 The photopic curve – average eye response

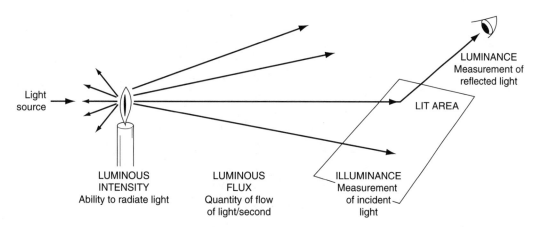

Figure 2.8 Light measurement parameters

- Luminous intensity (I) measures a source's ability to radiate light, in candelas (formerly candle power).
- Luminous flux (F) measures the flow of light/second from a light source in lumens.
- Illuminance (E) measures the incident light on a surface in Lux (lumens/m^2) or foot-candles (lumens/ft^2).
- Luminance (L) is a measure of the reflected light from a surface in Apostilbs (reflected lumens/ft^2) or foot lamberts (reflected lumens/ft^2).

Note: the term 'brightness' refers to how bright we see objects. This is a subjective effect and depends on their surroundings and background. The eye and the brain adapt to the prevailing visual conditions. In everyday usage the term 'brightness' is often used when, strictly speaking, 'luminance' should be used.

Luminous intensity (I)

This is measured by making a **visual** comparison with a known standard. Originally this was a **standard** candle, and the term **candlepower** evolved as a measurement of Luminous Intensity, e.g. 15 000 candlepower for a 1 kW Fresnel spotlight in full flood mode. Candlepower has been replaced by a modern standard of the **candela**, which is a more scientifically specified standard. However, candlepower and candela can be regarded as similar for most practical purposes.

Luminous flux (F)

This is measured in lumens and may be defined as shown in Figure 2.9. It is the luminous flux emitted into a unit solid angle from a point source of one candela. Strictly speaking, the element of time should be introduced, in which case the definition becomes 'luminous flux, per second, emitted into a unit solid angle from a point source of one candela'.

Luminous flux is measured as seen by the human eye, i.e. measurements are **weighted** by the **photopic curve.**

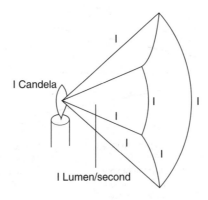

Figure 2.9 Definition of the lumen

Illuminance (E) or illumination

This is a measure of the total luminous flux per metre incident onto a surface and is measured in terms of lumens per unit area, i.e. lumens/m^2 or lumens/ft^2 (see Table 2.1). Figure 2.10 illustrates the basic unit. The **lux** is the preferred term in television (except the USA), but, the **foot-candle** has been around since the origins of film and is still used by many cinematographers. As a result many incident light meters are calibrated in foot-candles. To convert foot-candles to lux, simply multiply the foot-candles by 10.76, i.e.

1 foot-candle = 10.76 lux
(10.76 is the number of square feet in a square metre)

For most practical purposes it is sufficient simply to multiply by 10 when converting foot-candles to lux **or** dividing by 10 when converting lux to foot-candles. (Metric measurement is preferred in many parts of the world. However, with the film industry maintaining a strong presence in the world, the term 'foot-candle' will be found in use in many lighting applications for many years to come!)

Table 2.1 Typical illuminance values

	Illuminance (lux)
Sunlight on a bright sunny day, no clouds	100 000
Daylight on a overcast day	6500 (2000–10 000)
Daylight on an heavily overcast day (winter)	500
Interior lighting levels (day)	400
Interior lighting levels (artificial)	200–300
Office lighting (horizontal at desk height)	300–500
Offices with VDU	300
Drawing office	750
Typical supermarket	600–700
Dawn/dusk	<200
Street lighting	4–20
Moonlight – full moon!	0.1

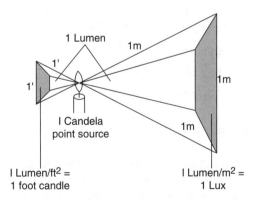

Figure 2.10 Definition of the units of illuminance

Table 2.2   Typical EVs (exposure values)

	EV
Blue sky	13–14
White clouds	15–16
Overcast sky	10–11
Face tone on a sunny day (Caucasian skin)	14–15
Face tone on overcast day	8–9
Typical face tone indoors (day)	7
Face tone indoors (artificial)	6
TV monitor peak white	7.0

Incident light meters usually have a very wide angle of acceptance. To measure incident light a diffusing disk is used over the photocell. However, when using the meter as an exposure meter it is more usual to use a diffusing hemisphere over the photocell. This integrates all of the light hitting the subject and gives a better indication of the total light onto the subject.

Luminance (L)

This is a measure of the amount of light reflected from a surface. When a surface reflects a **total** luminous flux of 1 lumen/m^2 it is said to have a luminance of 1 Apostilb. (Similarly, a surface reflecting a total luminous flux of 1 lumen/ft^2 is said to have a luminance of 1 foot-lambert.) These terms are not in general use because usually the point-by-point luminance of a scene is 'measured' by the television camera.

The amount of light reflected from a surface depends on its reflectance or reflectivity (ρ):

Luminance $= (\rho \times \text{illuminance})$ Apostilbs

e.g. if illumination is 600 lux, what is the luminance of a TV peak white surface $\rho = 0.6$ (60% reflectance)?

Luminance $= \rho \times \text{illuminance} = 0.6 \times 600 = 360$ Apostilbs

Luminance meters are normally a very narrow angle of acceptance, typically 1°, e.g. Pentax spotmeter or Minolta spotmeter. Most spotmeters are calibrated in **exposure values** (EV) where the exposure value increases by a factor of one when the luminance is doubled. Often, exposure values are thought of in terms of f-stops, e.g.

peak white gives a reading of 9 EV
black gives a reading of 4 EV (see Table 2.2)

This represents a contrast of 5 EV or 5 f-stops or a ratio of 2^5:1 $= 32$:1.

2.3   Inverse square law – Nature's law

The inverse square law is a fundamental law of Nature and is met in sound as well as in lighting. Light from a point source will diverge (spread out), consequently the further away from the light source, the greater will be the illuminated area (Figure 2.11) and the illuminance will be reduced.

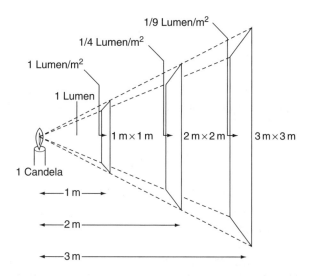

Figure 2.11 The inverse square law

At 1 m from the light source, 1 lumen is spread over 1 m² so illuminance = 1 lux
At 2 m from the light source, 1 lumen is spread over 4 m² so illuminance = 1/4 lux
At 3 m from the light source, 1 lumen is spread over 9 m² so illuminance = 1/9 lux

When the distance is doubled, the illuminance does not become 1/2, it becomes 1/4, i.e. $1/2^2$.

$$\text{Illuminance } (E) \propto \frac{1}{\text{distance}^2} \text{ lux}$$

When the distance is tripled, the illuminance does not become 1/3, it becomes 1/9, i.e. $1/3^2$, If the candlepower had been doubled, the illuminance would have been doubled. Similarly, if we had a light source of 1000 candelas, the illuminance would have been ×1000.
   The general equation for illuminance is therefore

$$\text{Illuminance } (E) = \frac{\text{candlepower}}{\text{distance}^2} \text{ lux}$$

Example 1

What illuminance would you expect at 5 m from a 1.2 kW HMI Fresnel spotlight, which has an effective candlepower of 50 000 candelas?

$$\text{Illuminance } (E) = \frac{\text{candlepower}}{\text{distance}^2} = \frac{50\,000}{5 \times 5} = 2000 \text{ lux}$$

Example 2

What illuminance would you expect from a 650 W Fresnel spotlight of 9000 candelas, at 3 m throw?

$$\text{Illuminance} = \frac{\text{candelas}}{\text{distance}^2} = \frac{9000}{3 \times 3} = 1000 \text{ lux}$$

Example 3

What would be the maximum 'throw' for a 5 kW Fresnel spotlight of 100 000 candelas if the required illuminance is 500 lux?

$$\text{Illuminance} = \frac{\text{candelas}}{(\text{distance})^2} \text{ so } (\text{distance})^2 = \frac{\text{candelas}}{\text{Illuminance}} = \frac{100\,000}{500} = 200$$

$$\therefore \text{ distance} = \sqrt{200} = 14.14 \text{ m} \cong 14 \text{ metres}$$

These examples illustrate how easy it is to estimate the **illuminance** at any given 'throw', provided the **effective candlepower** is known. The effective candlepower is normally quoted for 'centre beam' performance.

The inverse square law, strictly speaking, refers to the behaviour of light emitted from **point** sources, i.e. small area sources. See page 131 for the note on large area sources.

Example 4

Which luminaire would you use to provide 500 lux at 7 m throw?

$$\text{Illuminance} = \frac{\text{candlepower}}{(\text{distance})^2}$$

$$\text{So candlepower} = \text{Illuminance} \times (\text{distance})^2$$

$$= 500 \times 7 \times 7 = 24\,500 \text{ candelas}$$

From manufacturers' data, a 2 kW Fresnel spotlight (36 000 candelas) could be used.

Whilst discussing the inverse square law, it is worth mentioning the often-asked question 'Why doesn't the image of scene get brighter as the viewer/camera moves nearer to it?' Unless tracking the camera very close to an object and requiring the macro adjustment to focus, the subject will remain the same brightness/luminance. The reason is that although the camera will collect more light from the subject, the image of the subject is getting larger as the camera tracks in. So, on the one hand, more light is collected, and on the other, the light is 'spread' over a larger area on the camera image plane. The two 'effects' cancel resulting in a constant camera exposure.

2.4   Cosine law – or you don't get something for nothing!

In the discussion of the inverse square law it was assumed that the incident light was landing 'normal' to the surface, i.e. at right angles (Figure 2.12). This is rarely the case in practice; when a light beam lands obliquely the light is 'spread' over a larger area, conse-quently the illuminance (lumens/m^2) will be decreased.

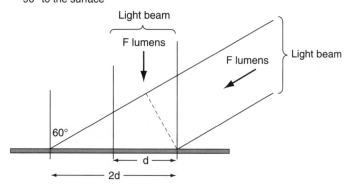

At 60° angle of incidence
the area covered is doubled!

Illuminance is halved
compared to illuminance at
90° to the surface

Figure 2.12 The cosine law

The illuminance is reduced by a factor equal to the cosine of the angle of incidence, i.e.

Illuminance ∝ cosine (angle of incidence)

The complete inverse square law equation becomes:

$$\textbf{Illuminance} = \frac{\textbf{candlepower}}{\textbf{(distance)}^2} \cdot \textbf{cos } \theta \textbf{ lux}$$

This may seem like an unnecessary complication. However, for angles of incidence less than about 25°, the effect of the cosine law is minimal and may be ignored:

Cos 25° = 0.9, i.e. only a 10% reduction!

However, with larger angles of incidence, the reduction in illuminance becomes significant, i.e.

Cos 45° = 0.7, this is a 30% reduction (−1/2 stop)

Cos 60° = 0.5, this is a 50% reduction (−1 stop)

Hence the sub-title to this section: a larger lit area can be achieved by lighting at a large angle of incidence, but a price will be paid in terms of reduced illuminance!

It should also be noted that in Figure 2.13 the illuminance will also suffer a shading from left to right. The angle of incidence and lamp 'throw' is different to each side of the lit area. This illustrates the need for some form of intensity control within the light beam if reasonably uniform illuminance is to be achieved (see use of wires/veils).

Fresnel spotlights are designed to achieve uniform illuminance over a wide beam. The design of the Fresnel lens is such that an element of compensation is introduced at the beam edges to take account of the effect of longer 'throw' and larger angle of incidence (Figure 2.14).

One should be aware of the cosine law when making incident light measurements. To measure the illuminance or illumination on a surface, the incident light meter should be held

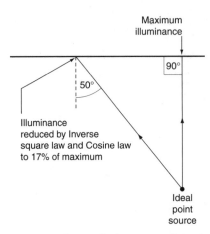

Figure 2.13 Effect of inverse square law and the cosine law

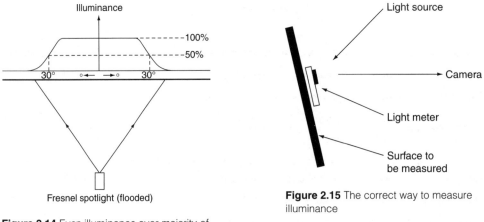

Fresnel spotlight (flooded)

Figure 2.14 Even illuminance over majority of
light beam

Figure 2.15 The correct way to measure
illuminance

parallel to the surface – not pointed at the camera or light source (see later section on the
use of meters) (Figure 2.15).

2.5   Reflection of light – direct/diffuse

An awareness of the nature and behaviour of light is a fundamental need for anyone
engaged in lighting. In lighting we make use of **reflected** light, and it is therefore important
that the different types of light reflection are understood and can be recognised. They are:

● direct or specular reflection
● diffuse reflection
● glare reflection.

Direct or specular reflection

This occurs when light is reflected from smooth **metallic** surfaces, e.g. conductors. Direct reflection follows the laws of physics, namely that:

Angle of incidence = angle of reflection, in the same plane

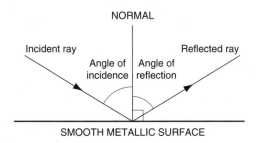

Figure 2.16 Direct or specular reflection

Figure 2.16 illustrates direct reflection, typical of reflection from a plane (flat) mirror. It should be noted that when objectionable direct or specular reflections appear in shot, any movements of a flat surface will cause the reflection to be moved by twice the angle, e.g. when a flat mirror is rotated by 10° the reflected beam is rotated 20° (Figure 2.17) (see later section on lighting shiny metallic objects).

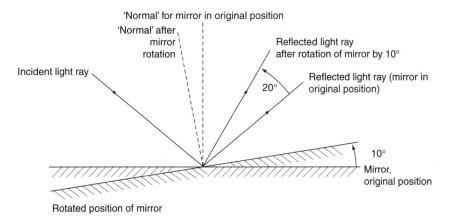

Figure 2.17 Effect of rotating a mirror

Diffuse reflection

This is the type of scattered reflection which occurs when light is reflected from a diffuse surface. Most everyday objects are diffuse reflectors, although some may exhibit a combination of direct and diffuse reflection.

It is important to note that light reflected from a perfectly diffuse surface behaves in a particular way (see Figure 2.18). The light is reflected according to a cosine law. The significance of this cosine law of reflection is that a perfectly diffuse surface will **appear equally bright** when viewed from **any angle**. Figure 2.19 demonstrates this very important result. Why is it important? Consider the consequences if light **reflection** from a diffuse surface was reflected equally in **all** directions. Objects would change their brightness according to the viewing angle!

Metallic reflectors with a textured surface give rise to a **spread** of the reflected light, but all in the general direction expected for a metal reflector. Each point on the textured surface will give rise to such reflections, thus creating a soft source (see section 9.7 Softlights – bounce, page 99).

Metallic surfaces with a 'brushed' texture result in the light being spread at right angles to the direction of the brushing.

Reflected light follows a cosine law of reflection, that is, the amount of light reflected in a particular direction is proportional to the cosine of the angle of reflection. It follows from this statement that the maximum light will be reflected at right angles to the surface (angle of reflection $= 0°$, cosine $0° = 1$) and that minimum light will be reflected parallel to the surface (angle of reflection $= 90°$, cosine $90° = 0$) (Figure 2.18).

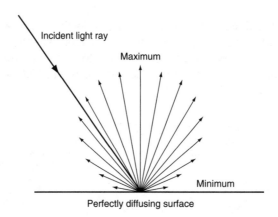

Figure 2.18 Diffuse reflection, illustrating the cosine law of reflection

Figure 2.19 shows that for visual control/exposure, the luminance of the object would be the same, whether viewed from A or B.

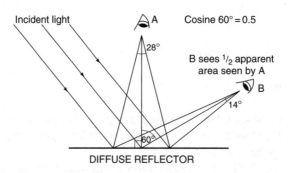

Figure 2.19 The principle of 'equal brightness' for diffuse reflectors

2.6   Reflection of light – glare reflection

This occurs when light is reflected from the surface of an **insulator**, e.g. polished wood, leather, plastics and glass. It has the appearance of a direct reflection of the light source and causes a desaturation of the colour of the surface. Glare reflection is the result of light being polarised when reflected off an insulator. Although we see light as a continuous 'stream', light occurs as **photons**, small 'packets' of energy. These have characteristics of an electromagnetic wave (radio wave), i.e. an associated magnetic field and an electric field at a fixed 90° to each other at 90° to the direction of propagation (Figure 2.20).

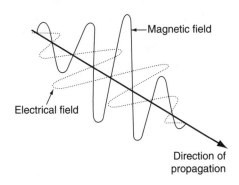

Figure 2.20 The 'photon' of light

Normally, light sources produce photons, which have a totally random polarisation of their electric and magnetic fields. However, when reflected from an insulator type material, all the electric and magnetic fields are aligned – this results in the appearance of a glare reflection. It is sometimes desirable to have some glare reflection. It is important to be able to recognise glare and to be able to control it to an acceptable level.

Polarising filters or polarisers can be used on a camera to control the glare reflections, provided the angle of incidence of the illuminance is large. They are most effective when the angle of incidence is 57°. When angles of incidence are small, the polarisers are not effective (Figure 2.21).

Note that the use of a polariser will introduce approximately 2 *f*-stops, of loss! A polarising filter may be used to:

1   reduce glare reflections from insulator-type objects
2   improve colour saturation (colour purity)
3   reduce reflections from glass windows when shooting through windows, display cabinets etc. Similarly with removing surface reflection when viewing objects in water
4   darken blue sky, thus improving the contrast of the sky to the clouds (blue sky is a form of polarised light).

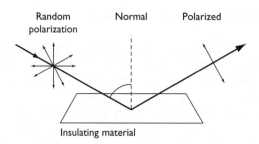

Figure 2.21 Glare reflection (polarisation of electric field only shown)

It is worth noting that (1) also includes control of light reflection when using a **kicker** light (see page 185), and the control of 'glare' from floors which have been strongly backlit. Experimentation with a polarising filter will yield its worth as an essential item of 'kit' on location. However, it will also reveal that is does nothing for direct or specular reflections. If one of the light sources is resulting in excessive direct reflections, they may be controlled by using a second polariser filter (not of optical quality) on the light source.

3
Television camera basics

3.1 The television signal

There is a need to be able to monitor the television signal amplitude to establish the quantity of picture signal. The principles of the television scanning system and television waveform are well documented, but they are reproduced here as a précis for reference.

Television is the process of transmitting moving pictures by 'scanning' a series of still pictures at a rapid enough rate so that the change from one picture to the next picture is seen as continuous movement. The persistence of vision of the eye/brain means that this is possible.

Aspect ratio – Ratio of picture width and picture height. Originally 4:3, gradually moving to 16:9 with 14:9 as an interim measure.

Scanning system – With an odd number of lines/picture, each picture is scanned as two interlaced fields to give an 'effective' picture frequency of 50 Hz or 60 Hz and thereby reduce flicker. (High definition digital cameras use progressive scanning at 24 pictures/frame, i.e. 1080/24P indicates 1080 lines/picture at 24 frames/second, progressively scanned. These pictures are subsequently processed to produce standard PAL/NTSC interlaced pictures for transmission.)

Pictures/second – Number of complete pictures transmitted/second. Rapid enough to see pictures as a continuous image. Originally linked to mains frequency 30 Hz (60 Hz mains frequency) in the USA and 25 Hz (50 Hz mains frequency) in Europe.

Lines/picture – Odd number for interlace (525, 625) with sufficient lines/picture to avoid the line structure being visible.

To display the scanned information from the camera in perfect synchronism at the receiver requires that the television signal needs to have two components, namely:

- picture information indicating the point-by-point scene 'brightness' and colour
- synchronising information to synchronise the displayed picture with the camera scanning process.

These components must be readily detected at the receiver/monitor. It is achieved by separating the two pieces of information:

● by voltage level
● in time.

This is illustrated in Figures 3.1 and 3.2; the basic monochrome television waveform for the European standard 625-line system and the US standard 525-line system. It has a standard amplitude of one volt. The important part of the waveform for lighting interests is, of course, the video or picture information, which is between black level and peak white, 0.7 V.

The major difference between the 525- and 625-line systems, apart from timing differences, is the introduction of a pedestal for black level of 7.5 IRE (a 'lift' of the black level of 7.5% of 0.7 V) to separate the black level and blanking level.

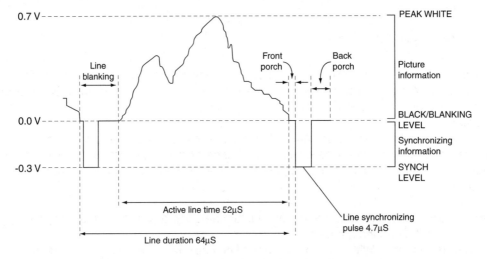

Figure 3.1 Typical television line waveform (625-line system)

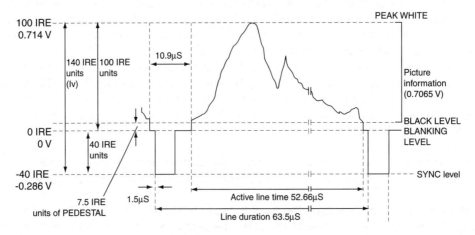

Figure 3.2 A 525-line waveform

Bandwidth requirements

To transmit fine detail in a picture requires a large system bandwidth (expensive). In the 625-line system we are able to transmit about 572 pieces of fine detail on each line, or 286 cycles of information within 52 µs. This equates to 5.5 MHz, the **bandwidth** of the system.

3.2   Tonal reproduction and gamma

The faithful reproduction of the tonal values in a televised scene is obviously one of the main objectives of any television system, i.e. no crushing or stretching of the tonal information – no tonal distortion. It would appear to be a desirable feature to have a completely linear system from camera to display device.

Unfortunately, this is not so, with the display tube having a non-linear characteristic. However, we shall see later that this has a significant advantage! The transfer characteristic of the display tube is shown in Figure 3.3.

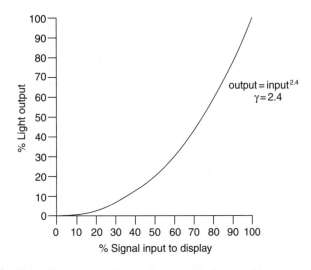

Figure 3.3 Television display tube transfer characteristic

Another way of expressing this characteristic would be to describe the curve as a mathematical law, for example (see Figure 3.4 on page 28):

Figure 3.4(a) illustrates a linear law $y = x$ or $y = x^1$
Figure 3.4(b) illustrates a square root law $y = \sqrt{x} = x^{1/2} = x^{0.5}$
Figure 3.4(c) illustrates a square law $y = x^2$

In each of these examples, the law can be described by the **index** associated with x. Extensive use is made of this concept in television to describe the relationship between the input and output of any part of a system. The term gamma (γ) is used to indicate the transfer characteristic, for example:

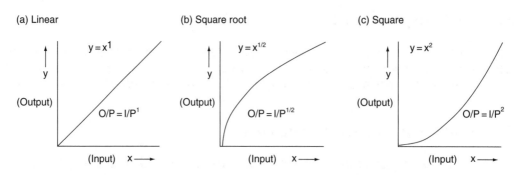

Figure 3.4 Basic mathematical laws

CCD camera chip	$\gamma = 1$
Video distribution amplifier	$\gamma = 1$
TV display tube	$\gamma = 2.4$

Note that the individual gammas are **multiplied** to derive the overall gamma (Figure 3.5).

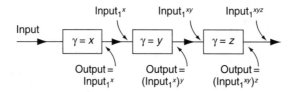

Figure 3.5 Derivation of overall gamma

Therefore in the case of the television system, if the signal derived from a CCD was to be applied directly to the display tube, severe 'black crushing' will occur together with 'stretching' of the highlight information, i.e.

Overall gamma $= 1 \times 2.4 = 2.4$ (Figure 3.6)

Clearly, this indicates the need for some extra processing to pre-distort the video signal prior to it being applied to the display tube. The basic requirement is for black stretch to alter the gamma of the signal. This will introduce extra noise to the **gamma correction**, so it takes place in the camera where the signal/noise ratio is much better than at the receiver.

Figure 3.7 illustrates a number of gamma laws, and typically a gamma corrector with a 0.45 law is used to give an overall gamma of 1.08:

$$1 \quad \times \quad 0.45 \quad \times \quad 2.4 \quad = \quad 1.08$$
$$(\text{CCD}) \quad (\gamma \text{ corr.}) \quad (\text{display}) \quad (\text{overall})$$

The gamma law is selectable in the camera.

The gamma correction curves shown in Figure 3.7 represent the ideal condition of a full gamma corrector. In practice full gamma correction is not applied to the extreme dark tones. An examination of the correction needed for a 1% signal to a 0.5 gamma reveals the reason why:

Output $= (\text{input})^{\gamma}$
for a 1% signal, output $= (0.01)^{0.5} = 0.1$

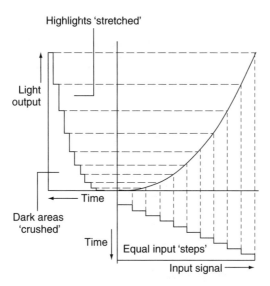

Figure 3.6 Black crush/white stretch of CRT display

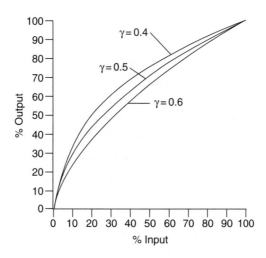

Figure 3.7 Typical camera gamma laws

i.e. the extra gain required is ×10. This will bring with it a lot of extra noise resulting in an unacceptable signal-to-noise ratio.

Usually, a compromise is made where the gamma correction applied to the 0–5% signal area is a fixed gain of ×5. It is worth checking that your camera has the recommended correction. In practice, some manufacturers operate with a reduced fixed gain to preserve the signal-to-noise ratio. The consequences of undercorrection are black crushing of dark tones, for example the detail seen in dark hair. Gamma correction, because it adds noise, is completed where the signal-to-noise ratio is at its best, i.e. at the camera.

Table 3.1 Typical video levels for 9-step grey scale at various gamma levels

Step	% Reflectivity	As % of Step 1 $\gamma = 1$	% TV signal $\gamma = 0.4$	% TV signal $\gamma = 0.5$
1	60	100	100	100
2	49	81	92	90
3	36	60	81	77
4	26	43	70	65
5	16	26	56	50
6	13	21	51	44
7	8	13	41	35
8	5	8	32	26
9	2	3	14	14
Background	16	26	56	50
Black patch	<0.5	<0.5	$\cong 3$	$\cong 3$

Often, a nine-step step-wedge chart is used to check the transfer characteristic of cameras, i.e. Table 3.1 (Figure 3.8). The basic test is to observe the difference between step 9 (2% reflectance) and the black patch (0.5% reflectance), i.e. expect about a 10% difference.

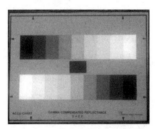

Figure 3.8 Nine-step grey scale with 60% peak white

If a 100% video signal is achieved with a surface reflecting 100% of the incident light the resulting video signal for European skin tones would look underexposed. A scene peak white reflectance of 60% is usually used to produce a 100% video signal (peak white). Typical European facetones are approximately half the reflectance of a peak white surface, resulting in a television signal of about 50% (before gamma correction). After gamma correction this becomes a 70–75% television signal, i.e. about 0.5 V (Figure 3.9). (Hence some ENG cameras set zebra patterns to onset at a 75% signal.)

Note: The need for gamma correction caused by the high gamma of the display tube is not all bad news. The 'crushing' of the signal at the display tube means that the 'noise' received at the receiver is also crushed, i.e. made less visible. This is clearly a bonus!

LCD and plasma screens have an inherent gamma of one, so they have to be fitted with a 2.4 gamma law to ensure correct display of the television signal.

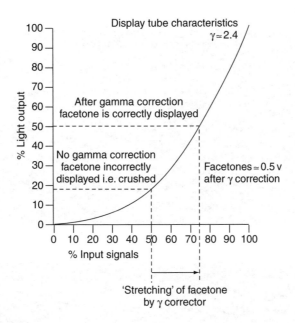

Figure 3.9 Typical facetone video levels after gamma correction

3.3   Tonal reproduction, dynamic range and knee

The range of tonal values over which full gamma correction is possible is sometimes referred to as the acceptable contrast ratio (ACR). This is typically about 32:1, which can be interpreted as a dynamic range of 5 exposure values (5 EV) or 5 f-stops.

Using the grey scale in Figure 3.8 this dynamic range can be easily confirmed by first lighting the grey scale so that it is correctly exposed at an aperture of f2.8. Then if the camera is stopped down by five stops the video signal is almost extinguished confirming the dynamic range as approximately 5 f-stops (Figure 3.10). This illustrates the problem which we have in the real world where the contrast ratio or dynamic range of a naturally lit scene may well often be in excess of the available 5-stop or 32:1 contrast handling of the camera (Figure 3.11). The average contrast out of doors is typically 150:1 (over 7 f-stops) can under the right circumstances be as high as 1000:1.

There are several ways in which the problem can be solved:

- add additional fill-light to shadow areas to reduce the contrast
- add light to a subject against a bright background, i.e. raise the exposure on the subject compared to the bright background
- reduce the luminance of the background by inserting a neutral density filter between the subject and the background
- introduce some form of black stretch to reveal more detail in the darker parts of the picture (provided additional noise is not a problem) or change the gamma in the darker parts of the picture (digital processing)
- use some form of 'knee' in the camera characteristic to extend the dynamic range.

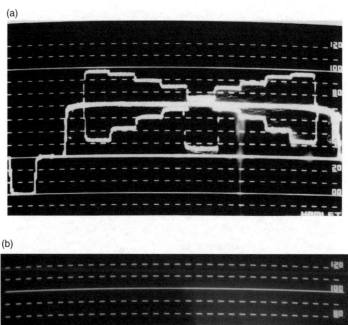

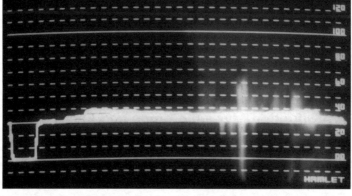

Figure 3.10 Confirming camera dynamic range. (a) Camera at $f2.8$; (b) camera at $f16.0$

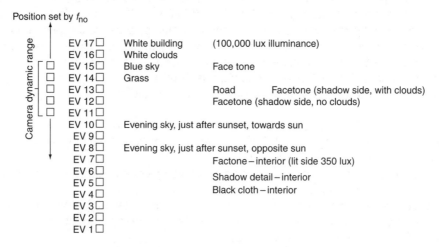

Figure 3.11 The wide dynamic range in the real world

CCDs (charge-coupled devices) have the advantage of a very large dynamic range of approximately 600% of the normal exposure (Figure 3.12) before the CCDs reach a 'saturation' point, the television picture signal must of course be limited to 0.7 V – the standard.

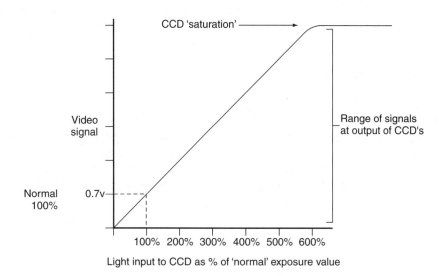

Figure 3.12 CCD dynamic range

However, by introducing signal **compression** above a pre-set onset value, the **knee**, it is possible to extend the signal handling beyond 100% of normal exposure.

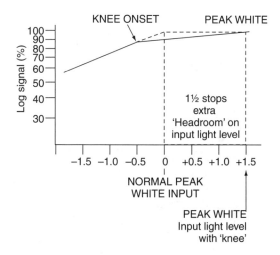

Figure 3.13 Basic 'knee' facility

This is illustrated in Figure 3.13. It should be noted, when using a 'knee':

● The tonal gradation above the knee will be 'crushed', i.e. the gamma will be reduced. For example, tonal values for sky and clouds become resolved but the contrast between the 'above-knee signals' will be reduced.
● The knee should be set to operate above normal facetone signal values. Compression of skin tones is generally not desirable.

3.4 Camera sensors – CCD basics

Most television cameras use Charge Coupled Devices(CCDs). The CCD is a solid-state device using special integrated circuitry technology, hence it is often referred to as a **chip** camera. The complete CCD sensor or chip has at least 450 000 picture elements or **pixels**, each pixel being basically an isolated (insulated) photodiode. The action of the light on each pixel is to cause electrons to be released which are held by the action of a positive voltage. Figure 3.14 illustrates how this charge may be moved, i.e. how scanning may be achieved.

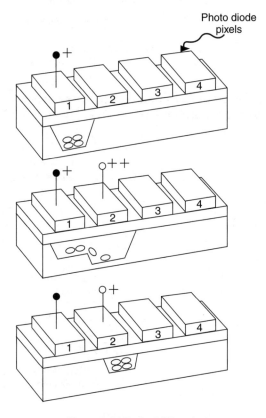

Figure 3.14 Basic CCD action

The charge held under electrode 1 can be moved to electrode 2 by changing the potential on the electrodes as shown. The electrons (negative charges) follow the most positive attraction. A repeat of this process would move the charges to electrode 3, hence charge-coupled device. A system of transfer clock pulses is used to move the charges in CCDs to achieve scanning.

There are three types of CCD device:

● frame transfer (FT).
● interline transfer (IT).
● frame interline transfer (FIT).

Frame transfer (FT)

Frame transfer was the first of the CCDs to be developed and it consists of two identical areas, an imaging area and a storage area (Figure 3.15). The imaging area is the image plane for the focused optical image, the storage area is masked from any light. The electrical charge image is built up during one field period, and during field blanking this charge is moved rapidly into the storage area. A mechanical shutter is used during field blanking to avoid contamination of the electrical charges during their transfer to the storage area. The storage area is 'emptied' line by line into a read-out register where, during line-time, one line of pixel information is 'clocked' through the register to produce the video signal.

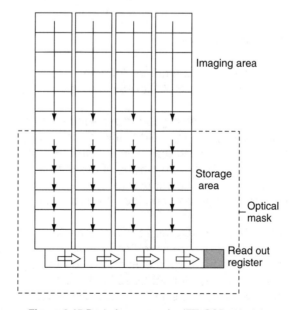

Figure 3.15 Basic frame transfer (FT) CCD principle

Interline transfer (IT)

Interline transfer CCDs were developed to avoid the need for a mechanical shutter (Figure 3.16). The storage cell is placed adjacent to the pick-up pixel; during field blanking the charge generated by the pixel is shifted sideways into the storage cell.

The read-out process is similar to the frame transfer device, with the storage elements being 'clocked' through the vertical shift register at field rate into the horizontal shift register, then the charges read out at line rate. Earlier forms of IT devices suffered from severe **vertical smear**, which produced a vertical line running through a highlight. This was caused by excessive highlights penetrating deeply into the semiconductor material, leaking directly into the vertical shift register. Later IT devices have improved the technology to make this a much less objectionable effect.

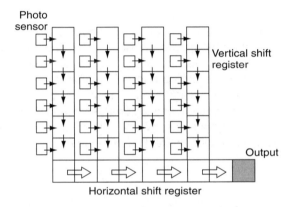

Figure 3.16 Basic interline transfer (IT) CCD principle

Frame interline transfer (FIT)

Frame interline transfer CCDs are a further development of the interline transfer device to overcome the problem of vertical smear. As its name suggests, it is a combination of both types (Figure 3.17).

The FIT sensor has a short-term storage element adjacent to each pixel (as IT) and a duplicated storage area (as FT). During field blanking the charges are moved from the pixels into the adjacent short-term storage element and then moved at 60 times field frequency into the storage area. This rapid moving of the charge away from the vulnerable imaging area overcomes the vertical smear problem.

Development in CCD technology has seen the introduction of:

- the hole accumulated Diode (HAD) sensor which enabled up to 750 pixels/line, with increased sensitivity and a reduction in vertical smear;
- the hyper HAD sensor, which included a microlens on each pixel to collect the light more efficiently (this gave a one stop increase in sensitivity over the HAD sensor);
- the power HAD sensor with improved signal-to-noise ratio which has resulted in at least half an f-stop gain in sensitivity; in some cases a full f-stop of extra sensitivity has been realized.

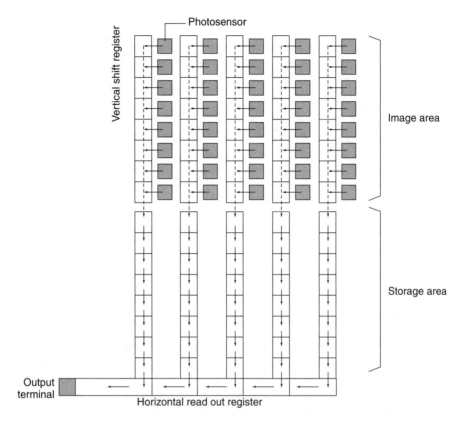

Figure 3.17 Frame interline transfer (FIT) CCD

3.5   Features of CCD processing

CCD output integration

The two interlaced fields may be obtained in one of two ways:

1   **Field integration** in which the signals from adjacent lines are averaged, i.e.
    Field 1 – (line 1 and line 2), (line 3 and line 4) etc.
    Field 2 – (line 2 and line 3), (line 4 and line 5) etc.
    This gives less motion blur than frame integration, but the vertical resolution is reduced.
    The effective exposure is 1/50th of a second
2   **Frame integration** reads out once every frame or picture period, 1/25th of a second.
    This results in more motion blur due to the larger integration time but should give better vertical resolution on static subjects (Figure 3.18).

Normally cameras are operated in the field integration mode, i.e. an exposure time of 1/50th of a second.

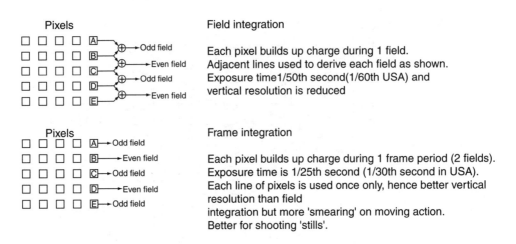

Figure 3.18 Field and frame integration

Electronic shutters

The integration time of CCDs can be shortened electronically by draining unwanted charges on each pixel during the 1/50th second exposure time, i.e. 1/60th, 1/125th, 1/250th, 1/500th, 1/1000th, 1/2000th second. This is particularly useful for 'still' shots of fast-moving objects (less blur), or simply reducing the camera sensitivity. Note, however, that live fast-moving action and short exposure times result in 'jerky' action – not to be recommended.

Enhanced vertical definition system

EVS refers to the technique of blanking out one field with the electronic shutter when in the field integration mode. This results in improved vertical resolution, no averaging of lines, and a reduction in sensitivity of one stop.

Resolution

Resolution of sensors, the ability to resolve fine detail, has increased as the technology has improved, e.g.

Sony BVP 50 – approx. 500 pixels/line
Sony BVP 70 – approx. 700 pixels/line
Sony DVW 790 WSP – approx. 1000 pixels/line (widescreen camera).
Sony HDW-750 – 1920 pixels/line (High Definition Camera). This is known as 2k resolution.

Switchable 4:3 and 16:9

Two techniques have been adapted by manufacturers.

1 Using a common height of CCD and switching the 'scanned' width of CCD (Figure 3.19(a)).
2 Using a common width of CCD and switching the scanned height of the CCD (Figure 3.19(b)) (referred to as Dynamic Pixel Management). These sensors use chips which have four times the number of pixels in the vertical direction. Hence the use of $\frac{3}{4}$ of the pixels for 16:9 operation, resulting in reduced height of the 'scanned' area. All of the pixels are used for 4:3 – each picture 'cell' uses 4 pixels in the vertical direction resulting in an increase in 'scanned' picture height.

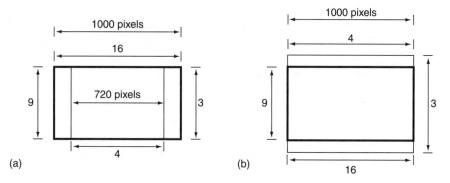

Figure 3.19 Switchable CCDs. (a) Conventional CCD, change of angle of view when switched to 4:3, horizontal angle reduced; (b) dynamic pixel management (DPM) uses three quarters of pixels for 16:9 to maintain *same* angle of view as for 4:3 and horizontal resolution

4
Television optics

An understanding of basic optics in relation to television is important in coping effectively with the needs of lighting on location. The basic television optical parameters are:

Focal length   *f*-**no.**   **angle of view**   **depth of field**

4.1 Focal length

The focal length of a lens indicates the 'bending' power of a lens, and it is usually quoted in mm. Figure 4.1 illustrates the bending of light rays to a focal point, due to the refraction of light through glass. A short focal length lens has a greater curvature in its surfaces and bends the light rays significantly. This results in a wide angle of view of the scene (Figure 4.1). A long focal length lens produces less bending of the light rays (shallower curvature of the lens surface) and results in a narrower angle of view (Figure 4.1(b)).

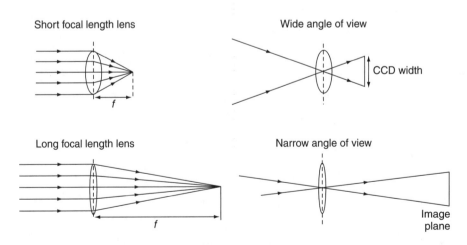

Figure 4.1 (a) Focal length; (b) angle of view/focal length

4.2 Angle of view (horizontal)

The angle of view for a given lens depends on its **focal length** and the **width** of the active sensor area (Figure 4.2). For planning purposes it is usually more meaningful to refer to lenses by their angle of view rather than their focal length:

$$\text{Angle of view} = 2\tan^{-1}\frac{\text{width of sensor }(w)}{\text{focal length of lens }(f)}$$

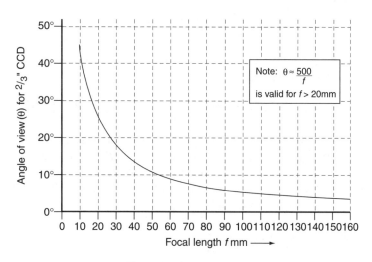

Note: $\theta \approx \dfrac{500}{f}$ is valid for $f > 20\text{mm}$

Figure 4.2 Angle of view/f

4.3 Lens aperture (f-number or f-stop)

Lenses are fitted with some form of exposure control usually a variable 'iris' mechanism to give a continuously variable lens aperture. Figure 4.3 shows that there are two factors which affect the luminance of the focused image:

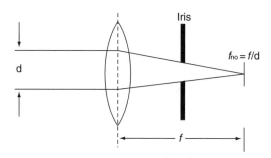

Figure 4.3 Illustrating the f-number

- focal length of the lens – the shorter the lens focal length, the more concentrated will be the image, i.e. small, but 'bright'
- effective diameter of the lens – the larger the effective lens diameter, the greater will be the amount of light passed by the lens in a given time.

Clearly, in the above situation, with the same lens diameter, the shorter focal lens will always produce a brighter image. To ensure that all lenses can be operated to give a constant exposure, irrespective of focal length, the lens aperture is calibrated in f-numbers or f-stops.

$$f_{no} = \frac{\text{Focal length of lens } (f)}{\text{Effective diameter of lens aperture } (d)}$$

All lenses at the same f-number will give the same exposure provided the transmission factors of the lenses are the same.

Typical f-number series: $f1.4$ 2.0   2.8   4.0   5.6   8.0   11.0   16.0

Note that this is a logarithmic series with a common multiplying factor of $\times 1.4$ when opening up, i.e. the effective lens diameter changes by a factor of $\times 1.4$ between f-numbers. This results in a change in the **area** of the lens aperture by a factor of $(1.4 \times 1.4) = 2$, giving a doubling of exposure. When stopping down the change is $1/1.4$ or 0.7 which when squared gives $1/2$, a halving of exposure:

$$\frac{1}{\textbf{Exposure}} \propto (\textbf{\textit{f}}_{no})^2 \text{ or } \textbf{Exposure} \propto \frac{1}{\textbf{\textit{f}}_{no}^2}$$

A change in exposure of 2 f-stops results in a 2^2 change $= \times 4$ (or 1/4) when stopping down. A change in exposure of 5 f-stops results in a 2^5 change $= \times 32$ (or 1/32) when stopping down.

   By having a logarithmic change in the lens aperture, the effect perceived by the eye/brain will be **linear** when the lens aperture is opened up/stopped down!

4.4   Depth of field

Depth of field refers to the range of object distances which appear to be within **acceptable** focus. It is a parameter which, with a small depth of field, can have a major impact on picture quality by:

- separating an artiste from the background
- concentrating attention to the subject in focus
- ensuring that all background objects in a close-up are well out of focus thus avoiding distractions in the picture
- allowing split-focus two-shots for dramatic effect

Equally, there are times when, for technical reasons, a large depth of field is required, for example for chroma key foreground shots.

Defining depth of field

When a lens is positioned to produce a sharply focused image of a subject there will be a range of object distances in front and behind the subject, which appear to be in **acceptable focus**. The distance between the two extremes within acceptable focus is known as the depth of field. Figure 4.4 illustrates this important parameter.

The depth of field depends on a number of factors:

Depth of field $\propto$ format size of sensor (relates to the height of one TV line)

$$\propto f\text{-number}$$
$$\propto (\text{angle of view})^2 \text{ or } \frac{1}{\text{focal length}^2}$$
$$\propto (\text{object distance})^2$$

When focused on object O, O_1 and O_2 are also within acceptable focus

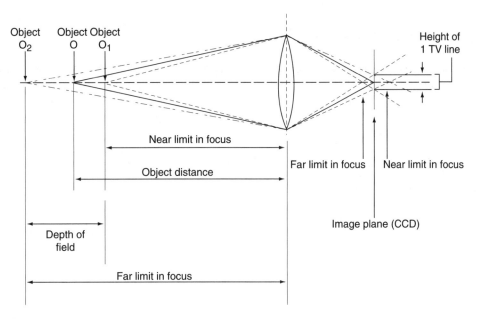

Figure 4.4 Depth of field. Image of O_1 and O_2 at the CCD (image plane) will appear within acceptable focus if the 'disc of light rays' is less than the height of one TV line. (This disc of light rays is sometimes called 'a circle of confusion'.)

Operating lens aperture

The depth of field and exposure will vary as the lens aperture is altered. The usual practice is to work with a particular lens aperture (or within a small range of lens apertures) which satisfies the depth of field requirements. This dictates the camera sensitivity and hence the illuminance requirements.

Table 4.1 Nominal lens aperture and camera formats

Camera format	Image size	Nominal f_{no}
30 mm ($1\frac{1}{4}''$)	17.1 mm × 12.8 mm	f4.0
25 mm ($1''$)	12.8 mm × 9.6 mm	f2.8
18 mm ($\frac{2}{3}''$)	8.8 mm × 6.6 mm	f2.0
12.5 mm ($\frac{1}{2}''$)	6.4 mm × 4.8 mm	f1.4

The 'nominal' lens aperture for different sensor formats is given in Table 4.1, where the nominal f-number is the lens aperture which gives an acceptable depth of field for a given angle of view and subject distance, i.e. the depth of field is the same for an 18 mm sensor (2/3 inch) at f2.0 as a 12.5 mm sensor (1/2 inch) at f1.4.

There is often the need with the current sensitivity of television cameras to reduce the sensitivity so that the lenses may be opened up to reduce the depth of field. This can be achieved by reducing camera gain and/or using neutral density filters in the camera filter wheel, or using the camera shutters to reduce exposure time.

High definition cameras

At the time of writing high definition television cameras use the 2/3-inch format. Consequently, with the extra lines/picture height the depth of field is reduced to about half that of normal television cameras.

5
Colour television

5.1 Principles

Colour television is based on the principle of **additive** colour mixing in which three suitable primaries (red, green and blue) can be mixed together to produce (synthesise) white and a wide range of colours. The colour seen is dependent on the relative amounts of red, green and blue light (Figure 5.1).

Mixtures between two of the primary colours can be plotted as points on the line joining the two primaries, e.g. a mixture of red and green produces yellow. When the three primary colours are mixed together the resultant colour 'mix' can be plotted inside the triangle. In colorimetry (the measurement of colour) it is a useful concept to consider white being made up of equal amounts of red, green and blue (see later notes), hence white plots at the centre of the triangle.

Hue is the term given to the **dominant** wavelength of any object and literally means the colour we see. **Saturation** is a measure of the **purity** of the colour, and is an indication of how diluted the hue is with the other wavelengths. The following important results should be noted:

Red and green and blue	≡ white	
Red and green	≡ Yellow	⎫
Green and blue	≡ Cyan	⎬ Secondary or complementary colours
Blue and red	≡ Magenta	⎭

i.e. primary colour plus its complementary colour produces white.

Red and cyan	≡ white
Green and magenta	≡ white
Blue and yellow	≡ white

When additive colour mixing, a colour may be desaturated by adding 'white' light or a suitable amount of the complementary colour. In colour television the display tube in the

(a) Colour triangle

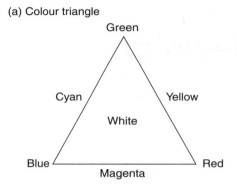

(b) Illustrating hue and saturation

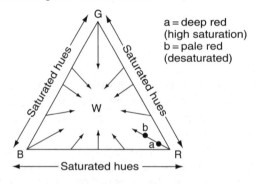

Figure 5.1 Additive colour mixing

colour monitor or receiver generates three separate red, green and blue pictures, and the viewer sees the appropriate 'mixture' colour (e.g. shadow mask tube – Figure 5.2 on page 47).

Having established how colours may be synthesised with suitable mixtures of red/green/blue light we need to turn our attention to the analysis of the scene to be televised to see how the appropriate red/green/blue signals may be derived. The inherent colour of an object is fundamental to the pigmentation of the surface of the object. For example, an object painted blue will have pigments which **absorb** all wavelengths except the blue ones. Note that this will be a **band** of wavelengths, not a single wavelength. The process of light absorption gives rise to subtractive colour mixing, which applies to paint pigments, and colour filters used in combination.

Note the reversal of colour roles, i.e. primaries are cyan, magenta and yellow and complementaries are red, green and blue. All three absorbent pigments present results in black. Remember when using water colours how all the colours when mixed gave black, or the brush cleaning water eventually became black! If three different red surfaces are examined, say, bright red, dull red and pale red, they can be illustrated as reflectance against wavelength to give the graphs shown in Figure 5.3 (page 47). Note that if the surface is white or a neutral grey there will be no colour present, i.e. no hue, and therefore no saturation measurement (Figure 5.4 on page 47).

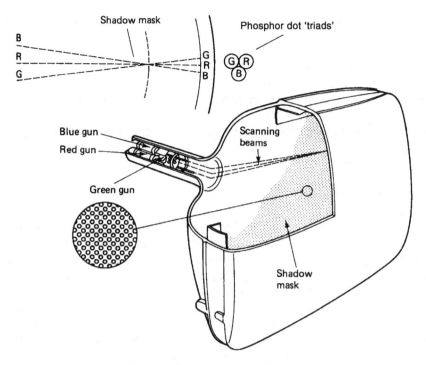

Figure 5.2 Shadow mask tube principle

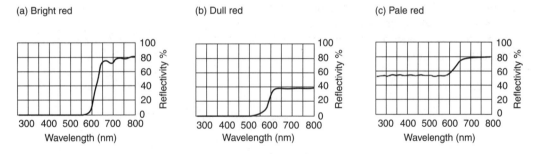

(a) Bright red

(b) Dull red

(c) Pale red

Figure 5.3 Reflectivity of three different red surfaces

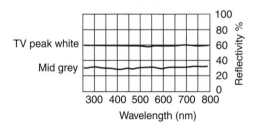

TV peak white

Mid grey

Figure 5.4 Reflectivity of neutral surfaces

If we are going to reproduce three colours we need to know three things about the 'colour':

- hue – the dominant wavelength, the colour perceived
- saturation – the purity of the colour
- luminance value – the total amount of light reflected from the colour.

(*Note*: 'light' here means visible light measured with a meter which has a photopic response (eye response) (p. 11).

5.2 Camera overview

The basic camera system is shown in Figure 5.5. The optical image of the scene to be televised is focused by the zoom lens onto the appropriate light sensor (CCD) via a light-splitting block which splits the light into a red image, a green image and a blue image. Dichroic layers are used in the light-splitting prism, which reflect a band of wavelengths (red or blue). Figure 5.6 illustrates the principle.

The action of the light sensor is to turn the optical image into an electrical charge pattern corresponding to the point-by-point scene luminance. The charge image is scanned to produce the appropriate red, green and blue video signals; these are processed in the camera to produce standard Red, Green and Blue signals of 0–0.7 V. A fundamental requirement in colour television is that the Red, Green and Blue signals are equal when focused on a white or neutral grey object (i.e. no hue and no saturation). This relationship is maintained throughout the television system, and only at the display tube are the proportions of Red, Green and Blue corrected for display (30% Red; 59% Green and 11% Blue) for a white or neutral area.

The signal processing provides the essential signal gain (amplification) requirements and includes the following:

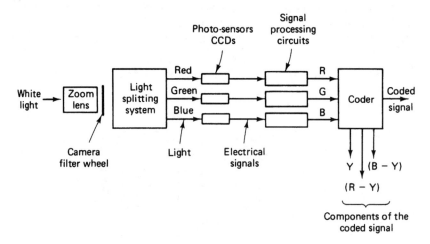

Figure 5.5 Basic camera system

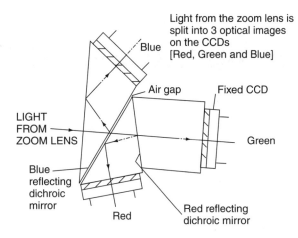

Figure 5.6 Light-splitting block

- The picture **black level** adjustment is used to establish the Black level in a picture by 'fixing' (clamping) the level of the picture signal with reference to the TV signal black level of 0.0 V.
- **Black balance** – setting of the individual 'black' levels of the Red, Green and Blue levels to be identical and unaffected by picture contrast.
- **Flare** correctors use the average picture signal to provide a correction signal related to 'flare' produced in the zoom lens. This is used to 'sit down' the black level.
- **Peak white clippers** ensure that the RGB signals are limited to a few per cent above 100%.
- **Linear matrix** improves the colour renditioning of the camera by correcting for deficiencies in the colour analysis system.
- **Detail** enhancement provides special high-frequency correction to improve the rendition of fine detail. Detail should be used with care, as overcorrection will result in 'edgy' looking pictures. Noise is increased with detail enhancement.
- **Gamma correction**, which pre-distorts the RGB signals to ensure that the signals are displayed correctly. This includes an option for a knee and selection of the required gamma. Cameras also have a black stretch and, more recently, an ability to adjust the gamma only in the darker parts of the picture.
- **Digital processing** involves the sampling of the analogue signals at a very fast rate, and converting the sample to a digital number for transmission as a series of digital data. Digital processing has the advantages of:

  - Stability of performance
  - High picture quality
  - Easy matching between cameras
  - Easy switching between format 4:3 and 16:9.

6
Colour temperature/ND filters

6.1   Colour temperature – defining white

Defining what we mean by 'white' is a major concern in colour television. The process of calibrating the colour camera 'white' point is known as **white balance**, in which the camera is exposed to a line-up chart or white card suitably lit with 'white' light. The camera's auto-white balance facility equalises the RGB signals (R and B matched to G) so that the line-up chart or white card looks neutral or white.

Our perception process accepts many sources of light as white, e.g. daylight, tungsten light, fluorescent light, metal halide discharge lights, xenon lights etc. So how can we define what is meant by white? One convenient way is to use the concept of colour temperature by comparing the colour of light from a light source with the colour of light from a full radiator (black body radiator, furnace or poker) which radiates light of differing colours according to its temperature. Taking a poker (an iron rod) as an everyday example, when it is cold it will look black (reflecting very little light). As the poker is heated, it will begin to **emit** light, first glowing red, then orange followed by yellow, white and ultimately blue as its temperature rises. The temperature at which the **colour** of the light source and the **colour** of the poker match is known as its colour temperature.

Colour temperature is measured in **Kelvin** after Lord Kelvin the physicist. The Kelvin scale of temperature is based on the absolute temperature scale which has 0 Kelvin at $-273\,°C$ (this avoids complications of minus values).

Tungsten and daylight

The most common colour temperatures in television work relate to tungsten lit scenes and daylight lit scenes, i.e.

Tungsten halogen	3200 K	(tungsten film)
Average summer sunlight	5500 K	(daylight film)

These are the 'white points' for colour film, and the film is 'balanced' to operate with these particular colour temperatures. The colour camera has the advantage that it has a moveable 'white point' and may be white balanced to a wide range of colour temperatures. Cameras also have a pre-set white balance to 3200 K or 5600 K which is factory set (see later section on the camera filter wheel), newer cameras have a pre-set white balance of 3200 K, 4300 K and 6300 K.

Tolerances

When using more than one light source it is important that the sources **match** each other in their colour rendition properties. **Tungsten light** sources will only have a colour temperature of 3200 K when

- the lamp is relatively new
- the mains voltage is correct.

Any reduction of mains voltage either by dimming or simply due to the voltage drop on cables will reduce the colour temperature (light becomes yellow–orange–red as it is dimmed) and also the light output. Typically, tungsten sources should be matched in colour temperature to within ±150 K. (See Figure 8.2 on p. 76.)

Sunlight

Note how sunlight has been modified on entering the Earth's atmosphere (Figure 6.2) – energy distribution is not identical to Figure 6.1. This is because the shorter wavelengths (blue) of sunlight are scattered by tiny particles of dust in the Earth's atmosphere. The scattered light (blue) creates the illusion of a 'sky', with some of the light scattered back to space. Figure 6.3 illustrates this.

'Sunlight' is therefore a combination of skylight and direct sunlight. Strictly speaking, the measurement of daylight/sunlight are correlated colour temperatures.

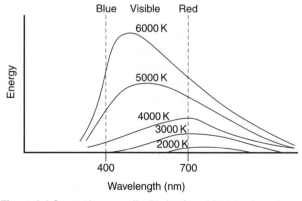

Figure 6.1 Spectral energy distribution for a black-body radiator

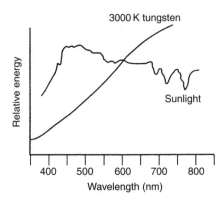

Figure 6.2 Relative spectral energy distribution for tungsten and sunlight

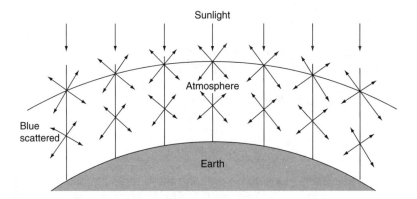

Figure 6.3 Scattering of blue wavelengths to give blue 'sky'

Daylight

This varies enormously in colour during the day. Average summer sunlight at 5500 K needs to be matched to ±400 K when additional light sources are used. This tolerance appears to be greater than that for tungsten, but the perceived colour shift in tungsten ±150 K and daylight ± 400 K will be the same! The change in colour for each 1 Kelvin shift is less as the colour temperature of the light source is increased.

If light sources are not within the colour temperature tolerance of the camera's 'white balance' then the sources have to be corrected with appropriate filters.

An important psychological/physiological difference should be noted. We associate red/orange with warmth and blue colours with cold, **but** with colour temperatures, as the source becomes physically hotter, the colour temperature increases and it becomes blue!

6.2   Colour temperature correction

For many location shoots there is a need to cope with the problem of mixed lighting, e.g. daylight and tungsten sources. Typically this would be when lighting indoors during daylight hours. There is a need to correct the light sources to a common colour temperature, by using appropriate filters:

- to correct the tungsten sources to daylight (5500 K)
- to correct the daylight to tungsten (3200 K)
- to correct both sources to an intermediate value, say 4300 K.

There are two basic colour correction filters, colour temperature blue (CTB) and colour temperature orange (CTO). The colour temperature blue (CTB) filters transmit more blue wavelengths than orange/red wavelengths, and the increase in the proportion of blue light and decrease in red light results in an increase in colour temperature (Figure 6.4).

Often it is necessary to make intermediate or minor adjustments to colour temperature and a range of CTB filters is therefore available for this purpose as shown in Table 6.1.

Note the transmission of a full colour temperature blue, often referred to as a 'full blue', is only about 33%! This represents a significant loss of light. For example, a 2 kW tungsten lamp effectively becomes a 660 W lamp. Often a compromise is made on correction and light loss by using a $\frac{1}{2}$CTB, or the recently developed $\frac{3}{4}$CTB.

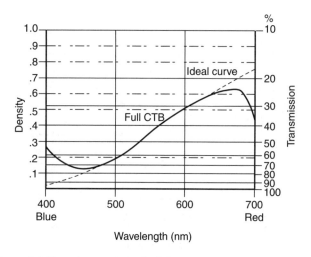

Figure 6.4 Filter characteristics for full colour temperature blue (CTB)

Table 6.1 Colour temperature blue (CTB) filters – basic conversion

Filter	Conversion (K)	Transmission (%)
Full CTB	3200–5700	34
$\frac{3}{4}$CTB	3200–5000	45
$\frac{1}{2}$CTB	3200–4300	55
$\frac{1}{4}$CTB	3200–3600	69
$\frac{1}{8}$CTB	3200–3400	81

Note: See later tables for complete data on conversion.

The CTO filters behave in the opposite way to the CTB filters. They transmit more orange/red wavelengths than blue, consequently the colour temperature is decreased (Figure 6.5). A similar range of CTO filters is available to make possible intermediate or minor adjustments to colour temperature (Table 6.2).

Note the transmission of a full CTO (full orange) is 55%, significantly more than a full blue. When using CTO filters on 'in-shot' windows, the filter must be placed on the outside of the window, otherwise the window glazing bars will be changed in colour by the filter. With large plate windows it may be possible to squeegee the filter onto the window. Ideally the CTO filters should be stapled to wooden frames and wedged in place. Care should be taken to avoid any wrinkles in the filter as these will cause reflection of lights. Acrylic filters, 3 mm thick, are available which overcome the problem of maintaining a rigid, wrinkle-free filter. These are more expensive than the normal flexible filters (polyester).

It should be noted that average summer sunlight (5500 K) is an 'average'. There will be occasions when the daylight colour temperature is higher than this value and any additional artificial lighting will need to be corrected to a higher value. This is a situation where an HMI/MSR source may require, say, $\frac{1}{4}$CTB to match with daylight.

Similarly, on a winter's day with a low-elevation sun, an HMI/MSR may require a $\frac{1}{4}$CTO to make a good match to the daylight. In both these cases it will be fairly obvious by eye that there is a need for correction to be applied to the artificial sources.

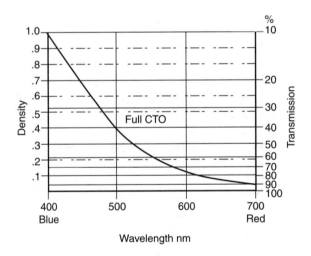

Figure 6.5 Filter characteristics for full colour temperature orange (CTO)

Table 6.2 Colour temperature orange (CTO) filters – basic conversion

Filter	Conversion (K)	Transmission (%)
Full CTO	6500–3200	55
$\frac{3}{4}$CTO	6500–3600	61
$\frac{1}{2}$CTO	6500–3800	71
$\frac{1}{4}$CTO	6500–4600	79
$\frac{1}{8}$CTO	6500–5500	85

Note: See later tables for complete data on conversion.

Filters are also available for correcting CSI/CID and HMI sources to tungsten lighting. When required to obtain an accurate match between two sources the procedure illustrated in Figure 6.6 is recommended.

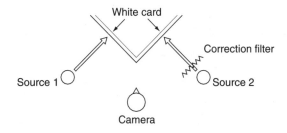

Figure 6.6 Method for matching two light sources

6.3 MIRED

Often it is required to estimate which filter to use for a particular application. Unfortunately the change in colour temperature produced with a particular filter is not a constant value. It depends on the starting colour temperature; the higher the starting colour temperature, the greater will be the change.

A full colour temperature blue filter causes a bigger change on a 4000 K source than a 2800 K source, i.e.

2800 K + full blue = 4600 K (2000 K shift)

3200 K + full blue = 5700 K (2500 K shift)

4000 K + full blue = 8850 K (4800 K shift)

Fortunately it is possible to predict the effect of a filter by using the concept of MIREDs. These are based on the observation that a given filter causes a **constant** shift in the **reciprocal** value of the colour temperature of a light source. However, the reciprocal value of a colour temperature will give a very small number, so to make the numbers easier to handle we take a millionth of the colour temperature (its 'micro' value), hence MIREDs where MIRED stands for **MI**cro **RE**ciprocal **D**egree.

$$\text{The MIRED value of a light source} = \frac{1}{K} \times \frac{1}{10^{-6}} = \frac{10^6}{K}$$

$$\text{e.g. the MIRED value for } 5000\,K = \frac{10^6}{5000} = 200 \text{ MIREDs.}$$

Manufacturers quote the MIRED shift for all colour temperature correction filters, CTB filters reduce the MIRED value of the colour temperature and therefore have a negative sign (Table 6.3).

Using this concept we can estimate the filter required to cause a particular change in colour temperature, or predict the new colour temperature when using a particular filter.

Table 6.3 MIRED shift of CTB/CTO filters

Filter	MIRED shift	Filter	MIRED shift
Full CTB	−137	Full CTO	+159
$^3/_4$CTB	−113	$^3/_4$CTO	+124
$^1/_2$CTB	−78	$^1/_2$CTO	+109
$^1/_4$CTB	−35	$^1/_4$CTO	+64
$^1/_8$CTB	−18	$^1/_8$CTO	+26

Note: A word of caution: the description FULL, $^3/_4$, $^1/_2$ etc. is a very loose description. The addition of 2 fractional filters to make up a filter usually produces a larger MIRED shift, e.g. $2 \times {^1/_2}$CTB = −156 MIREDs, 19 MIREDs away from a FULL CTB filter. Similarly $2 \times {^1/_2}$CTO = +218.

Example 1

What filter is required to simulate Moonlight (4100 K) when using a 3200 K Tungsten source?

$$\text{MIRED value of 3200 K} = \frac{10^6}{3200} = 312$$

$$\text{MIRED value of 4100 K} = \frac{10^6}{4100} = 243$$

$$\text{Required MIRED shift} = -69, \text{ i.e. } {^1/_2}\text{CTB } (-78 \text{ MIREDs})$$

Note that the tolerances of 3200 K ± 150 K and 5500 K ± 400 K, discussed earlier, represents a MIRED shift of approximately 14 MIREDs, consequently use of the $^1/_2$CTB filter would be within this tolerance.

Example 2

What is the new colour temperature if a $^3/_4$CTO is used on a 3200 K source?

$$\text{MIRED value of 3200 K} = \frac{10^6}{3200} = 312$$

$$\text{MIRED shift of } {^3/_4}\text{CTO} = +124$$

$$\text{New MIRED value} = 436$$

$$\text{New colour temperature} = \frac{10^6}{436} = 2293 \text{ K} \simeq \textbf{2300 K}$$

i.e. a colour temperature shift of 900 K.

Note the difference in colour temperature shift if used on a 5000 K light source:

$$\text{MIRED value of 5000 K} = \frac{10^6}{5000} = 200$$

$$\text{MIRED shift of } {}^3\!/_4\text{CTO} = 124$$

$$\text{New MIRED value} = 324$$

$$\text{New colour temperature} = \frac{10^6}{324} = \textbf{3086 K}$$

i.e. a colour temperature shift of 1914 K.

This confirms the opening statement: the higher the initial colour temperature, the greater the effect of a colour temperature correction filter.

Note: There can be slight colour differences between filter batches and between manufacturers.

Colour temperature correction filters are often used to create appropriate lighting effects, e.g. moonlight, sunset etc. Tables 6.4–6.6 give the appropriate colour temperature change introduced when using them.

Table 6.4 Tungsten light conversion

Filter	Conversion (K)	MIRED shift	Transmission (%)
Full CTB	3200–5700	−137	34
³⁄₄CTB	3200–5000	−113	45
½CTB	3200–4300	−78	55
¼CTB	3200–3600	−35	69
⅛CTB	3200–3400	−18	81
Full CTO	3200–2100	+159	55
³⁄₄CTO	3200–2300	+124	61
½CTO	3200–2400	+109	71
¼CTO	3200–2650	+64	79
⅛CTO	3200–2950	+26	85

Table 6.5 Daylight conversion

Filter	Conversion (K)	MIRED shift	Transmission (%)
Full CTO	6500–3200	+159	55
³⁄₄CTO	6500–3600	+124	61
½CTO	6500–3800	+109	71
¼CTO	6500–4600	+64	79
⅛CTO	6500–5550	+26	85
Also			
³⁄₄CTO	5300–3200	+124	61
½CTO	4900–3200	+109	71
¼CTO	4000–3200	+64	79
⅛CTO	3700–3200	+26	85

Table 6.6 Average summer sunlight conversion

Filter	Conversion (K)	MIRED shift	Transmission (%)
Full CTB	5500–22 000	−137	34
$^3/_4$CTB	5500–14 500	−113	45
$^1/_2$CTB	5500–9600	−78	55
$^1/_4$CTB	5500–6800	−35	69
$^1/_8$CTB	5500–6100	−18	81
Full CTO	5500–2950	+159	55
$^3/_4$CTO	5500–3270	+124	61
$^1/_2$CTO	5500–3450	+109	71
$^1/_4$CTO	5500–4100	+64	79
$^1/_8$CTO	5500–4800	+26	85

- Beware of using filters in combination on luminaires. The heat absorbed by the filters becomes trapped between them, resulting in a short filter life.
- When using diffusion and correction filters, always use the correction filter on the outside of the diffusion. This is to allow the heat absorbed in the filter to dissipate. Placed inside the diffusion it will result in a shorter life due to the trapped heat.

6.4   Change of camera white point

Colour temperature correction filters may be used to change the white balance or white point on the camera. For example, to have warmer pictures, say in a tungsten-lit scene, rather than putting $^1/_4$CTO filters on all the light sources, simply move the white point to $^1/_4$CTB by holding a $^1/_4$CTB filter over the lens at the time of white balancing the camera. A 3200 K lit scene would then look warm, only scene elements lit with 3600 K (3200 K + $^1/_4$CTB) would look 'normal' (Figure 6.7).

The MIRED scale is approximately linear in its perceived effect (for sources of greater than 1800 K). So if one wished to have twice the effect of a certain filter, say +50 MIREDs, a filter with a +100 MIRED shift would be used.

Note that colour temperature correction filters may be used in combination. Simply add the MIRED shift of each filter to determine the effect of a combination, and multiply the transmission factors to determine the overall transmission, e.g.

$$^1/_2\text{CTB} + ^1/_2\text{CTB} = \text{full CTB}$$

$$(-78) + (-78) = -156 \text{ MIREDs}$$

Note that this is about 19 MIREDs greater than a full CTB (−137), i.e. a noticeable departure from average daylight. Some cameramen only carry $^1/_2$CTB as a compromise on correction/ transmission; this is usually satisfactory, but be aware of the overcorrection when used together to produce full CTB. Similarly, overall transmission factor = 0.55 × 0.55 = 0.30, i.e. 30% transmission.

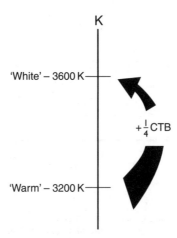

Figure 6.7 Change of 'white' point

6.5 Colour temperature measurement

Colour temperature meters fall into two basic categories:

● Simple meters which base their measurement on the smooth spectral energy distribution curve for incandescent sources and make two comparison measurements, one in the blue end of the spectrum and one in the red end of the spectrum (Figure 6.8, page 60).
● Digital meters which calculate the colour temperature from the analysis of the light source with three photocells, each filtered to examine a different part of the spectrum, e.g. Minolta Chroma Meter, Thoma TF5 Colormeter.

Digital meters may also have the facility to measure the actual chromaticity (colour) of the light source, e.g. Minolta Chroma Meter, Thoma TF5 Colormeter. Colour cameras also have a colour temperature indicator, generally not as accurate as the meters.

CIE Chromaticity Chart

The basic principle of colour synthesis using three suitable colours (R, G and B) has already been discussed. Using this system we can specify a particular colour in terms of R, G and B. However, this would only apply to colours that fall within the triangle. In practice, many colours in the real world, especially saturated and spectral colours, fall outside this basic triangle and require the use of negative values to specify them. The CIE, in 1931, introduced the CIE Chromaticity Chart using very special 'primary' colours. These are super saturated primaries, and do not exist in practice, but as a mathematical concept enable a colour to be specified in terms of X, Y and Z instead of RGB. The triangle produced by these three primaries embraces all known colours, including spectral colours. In this system, the three coefficients x, y and z are equated to 1, so only two coefficients are required to specify a particular colour; hence the 'triangle' can be redrawn as a right-angled triangle using coefficients of x and y only to plot a particular colour. If x and y are zero, then

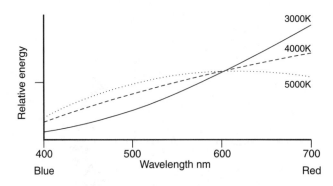

Note: (a) The curves are continuous and smooth.
      (b) Relative decrease in red radiation and relative increase in blue
          radiation as colour temperature is increased.
      (c) Within the visible spectrum the radiation curves are almost linear

Figure 6.8 Relative spectral energy distribution for incandescent sources.

the coordinates 0, 0 must indicate $z = 1$, so the diagram represents all three 'primaries' (Figures 6.9 and 6.10).

Chroma Meters, such as the Minolta Meter, include a plastic card showing the CIE diagram and the locus of the 'black-body radiator' (colour plot of increasing colour temperature for a 'full' radiator). This can be used to plot values of x and y if required. An enlarged version of the 'black-body locus' is included on the reverse of the plastic card for checking correlated colour temperature.

The Thoma Colormeter TF5 is similar to the Minolta but has more facilities, i.e. as well as measuring colour temperature it also indicates departures from the 'ideal colour temperature curve', plus chromaticity in u, v and u', v' terms.

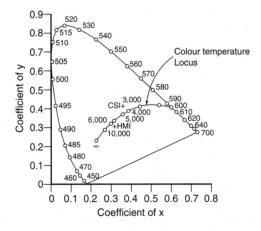

Figure 6.9 The CIE Chromaticity Diagram

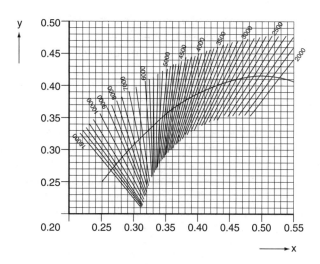

Figure 6.10 CIE diagram showing isotemperature lines

When measuring 'spikey' light sources the fact that meters are calibrated against a continuous, smooth incandescent source can lead to measurement errors. The Thoma Colormeter TF5 is recommended by a leading light source manufacture for measuring discharge lights.

The important point to remember is to test any light source combination plus corrections **on-camera** – do not rely totally on meters!

6.6 Correlated colour temperature and colour compensating filters

Strictly speaking, the term 'colour temperature' should only be used for incandescent sources, i.e. sources which are glowing by virtue of their temperature – sun, tungsten, tungsten halogen, carbon arc, oil lamps, candles.

The **shape** of the spectral energy distribution for these sources is very similar to that of a full radiator (poker), and a good 'match' can be made. Light sources which produce light from an electrical discharge tend to have a 'spiky' spectrum and may not give a good match to a full radiator (incandescent source), e.g.

Fluorescent sources
Low-pressure sodium
High-pressure sodium
High-pressure mercury   CSI
                                  CID
                                  HMI
                                  MSR
Xenon
CDM

There is, however, still a need to be able to describe the white point of such sources. This is done by quoting the correlated colour temperature for each source. This is the colour temperature which best describes the colour, i.e. looks closest to the colour. The term 'correlated' is dropped in everyday usage.

The CIE Chromaticity Chart can be used to determine the correlated colour temperature by plotting the value of x and y for non-incandescent sources and reading off the lines of isotemperature curves.

This is also a useful guide to the need for correction. Correction in the blue–orange direction has been discussed. However, few discharge sources will plot exactly on the colour temperature 'locus', they will plot either side of the locus representing a green or magenta bias (Figure 6.11).

Colour compensating filters are used to provide the required correction in the magenta or green direction (Table 6.7) to help correct a discharge source onto the colour temperature locus, or simply to make correction between two discharge sources, say HMIs, to achieve a good colour 'match'! See Figure 6.12.

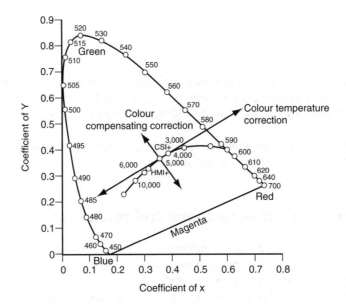

Figure 6.11 The colour correction 'axis' for correction filters

Table 6.7 Colour compensating filters

Filter	Value
Plus Green	CC 30 Green
Half Plus Green	CC 15 Green
Quarter Plus Green	CC 075 Green
Eight Plus Green	CC 0375 Green
Minus Green	CC 30 Magenta
Half Minus Green	CC 15 Magenta
Quarter Minus Green	CC 075 Magenta
Eight Minus Green	CC 00375 Magenta

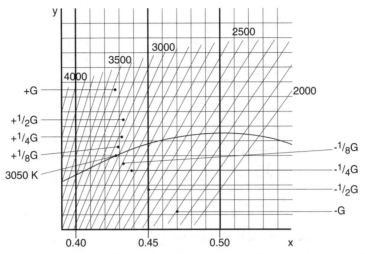

Note change in colour temperature as well as movement in the Green/Magenta axis.
Filter applied to a 3050k source.

Figure 6.12 Effect of colour compensating filters (on a tungsten source)

Meters are available which can measure the green/magenta error, in addition to providing an indication of the blue–orange correction required – usually specified in MIREDs, e.g. Minolta Colour Meter III. Note the observations made on measuring non-incandescent sources also apply – always check light source/filter combinations on camera!

6.7 Neutral density filters

Neutral density filters (ND filters) have very little colour bias and simply reduce the light equally throughout the spectrum (Figure 6.13).

The density of a filter is given by the formula:

$$\text{Density} = \log_{10} \frac{1}{\text{Transmission factor}} = \log_{10} \text{ opacity}$$

For a filter with a 50% transmission or 0.5 transmission factor,

$$D = \log_{10} \frac{1}{0.5} = \log_{10} 2 = 0.3$$

It is useful to think of the change in exposure introduced by an ND filter in terms of *f*-stops. The 0.3 ND filter would therefore introduce a one *f*-stop loss.

A range of ND filters is available (Table 6.8). Note that ND filters may be used in combination, e.g. $0.3 + 0.6 = 0.9$ ND.

The density scale is obviously a logarithmic scale so equal changes in density are perceived equally by the eye/brain, i.e. 0.3, 0.6, 0.9, 1.2.

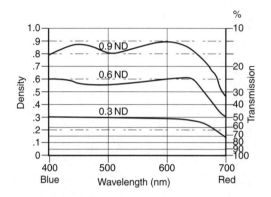

Figure 6.13 Characteristics of typical ND filters

Table 6.8 Properties of ND filters

Neutral density (ND)	Transmission (%)	Loss in f-stops
0.15	70	$\frac{1}{2}$ stop
0.3	50	1 stop
0.6	25	2 stops
0.9	12.5	3 stops
1.2	6.25	4 stops

Neutral density filters may be used:

● on windows, to reduce contrast between interior and exterior scenes
● on cameras, to adjust camera sensitivity as required, i.e. to help with excessive illumin-ance levels and/or help to work at wide apertures for depth-of-field considerations
● on luminaires, to assist in obtaining an appropriate lighting balance.

Neutral density filters are also available as 3 mm thick acrylic sheets (6 ft × 8 ft). These have the advantage of being completely rigid and therefore do not flap about in the wind or buckle.

Camera manufacturers use a different method for describing the neutral density filters used in camera filter wheels, i.e.

$\frac{1}{4}$ND is used to indicate a transmission of $\frac{1}{4}$ or 25% (2-stop loss) – filter position 2
$\frac{1}{16}$ND is used to indicate a transmission of $\frac{1}{16}$ or 6.25% (4-stop loss) – filter position 4

Neutral density in combination

Combination filters are available which provide full CTO correction and ND, e.g.

[0.3 ND + full CTO] provides $1\frac{1}{2}$ stops of light loss
[0.6 ND + full CTO] provides $2\frac{1}{2}$ stops of light loss

Note: When using diffusion and ND filters in combination always put the ND on the **outside** of the diffusion to avoid the ND filter becoming excessively hot.

7
Camera sensitivity – how much light do we need?

7.1 Defining sensitivity

Camera sensitivity links three interrelated parameters, namely lens aperture (*f*-number), illuminance (lux) and signal-to-noise ratio (dB). This is illustrated in Figure 7.1.

Camera manufacturers use a standard light source and line-up chart which equates to an illuminance of **2000 lux** and a peak white reflectance of **89.9%**. The variables in the test are the **lens aperture** and the **signal-to-noise ratio**, both of these will depend on the CCD sensitivity and the amount of camera gain required.

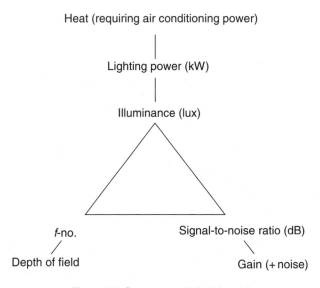

Figure 7.1 Camera sensitivity 'triangle'

A typical CCD camera sensitivity would be:

ƒ8.0 with 2000 lux for an 89.9% peak white, 60 dB S/N ratio

This, of course, is not an instruction on how to use the camera but simply a useful engineering definition that enables direct comparison of camera-to-camera sensitivity to be made. The 89.9% reflectance peak white is the standard used in Japan, a country of very fair skin tones, especially those of females. The rest of the world generally favours the use of a test chart with 60% reflectance peak white. This is based on the need to correctly expose the darker skin tone without overexposing on a peak white area. Clearly, the 60% reflectance surface will only reflect two-thirds of the light that the 89% (approx. 90%) surface reflected, so the illuminance has to be increased to 3000 lux, i.e.

ƒ8.0 with 3000 lux, 60% peak white reflectance, 60 dB S/N ratio

The operating lens aperture is clearly going to be the deciding factor in determining the illuminance required, unless gain adjustment is made which will increase the noise, thus reducing the signal-to-noise ratio. Opening up the lens aperture results in a significant drop in illuminance requirements, i.e. Table 7.1 (see Figure 7.2).

Table 7.1 Camera sensitivity and illuminance requirements

Lens aperture	Scene illuminance (60% peak white reflectance) (lux)
ƒ8.0	3000
ƒ5.6	1500
ƒ4.0	750
ƒ2.8	375
ƒ2.0	187.5

Depth-of-field is proportional to f-number, and, in fact, is usually the deciding factor for the f-number. Custom and practice over the years has led to the concept of 'nominal' lens apertures based on camera sensor format, i.e. Table 4.1 (p. 44). Using cameras at the nominal aperture results in similar depths of field for a given shot size and camera distance.

Lens sharpness decreases as the lens is opened up. This would appear to be a conflict in operating at an ƒ2.0 aperture. Fortunately, with the evolution of the high resolution CCD camera with an excess of 1000 pixels/line (within the 8.8 mm format) lenses have to be capable of superior resolution compared with lenses for tube cameras. Consequently, good-quality modern lenses produce good optical sharpness even at ƒ2.0. This means that lenses can be used in the ƒ2.0–ƒ2.8 region – this results in pictures with good 'optical separation' of the subject and background. This is so vital to good picture quality if the artiste is to be 'unstuck' from the background. Close-ups should be free from the distraction of a sharply focused background. Unless other criteria exist, aim to be in this 'ballpark'.

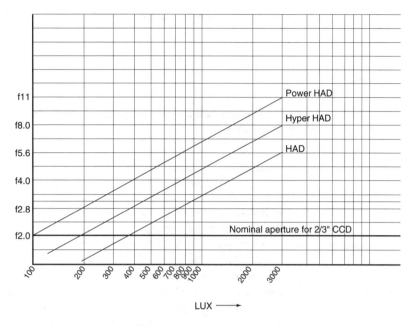

Figure 7.2 CCD sensitivity – illuminance/f-number

7.2 Factors affecting sensitivity

The camera sensitivity can be affected by a number of factors:

- use of teleprompter
- use of range extenders
- zoom ramping
- camera minus blue filter
- camera neutral density filters
- electronic gain
- electronic shutter
- camera frame rate.

Use of teleprompter

When used on location, expect a reduction in exposure of approximately $\frac{1}{2}f$-stop, i.e. ×0.7 or $1/\sqrt{2}$. Consequently there will be a need to increase illuminance by a factor of $\frac{1}{0.7}$ or $\sqrt{2} = 1.4$, e.g. with hyper HAD camera at $f2.8$, increase illuminance from 375 lux to 525 lux.

Use of range extenders

This causes a significant reduction in sensitivity. For example, a ×2 range extender will double the focal length, which means that the f-number is also doubled. A lens operating at $f2.8$ becomes effectively $f5.6$, a reduction in sensitivity of 2 stops, i.e. sensitivity is reduced to 25%.

Zoom ramping

This may occur when using large lens apertures at the long focal length end of the zoom, causing a reduction in effective f-number.

$$\text{Lens aperture or } f\text{-number is given by:}\ \frac{\text{Focal length } (f)}{\text{Diameter of lens aperture } (d)}$$

However, it is not the physical iris diameter which is important, but 'the diameter of the lens aperture seen from the object space' which determines the exposure (Figure 7.3). The action of a zoom lens is such that when zooming in (f increasing) the size of the aperture optically increases (iris is magnified). Thus, the f-number remains constant. However, when a large ratio zoom lens at its maximum sensitivity is zoomed in, a point is reached where the diameter of the lens front element is not large enough to give the required d. Any subsequent 'zooming in' results in a change in f but no change in d. The effective f-number gradually increases, resulting in a decrease in sensitivity. This is known as zoom ramping (e.g. Figures 7.3–7.5).

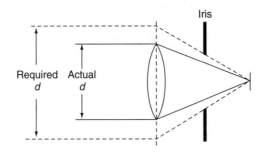

Figure 7.3 Zoom ramping

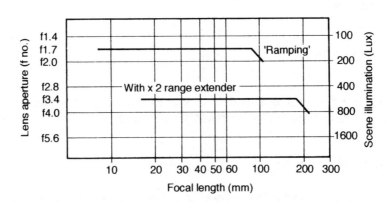

Figure 7.4 Camera sensitivity, zoom ramping and range extenders (14 × 9 zoom lens)

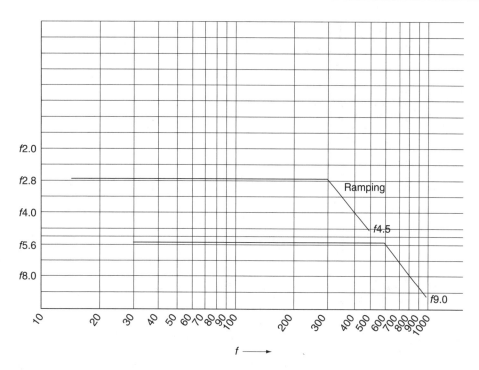

Figure 7.5 Ramping effect with a 33:1 zoom lens

Camera minus blue filter

Colour cameras are designed to operate in a tungsten-lit environment. Consequently, when exposed to daylight there is a significant increase in light at the blue end of the spectrum. The minus blue filter ($^3/_4$CTO) in the camera filter wheel (position 3) removes the excess of the blue light to equalise the daylight to tungsten values. The loss introduced by this filter is almost one stop. Historically, the minus blue filter was needed on tube cameras to avoid the overloading of the blue tube (tubes became overloaded very easily), and to reduce the significant changes in red and blue gain required when white balancing to daylight.

It should be noted that most CCD cameras can cope with white balancing to daylight even on filter 1 (Table 7.2). In conditions of low daylight this can be useful to maintain a good f-number, i.e. f2.0–f2.8 instead of f1.4.

CCD cameras have excellent highlight handling capabilities. CCDs overload at approximately 600% of normal input lighting level. Consequently, the need for a minus blue filter has diminished and many of the latest CCD cameras do not have this facility, all adjustments for white balance are achieved electronically.

Camera ND filters

Often it is desirable to reduce the camera sensitivity to cope with excessively bright conditions or as a means of reducing depth of field. Usually a combination of minus blue

Table 7.2 Camera sensitivity for different CCDs ($\frac{2}{3}''$ format)

	Standard sensitivity for 2000 lux and 89.9% peak white	Illuminance required at $f2.8$ for 60% peak white (lux)	Signal-to-noise ratio (dB)
HAD CCD cameras	$f5.6$	750	59
Hyper HAD CCD cameras	$f8.0$	375	60
Power HAD CCD cameras	$f11.0$	188	61

Table 7.3 Camera filter wheel: single wheel

Filter wheel position	Colour temperature	Loss
1	3200 K	0
2	5600 K + $\frac{1}{4}$ND	as filter 3 + 2 stops
3	5600 K	approx. 1 stop
4	5600 K + $\frac{1}{16}$ND	as filter 3 + 4 stops

Note: Preset White Balance follows position of the filter wheel. $\frac{1}{4}$ND means $\frac{1}{4}$ transmission, i.e. 25% transmission, not 0.25 ND. $\frac{1}{16}$ND means $\frac{1}{16}$ transmission, i.e. 6.25% transmission, not 0.0625 ND.

filters and neutral density filters have been included in the camera filter wheel – typically as shown in Table 7.3.

The high sensitivity of current cameras has created a need for neutral density filters in tungsten-lit environments. The arrangement of Table 7.3 is rapidly being replaced in these cameras with two filter wheels allowing independent adjustment of colour temperature filter and neutral density filter (Table 7.4).

Table 7.4 Camera filter wheel: double wheel

Filter wheel 1 position	Colour temperature (K)	Loss	Filter wheel 2 position	ND	Loss
A	Cross	0	1	Clear	0
B	3200	0	2	$\frac{1}{4}$ND	2 stops
C	4300	$\frac{1}{2}$ stop	3	$\frac{1}{16}$ND	4 stops
D	6300	1 stop	4	$\frac{1}{64}$ND	6 stops

Note: 'Cross' provides a simple four-point star filter, an older camera's ND may be $\frac{1}{4}$ND, $\frac{1}{8}$ND and $\frac{1}{16}$ND.

Electronic gain

This may be used to maintain signal levels when operating in difficult circumstances. Usually, this is switched to give discrete increments in gain (i.e. Table 7.5). The precise amounts of switched gain available differ from camera to camera. Sony, for example, use +6 dB and 12 dB on single-sensor cameras and +9 dB and +18 dB on three-sensor cameras. Remember, extra gain will result in an increase in noise and a consequent reduction in signal/noise ratio.

Minus gain is useful when less sensitivity is required, i.e. needing to operate at a wide aperture $f2.0$–$f2.8$. It has the advantage over neutral density filters of reducing the noise. Minus gain adjustments are also more subtle than ND filter adjustments, i.e. $\frac{1}{2}$ f-stop and 1 f-stop compared to 2 f-stops and 4 f-stops. The equivalent change in sensitivity with gain is shown in Table 7.5.

Table 7.5 Camera gain/sensitivity

Selection (dB)	Change in gain	Equivalent change in sensitivity
−6	×0.5	−1 f-stop
−3	×0.7	−$\frac{1}{2}$ f-stop
0	×1.0	0
+3	×1.4	+$\frac{1}{2}$ f-stop
+6	×2.0	+1 f-stop
+9	×2.8	+1$\frac{1}{2}$ f-stops
+12	×4.0	+2 f-stops
+15	×5.6	+2$\frac{1}{2}$ f-stops
+18	×8.0	+3 f-stops

Electronic shutter

Most CCD cameras have the facility of an electronic shutter, which enables the exposure time to be reduced. For example:

1/60, 1/125, 1/250, 1/500, 1/1000, 1/2000 second

The shutter can be used to help with problems of large depth of field by reducing the camera sensitivity, thus requiring the lens to be opened up to compensate. Note that when using short exposure times fast subject movement will appear 'jerky'. Short exposure times are often used to obtain a single clear image of a fast-moving subject as a graphic or still store picture. (See later note on HMIs and shutters.)

7.3 ASA rating and video cameras

It can sometimes be useful to think of video camera sensitivity in terms of film speeds, i.e. give the video camera an ASA rating (without 'knee' operational).

$$\text{ASA rating} = \frac{1250 \times f\text{-no.}^2}{\text{Illuminance}}$$

where illuminance is in foot-candles, and exposure is 1/50th second. So for a hyper HAD camera ($f8$, 2000 lux for 89.9% P.W, 60 dB) such as the Sony DVW 700P operating with 60% peak white, we have a need for 187.5 lux (or 17.4 foot-candles) at $f2.0$. Therefore

$$\text{ASA rating} = \frac{1250 \times 2 \times 2}{17.4} = 287$$
$$\cong 280 \text{ ASA}$$

Table 7.6 Camera gain/ASA rating/illuminance requirements

Gain (dB)	HAD		Hyper HAD		Power HAD	
	ASA rating	Illuminance for $f2.0$ (lux)	ASA rating	Illuminance For $f2.0$ (lux)	ASA rating	Illuminance for $f2.0$ (lux)
−6	70	750	140	375	280	188
−3	100	530	200	265	400	132
0	140	375	280	188	560	94
+3	200	265	400	132	800	66
+6	280	188	560	94	1120	≅48
+9	400	132	800	66	1600	33
+12	560	94	1120	≅48	2240	≅24
+15	800	66	1600	33	3200	16
+18	1120	≅48	2240	24	4480	≅12

Camera frame rate

Slow-motion facilities are achieved by shooting at three times normal rate and replaying at normal speed. The exposure time is thus shortened so there is a need for a higher lighting level, e.g. $f4.0$ for 2000 lux, 89.9% peak white; for a 60% peak white this equates to 3000 lux at $f4.0$, i.e. ASA 70.

High definition cameras usually offer a choice of scanning system, i.e. 24P, 25P or 50i. The reader is recommended to refer to the manufacturer's data on sensitivity to determine the lighting illuminance needed at the appropriate scanning rate/shutter combination. Note the signal/noise ratio will be less than standard cameras because of the wider bandwidth occupied by high definition video signals.

Current sensitivities are better than $f10.0$ for 2000 lux, 89.9% reflectance peak white and signal/noise ratio of 54 dB.

8
Light sources

8.1 Choice of light source

The decision on choice of light source is mainly influenced by:

- efficacy or lumens/watt
- lumens package
- colour temperature
- colour rendition index, R_a.

Other considerations are:

- ability to dim the source electronically (or mechanically)
- lack of auxiliary equipment
- stability of light source colour – with dimming and with lamp life
- lamp life
- compactness of light source – ability to collect the light and project it
- weight of luminaire.

Lamp efficacy

This is a measure of the ability of the light source to convert electrical energy into visible light. It is expressed simply as lumens/watts. One watt of electrical power converted into light of a single wavelength at 555 nm would provide 680 lumens/watt (this is an alternative definition of the lumen). This, however, is not particularly useful for comparisons because the light is of a single wavelength. A more realistic comparison can be achieved with 240 lumens/watt, an efficacy achieved if 1 watt of electrical power is converted totally into an equal energy visible spectrum.

   Domestic tungsten lamps have an efficacy of 12 lumens/watt, tungsten halogen about 25 lumens/watt and HMIs have efficacies in the region of 100 lumens/watt for the higher wattage lamps.

Lumens package

This indicates the total lumens available from a light source and is the product of lamp wattage and efficacy. For example, a 4 kW HMI would produce a total lumens package of $4000 \times 100 = 400\,000$ lumens whereas a 55 W high-frequency PL-L fluorescent lamp only produces $55 \times 87.5 = 4812$ lumens. The PL-L lamp therefore has to be used in multiples to produce a luminaire capable of delivering a useful light output.

Colour temperature

This has been discussed fully elsewhere in this book (p. 50). It is a convenient way of describing the 'whiteness' or white point of a light source. If the source has to be corrected with filters to match the natural lighting (or tungsten lighting) there will be some loss of light output. Effectively, this reduces the efficacy so a tungsten halogen source filtered for daylight becomes approximately 8 lumens/watt! Where possible use sources which match the natural lighting with little or no requirement for filters.

Colour rendition index, R_a

Faithful reproduction of scene colour is obviously important in television, it is therefore essential that the colour rendition or colour fidelity of light sources used in television is acceptable. Tungsten sources and daylight are regarded as excellent. The visible spectrum from these sources is continuous, with a smooth transition of light output between adjacent wavelengths resulting in the source being totally acceptable. All discharge sources have 'spikey' spectrums, and it is therefore necessary to give an indication of the colour fidelity achieved by such sources.

The colour rendition index, R_a, uses an arbitrary scale of 0 to 100, calibrated to give the original warm white fluorescent tube an R_a of 50. Generally, an R_a of 70 is regarded as the lower limit of acceptability for colour television.

The R_a for a light source is calculated by equating the colour errors when illuminating eight test colours, compared with the colours measured when the eight test colours are illuminated with a tungsten light of the **same** colour temperature. If the lamp under test is of a colour temperature greater than 5000 K, then a re-constituted daylight source of the same colour temperature is used, using computer data.

It should be noted that R_a is only a guide. The R_a gives no indication of the direction of error so two different sources of identical R_a and at the same colour temperature may not look identical. When considering the colour rendition of each colour test individually, R_i, a shift in the index of 5 is just discernible (Table 8.1, page 75).

8.2 Tungsten and tungsten halogen sources

These are the most commonly used light sources and very simple in operation. They are based on the principle of using the heating effect of an electric current to heat a tungsten

Table 8.1 Colour temperature/R_a efficacy for television sources

	Colour temperatures (K)	Colour rendition index (R_a)	Efficacy lumens/(W)
Tungsten, Domestic	2760	100	12
Tungsten, Studio	3200	100	25
Tungsten halogen	3200	100	25–29
CSI	4000 +/− 400	80	90
HMI	6000 +/− 400	95	70–105
CID	5500 +/− 400	70	70–80
MSR	6000 +/− 400	90	95
XENON	6200	98	15–50
CDM	3000	81–85	83–93
CDM	4200	90–95	78–80
Fluorescent – Warm white halophosphate (Domestic)	3000	58	78
HF Fluorescent – 55 W PL-L (colour 830) Tri-phosphate	3000	85	87
HF Fluorescent – 55 W PL-L (colour 930) deluxe	3000	95	55
HF Fluorescent – 55 W PL-L (colour 950) deluxe	5000	95	55

Note: HMI/MSR previously quoted as 5600 K (on leaving luminaire). 6000 K is actual lamp colour temperature, unaffected by luminaire optics.

filament to incandescence, i.e. until it glows. Fundamental to its operation is the fact that when it is dimmed the colour of light changes. However, if the changes are restricted to about ±150 K they are not normally perceived on skin tones. Unfortunately, operation of a tungsten source results in the filament gradually evaporating and condensing on the envelope. This darkens the envelope and reduces the lamp life. Tungsten halogen sources overcome this by introducing a halogen into the envelope (Figure 8.1). They are characterised

At normal operating temperatures Tungsten evaporates from the lamp filament – this combines with halogen at the envelope (250 °C–800 °C) to give Tungsten Halide, at temperatures in excess of 1250 °C this 'dissociates' to give halogen released and Tungsten deposited on the cooler parts of the filament

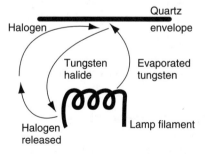

Figure 8.1 Halogen cycle to keep quartz envelope clean

by small, tough quartz glass envelopes, which have led to the development of many new small luminaires, i.e. compact and bambino ranges.

Operating notes: Tungsten halogen sources should be burnt within the range of tilt angles recommended by the manufacturer, otherwise the lamp life will be reduced significantly. The plastic glove or sleeve supplied by the manufacturer should always be used when handling **quartz** glass envelopes and subsequently removed. Touching the envelope of a tungsten halogen lamp results in harmful body acids being deposited. When heated, the acids attack the quartz glass envelope causing it to become opaque. Light and heat are then not transmitted, so the lamp overheats and destroys itself.

Typical operational practices

The inclusion of an electronic dimmer in series with a tungsten light source makes the control of light intensity very flexible, i.e. allowing swift balancing of light sources and motivated lighting changes. The dimmer is usually controlled via a fader calibrated with a 0–10 scale or 00 to 100% scale. A fader setting of 7 is usually adopted as a 'nominal' setting. This corresponds to 50% light output (see **Dimmer Law**) and a theoretical colour temperature of 2960 K, i.e. cameras are white balanced to 2960 K.

The value of working in this way is that the light output may be increased or decreased about this nominal value, within the accepted tolerances ($\pm$150 K), providing a useful range of intensity change. This is illustrated in Figure 8.2.

It should be noted that because of cable and dimmer losses it is usually not possible to reach 3200 K, consequently, moving the fader to 10 provides light within the specified colour temperature tolerance.

Operating at fader 7 results in a significant increase in lamp life, i.e. $\times$10. Running cooler results in less filament evaporation thus prolonging the life of the lamp. Typically, a lamp rated at 150 hours life at full mains voltage would last approximately 1500 hours at fader 7!

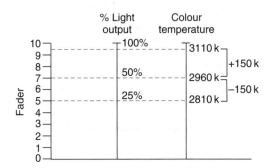

Figure 8.2 Fader setting versus percentage light output and colour temperature

8.3 Discharge sources – general

These are either low or high pressure discharge sources. They produce light as a by-product of an electrical discharge (current) through a gas. The colour of the light is characterised by the particular mixture of gas present in the quartz glass envelope or the nature of the tubular phosphor coating with the fluorescent lamp.

Discharge light sources used in television are:

- Compact source iodide (CSI)
- Mercury (Hg), medium arc gap, iodides (HMI)
- Compact iodide daylight (CID)   } High pressure
- Medium source rare-earth (MSR)
- Xenon
- Fluorescent   Low pressure
- CDM   High pressure

CSI, CID, HMI and MSR

These are basically mercury vapour discharge sources with added iodides to give the correct colour temperature and colour rendition. Their merit lies in:

- Greater efficacy than tungsten, approximately three to four times, thus less power required
- Compact light source, easy to collect (condense) and project the light
- Depending on type, can produce light which approximates to daylight
- Produce less infrared radiation than tungsten, i.e. cooler in operation
- Available from 24 W through to 18 kW (HMI).

The HMI and the MSR source are the most common of the discharge sources. Their disadvantages are that they:

1   Require an EHT supply, typically 27 kV, to ionise the gas and so produce an electric current.
2   Require a current limiting device, which may be a wire-wound choke, or an electronic ballast. The electronic ballast is associated with 'flicker-free' operation which results in a constant light output, i.e. it is operated with, typically, a 166 Hz square wave voltage so the light does not extinguish on each half cycle.
3   Require a warm-up period of 1–2 minutes before full output and correct colour is reached.
4   May not have a hot re-strike facility.
5   In many cases, may not be dimmed electronically. However, some of the later sources using an electronic ballast do have a dimming capacity down to approximately 50% maximum light output.
6   Operate at a high bulb pressure and are **liable to explode**.
7   Produce an output which is rich in **harmful ultraviolet radiation**. This is transmitted by the quartz envelope, therefore all discharge sources **must** be operated with a glass filter, i.e. lens or safety glass.
8   Are not as flexible in use as tungsten sources, they need to be fitted with mechanical shutters if it is required to fade-up from a black-out condition.
9   Are more expensive than tungsten sources.
10 Colour of the light changes with life.

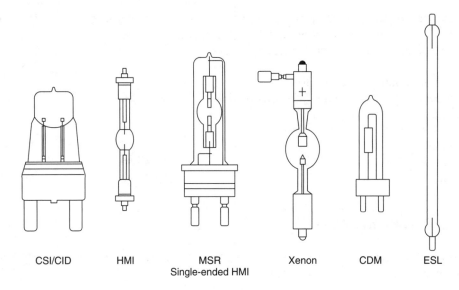

CSI/CID   HMI   MSR   Xenon   CDM   ESL
Single-ended HMI

Figure 8.3 Discharge light sources

Principle of operation

Gases are normally good insulators and need to be 'ionised' to produce an electric current. This process is started by applying an EHT voltage in excess of 27 kV. A few free electrons in the envelope are accelerated and collide with the gas atoms, and one of three events may take place (Figure 8.4):

1 An elastic collision giving rise to an increase in temperature.
2 An electron receives a discrete amount of energy to raise it to a higher energy level. It however, must fall back to its proper energy level and gives up the extra energy as electromagnetic radiation (a photon) of frequency proportional to the energy released. This may be visible!

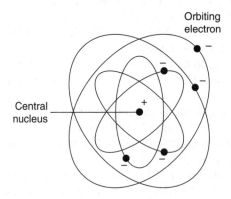

Figure 8.4 Basic atom – all electrons have a prescribed location, for a given element, represented by their energy level

3   An electron receives enough energy to break away from the parent atom. This results in
     a 'free' electron (−ve ion) and the gas atom becomes positively charged (+ve ion). The
     gas is ionised.

The most important aspect is 2, where the colour of the radiation produced is a function of
the gas elements and the gas pressure (Figure 8.5).

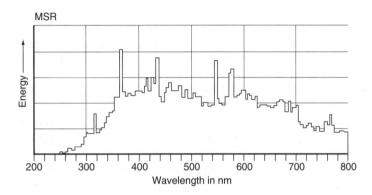

Figure 8.5 Spectral energy distribution MSR

8.4   Discharge sources – operating practices and safety

Operators of high-pressure discharge sources must be aware of the safety aspects and
potential hazards:

1   Extra high tension (EHT) starting voltage 27 kV (dangerous electric shock hazard) –
     correct earthing of all metalwork.
2   Harmful ultraviolet radiation (severe sunburn, headache and blindness hazard) –
     correct optical filter in place and undamaged, i.e. lens or protective glass. No leakage
     of light directly from the light source.
3   High operating pressure (exploding of lamp hazard) – restrict mechanical movement to
     a minimum when lamp is hot – use safety goggles when changing lamps – avoid
     changing hot lamp.
4   Mercury vapour (inhalation of mercury vapour hazard) – if lamp explodes harmful
     mercury vapour will be released.

The colour of the light from these sources is not stable – it is affected by temperature and
lamp life. Typically, the correlated colour temperature reduces by 1 K for each hour or life,
and, in addition, the colour of the light shifts along the green/magenta colour axis. Consequently, operators should be prepared to apply colour correction when using several HMIs
together. There may be a need to apply correction in the blue–orange direction **and** in the
green–magenta direction, i.e. use ⅛CTO and ⅛CTB filters and ⅛ plus green and ⅛ minus
green filters.

These sources have been designed to match average summer sunlight of 5500 K, but there will be occasions when daylight is not 'average' so be prepared to use ¼CTO or ¼CTB filters to correct these sources. When it looks right, it is!

When operating with daylight sources, typically they need to be within 400 K to look 'matched', i.e. ±400 K.

Operating notes

1 The operating current for these sources is larger than indicated by the lamp wattage, e.g. a 4 kW HMI operates at 21 A, and its starting current is 35 A! However, discharge sources using electronic ballasts have a controlled starting current and, consequently, do not have this characteristic of high initial current.
2 Non-flicker-free HMIs should **not** be used with CCD cameras when a shutter speed of less than 1/50th second is required. This is because the output signal suffers a 'breathing' effect. The shorter the exposure time, the greater is the effect.
3 Generators supplying to a mainly discharge source load should be under-rated by a factor of 0.7 to take account of the effect of the ballast chokes, i.e. a 100 KVA generator should be rated as 70 KVA. Recent developments have produced a unity power factor ballast which, when used, removes the need to down-rate generators.
4 Use flicker-free HMI/MSRs when shooting at a different field rate to mains frequency, e.g. shooting NTSC 60 Hz in a 50 Hz mains frequency environment.

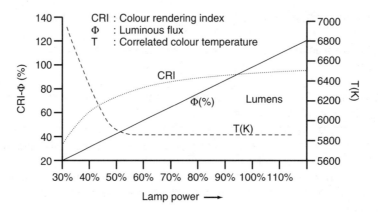

Figure 8.6 Characteristics of dimming HMI/MSR sources

8.5 Discharge sources – xenon

Xenon (100 W–10 kW)

Xenon produces an excellent 'white light', with a colour rendition index (R_a) of 98, which is **very** stable. It is known as the 'Queen of Lights'. This compact light source is ideal:

(a) For long throw applications (the light can be collected easily), e.g.

- Film projection in cinemas
- Follow spot applications (Super-Trouper)
- Narrow-beam 'searchlight' type application (Space Cannons).

(b) As an intense light beam in a xenon torch for lighting effects.

It should be noted that the xenon lamp, even when **cold**, has an internal gas pressure **greater** than atmospheric pressure, and it is likely to **explode** if disturbed mechanically. Special safety precautions should be taken when handling xenon lamps, i.e. face mask, gauntlets (to protect wrists) and body protection.

Xenon lamps have the following characteristics:

- Lamp efficacy can be as high as 50 lumens/watt
- Very good colour rendition (R_a 98)
- Very stable colour, with life and with operating temperature
- Correlated colour temperature 6000 K
- Very compact source
- Operates on DC voltage
- Liable to explode
- Output has a UV content (6% of input power)
- Can be dimmed electronically
- Long life.

ESL (enhanced spectrum long arc) lamps

The Xenon based linear/circular lamp is a relatively new light source. It has an excellent colour rendition, with an R_a of 96, luminous efficacy of 50 lumens/watt and a colour temperature of 5400 K. The colour of the light is very stable, with no change during life, and it is easy to match with other ESL sources. The light may be dimmed to 5% output with very little colour change (100 K).

The Alternating Current ESL Lamp is available from 3.3 kW to 100 kW! It requires no warm-up, and re-strike is available after one minute. Unlike Xenon lamps, the ESL lamp does not have an explosion hazard. It is silent in operation and available as flicker-free or non-flicker-free. Dimmer control is by DMX.

These sources are used in Soft Sun systems providing units, which give a softlight than readily matches with sunlight. ESL Direct Current lamps are available from 400 W to 15 kW.

8.6 Discharge sources – CDM

CDM source (35–250 W) (ceramic discharge metal halide lamp)

This is a relatively new high-intensity discharge light source which uses the PCA (Polycrystalline alumina) discharge tube technology developed for high-pressure sodium lamps. The discharge takes place within a ceramic tube, inside a quartz envelope.

CDM lamps have the following characteristic (see Figure 8.7):

- Very good colour rendering, R_a 85–95
- Stable colour during lifetime, unlike conventional metal halide lamps which have a shift towards blue/green (due to migration of the sodium ions through the quartz envelope – this does not happen with a CDM lamp)
- Available in 3000 K or 4200 K correlated temperature
- Lamp efficacy up to 95 lm/W
- 35 W, 70 W, 100 W, 150 W and 250 W lamps are available
- Compact source with a high luminous flux
- Single-ended version may be burnt at any angle
- Ceramic tube acts as a UV block reducing UV output by 60%
- Consistent colour performance between sources
- Electronic dimming of CDM lamps is not recommended because it has an adverse effect on the mechanical construction of the lamp and results in a significant change in R_a with the colour moving towards blue/green.
- Although the CDM source does not have a history of envelope explosion it is still recommended to operate the lamp within an enclosure, i.e. safety glass or lens included. A triple envelope on the CDM-TC lamp means that it may be operated in an open luminaire.
- Lamp life in excess of 12 000 hours!

These sources are becoming very popular in shops, public areas, street lighting and airports as well as being available in Fresnel spotlights, profile spotlights and PAR lights for television.

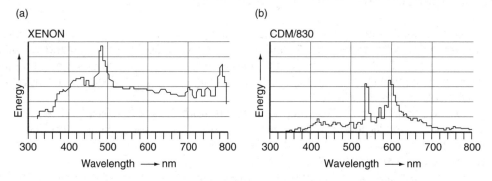

Figure 8.7 Spectral energy distribution. (a) Xenon lamp; (b) CDM lamp

8.7 Discharge sources – fluorescent sources

Fluorescent lights (coldlights) have recently become a viable option in television lighting, with similar efficacies to high-pressure discharge lights, and offer good savings in power requirements, especially in small/medium studios.

The wide range of colour temperatures available makes them particularly attractive when on location or when there is a need for light sources to match in-shot monitors or daylight in studio environments. The merits of the fluorescent lights source are:

1 Good efficacy (three to four times better than tungsten)
2 Consequence of 1 is significant power savings in lighting power and air-conditioning power
3 No radiant heat (tungsten sources have 55% of the electrical power as radiant heat in the light beam), hence the term 'coldlight' for fluorescent sources
4 Large area source – kinder modelling
                 – less glare for artistes (more comfortable)
5 Long life (approximately 10 000 hours)
6 High-frequency operation at greater than 40 kHz, no flicker
7 Dimmable 100–1% with little colour change
8 Choice of colour temperature – 2700 K/3000 K/3200 K/4100 K/5000 K/5500 K.

Safety

- These are low-pressure mercury vapour sources and, as such, do not have the safety hazards of the high-pressure sources. However, care should be taken in dispensing with old or broken tubes to ensure than none of the chemicals inside get into any cuts or damaged skin areas.

Control

- The integrated high-frequency ballast is easily controlled with a 0–10 V analogue signal for dimming purposes.
- The digital data signal (DMX) from modern lighting consoles needs to be converted to 0–10 V. This is done either with an integral DMX demutliplexer or a separate multi-channel DMX demultiplexer.
- Special ballasts are available for direct mains dimming, i.e. thyristor dimmers.
- *Note*: as with all discharge lights, these sources require a few minutes' warm-up time before full light output is achieved.

Colour

- The colour temperature and colour rendition properties of these sources are dictated by the phosphors used for the tube coating. They are indicated by the manufacturer's coding (Table 8.2).
- Colour 830 lamps, with R_a better than 80, at 3000 K have an efficacy of 87.5 lumens/watt. Consequently, these are recommended for all studios, using an 'all' coldlight solution to take advantage of the high light output. If tungsten sources are used for set lighting they should not pose any colour matching problems.
- Colour 930 lamps, with R_a better than 90, at 3000 K have a reduced efficacy of 50–70 lumen/watt (depending on manufacture). These are recommended for 'hybrid' installations where mixing of coldlight and tungsten light is required on faces, i.e. where coldlight is being used for fill-lights and tungsten sources are being used as keylights (Figure 8.8).

Table 8.2 Typical manufacturers coding to indicate R_a and K for fluorescent lamps

Code	Colour rendition index (R_a)	Colour temperature (K)
Colour 830	>80	3000
Colour 930	>90	3000
Colour 950	>90	5000

Notes:
1st digit of code indicates R_a.
2nd/3rd digits indicate first two digits of colour temperature.
Lamps of 2700 K, 3000 K, 3200 K, 4000 K, 5000 K and 6500 K are available.

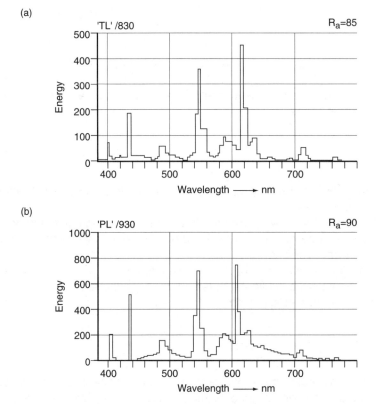

Figure 8.8 Spectral energy distribution for colour 830 and colour 930 lamps

Basic principle of the fluorescent light source (low-pressure mercury vapour)

The fluorescent light source relies on the principle of luminescence, whereby visible light is produced when phosphors are exposed to ultraviolet radiation (Figure 8.9). An electrical discharge is set up in the fluorescent tube, producing mainly harmless long wavelength ultraviolet radiation (60% of the input power), plus a single wavelength of green light (3% of the input

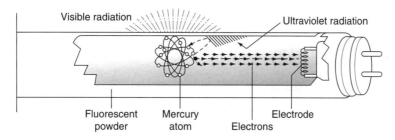

Figure 8.9 Basic principle of the fluorescent light source

power). The ultraviolet radiation (energy) is absorbed by the phosphors and re-radiated at a longer, visible wavelength (40% of the UV energy). Hence the colour of the light (colour temperature) and colour fidelity (R_a) are very much dictated to by the chemical make-up of the phosphors.

Note: The above description shows that the overall efficacy is about 27% (input power $\times$ 60% $\times$ 40% + 3%); this is improved by 10% on light output and a reduction on ballast losses of 10%, when operating at high frequency (40 kHz), i.e. light output is approximately **32%** of input power (compare tungsten at approximately 8%).

Table 8.3 Discharge sources, comparison of features

	Range of wattages	Correlated colour temperature (K)	Lumens/ wattage	R_a	Harmful UV	Liable to explode	Dimmable electronically
CSI	400 W–1000 W	4000 ± 400	80–90	80	✓	✓✓	No
CID	200 W–2500 W	5500 ± 400	70–80	85	✓	✓✓	No
HMI	24 W–18 kW	6000 ± 400	80–96	>90	✓	✓✓	To 50% with electronic ballast
MSR	125 W–12 kW	6000 ± 400	75–95	>90	✓	✓✓	To 50% with electronic ballast
Xenon	75 W–10 kW	6200	15–50	98	✓	✓✓✓	✓
High-frequency fluorescent	11 W–55 W	2700–6500	55–88	>80	No	No	✓
Mastercolour CDM	35 W–150 W	3000–6500	78–93	81–95	✓	✓	No

Notes:
HMI also available as single-ended option – HMI(SE).
HTI and HSR are compact versions. HSR is single-ended version of HTI.
Power rating is the power dissipated in the lamp excluding auxiliary equipment.

9
Luminaires

9.1   Luminaires – general

Over the years many different types of luminaire have been developed to satisfy specific needs of lighting:

- Fresnel spotlights (soft-edged projectors)
- Softlights, including fluorescent lights
- Dual source
- Hard-edged projectors, including follow-spotlights
- Cyclorama top lights
- Ground row
- PAR lights
- Intelligent lights (moving lights)
- Open-faced luminaires.

Luminaires are often referred to as a 'hard' or 'soft' depending on the type of shadow they produce, i.e. hard-edged or soft-edged. **Hard sources** are point sources, i.e. small area sources (Figure 9.1) and:

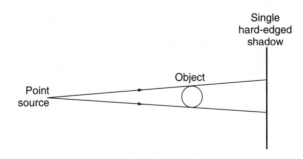

Figure 9.1 Definition of a hard source

- Produce a single hard-edged shadow
- Are usually a point source or of a small area
- Reveal surface texture to a maximum
- Can either be a focused source or an open-faced luminaire
- Have their beam shape controlled with barndoors
- The sun and moon are examples of natural hard sources.

All the light sources discussed earlier, except for fluorescent lights and ESL lights, can be considered as point sources. The tungsten/tungsten halogen source obviously gets larger as the wattage is increased but at the normal lamp throws it is viable to think of it as a hard source. The fluorescent lamp is **not** a point source and never will be. It is an **extended** light source, usually used in groups to obtain a large area and a practical level of illuminance.

Soft sources are effectively large area sources, which can be thought of as many point sources (Figure 9.2).

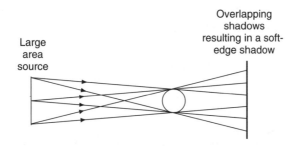

Figure 9.2 Definition of a soft source

- They produce multiple overlapping shadows which result in a soft-edged shadow
- They need to be of a large area to be truly soft
- They tend to destroy texture
- They produce light which cannot be controlled as easily as a hard source, it usually goes everywhere!
- A soft source can be created by **bouncing** a hard source off a suitable large area reflector
- A completely overcast sky is an example of a very good source producing almost shadowless lighting.

Fundamentally, it is the angle that the light source subtends at the subject, which determines whether it will behave as a hard or soft source, i.e. it is a function of area of light source and luminaire throw (Figure 9.3).

Note that when an object is very close to a background, a soft source will result in a harder shadow (Figure 9.4).

9.2 The Fresnel spotlight or soft-edged spotlight

This spotlight takes its name from the Fresnel lens used in its construction and the soft-edged nature of the disc of light it projects. It is a good modelling light and may be used as

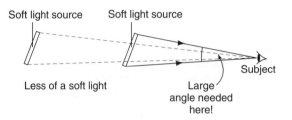

Figure 9.3 Requirements of a soft source

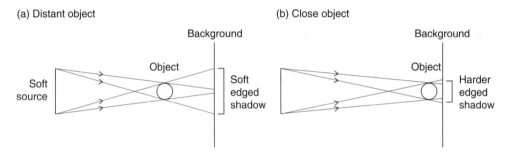

Figure 9.4 Harder shadow from a soft source when subject is near a wall

a keylight, backlight, set-light or whenever a hard fill-light is required. It is generally recognised as the main 'work-horse' luminaire, being a general-purpose variable beam angle luminaire, with a wide range of operating wattages, i.e. tungsten light sources – 100 W; 150 W; 300 W; 500 W; 650 W; 1.0 kW; 1.2 kW; 2 kW; 5 kW; 10 kW; 20 kW and 24 kW. There are also twin-filament versions giving $1^1/_4 /2^1/_2 /3^3/_4$ kW, $1^1/_4 /2^1/_2$ kW and $2^1/_2 /5$ kW. Fresnel spotlights are also available from 200 W to 18 kW with HMI/MSR sources. The construction of the Fresnel spotlight is illustrated in Figure 9.5.

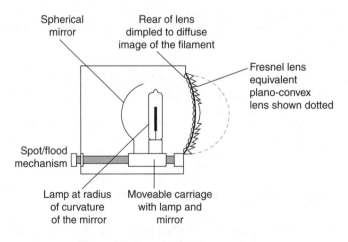

Figure 9.5 Fresnel spotlight construction

Use of the Fresnel lens (cut away lens) results in:

(a) A thin lens compared to a plano-convex lens
(b) Less weight than a plano-convex lens
(c) A lens which is less likely to crack than a plano-convex lens.

The reflector/lamp assembly can be moved to alter the beam angle from wide angle (full flood) to narrow angle (full spot). When fully flooded it behaves like a point source producing hard-edged shadows. When spotted, the lens acts as a magnifying glass so that the light source appears larger, i.e. a softer source (Figure 9.6).

All Fresnel spotlights should be fitted with **barndoors** which are essential in controlling the beam shape. They should be captive, i.e. not fall out easily, and rotate freely, even when hot!

Normally the Fresnel spotlight is used in the full flood mode, producing:

● Uniform illuminance over a wide beam angle
● The 'hardest' condition of light source, i.e. small source area
● Best condition for luminaire efficiency, 32% of the light leaves the luminaire
● Most effective barndooring (effective light source is small), with the barndoor edge producing the sharpest shadow when furthest from the lens.

Generally the spot/flood mechanism will be used when requiring more illuminance. The ratio of on-axis illuminance will change by about a factor of 6–8 depending on the particular unit, with the beam angle changing by a similar factor, i.e. 6–8. This may seem correct, but

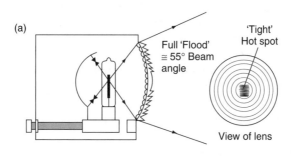

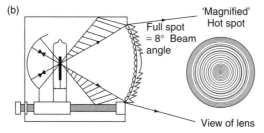

Figure 9.6 (a) Fresnel spotlight in full flood mode, lamp close to lens, approximately 32% efficient at collecting and projecting the lamp light; (b) Fresnel spotlight in full spot mode, lamp furthest from lens, approximately 8% efficient at collecting and projecting the lamp light

it should be remembered that the beam angle is not a single-dimension change but a two-dimensional change and if all things were equal the change should be about 57:1 (the difference in area covered by 56° and 8° beams)! In practice, when the Fresnel spotlight is spotted, when the lamp and reflector move away from the lens, a large proportion of the beam is no longer 'collected' by the lens (see Figure 9.6, shown shaded).

Note that:

- The barndoors cease to operate when they 'touch' the hot spot. The barndoors change from a beam-shaping role to one of dimming when this condition is reached. Consequently, when in the spot mode, apart from controlling light scatter from the lens, there is very little beam control with the barndoors.
- The luminaire efficiency is only 8% when in the spot mode! The Fresnel spotlight should always be used in the flood mode when requiring maximum light output for 'bounce' applications (see Section 9.7 Softlights – bounce).
- The fully spotted Fresnel spotlight is often used to create a more natural-looking 'spot' of light with no hard edges of barndoors showing.
- Anything placed close to the Fresnel lens will not create a hard shadow, as an object is moved away from the lens so the shadow created will become harder.

9.3   Luminaire performance

Manufacturers usually publish data which gives the illuminance and width of coverage at various distances from the luminaire. While these are useful in determining performance, reference to the beam angle and the effective luminous intensity in candelas (candlepower) is all that is needed to work out the illuminance and coverage at any distance. The beam angle is the angle between the 'half intensity' points (Figure 9.7). This is an angle which can be measured easily, but it does of course indicate where the light has dropped to 50%. In order to get a more useful figure which gives uniform coverage, the beam angle should be reduced by 10°, e.g. typical beam angle for a Fresnel spotlight is 55°, so useful beam width would be 45°.

The inverse square law can be used to estimate the illuminance:

$$\text{Illuminance} = \frac{\text{Candlepower (candelas)}}{(\text{distance})^2} \text{ lux}$$

(Distance is expressed in metres. If distance is expressed in feet, the illuminance will be in foot-candles.)

Taking a 2 kW Fresnel spotlight, with a candlepower of 30 000 candelas, the illuminance at 5 metres would be:

$$\text{Illuminance} = \frac{30\,000}{5 \times 5} = 1200 \text{ lux}$$

This is the illuminance at full mains voltage, at fader 7 it would be 50%, i.e. 600 lux.

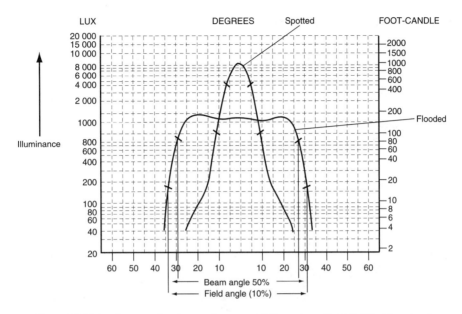

Figure 9.7 Polar diagram showing performance of Fresnel spotlight (1 kW at 3 metres)

Manufacturers publish data based on a new clean luminaire, a new lamp and full mains voltage. To take account of lamp ageing, tarnished optics and possible reduced mains it is recommended to reduce manufacturers' data by approximately 15–20%.

Manufacturers will also quote a field angle, the angle between the points where the illuminance has dropped to 10% of centre beam value. The field angle is useful in indicating how quickly the light is falling off at the beam edge. Typically the field angle is about 10° more than the beam angle for a Fresnel spotlight.

The performance will be affected by the lens diameter and the beam angle. Clearly if the light is spread over a larger area it will result in a lower luminance. These are factors to be taken into account when comparing different manufacturers' data (Table 9.1).

9.4   Control of beam shape

Control of light is a major part of lighting, and much that happens in a television production is not within the control of the Lighting Director, but basic control of light intensity and beam shape is paramount.

Generally, Fresnel spotlights are used in the full-flood mode to provide uniform coverage over a wide area, and the basic beam shape can be modified from a circular beam to a rectangular beam using the barndoors. Barndoors are normally fitted as a pair of short and a pair of long doors; the smaller doors when tucked inside the larger doors give 'tighter' control (Figure 9.8). So, for example, when lighting a seated subject, keeping the light off the background is best achieved by:

- Rotating barndoors to give small doors top and bottom.
- Setting the luminaire on the artiste position.

Table 9.1 Typical Fresnel spotlight performance

Wattage	Lens diameter mm	Candlepower (flood) (cd)	Flood beam angle	Spot beam angle	Candlepower (spot) (cd)	Weight (kg)
Tungsten						
300 W	120	3 000	57°	8°	27 000	2.7
500 W	120	6 000	57°	8°	42 000	2.7
650 W	120	11 000	57°	8°	75 000	2.7
1 kW	150	12 000	55°	7.5°	120 000	7
2 kW	250	36 000	54.5°	8.8°	360 000	13.4
Bambino 2 kW	150	29 000	49°	10°	160 000	8
5 kW	300	100 000	56°	5.6°	730 000	21
Bambino 5 kW	250	150 000	34°	13°	430 000	15
10 kW	500	160 000	50°	10°	990 000	48
12 kW	500	170 000	50°	10°	1 000 000	48
20 kW	625	360 000	51°	13°	2 200 000	63
24 kW	625	421 000	51°	13°	2 490 000	63
Discharge (MSR)						
200 W	120	10 000	48°	6°	100 000	2.9
575 W	150	50 000	47°	5.8°	400 000	7.1
1200 W	250	85 000	51°	6.5°	1 000 000	14.0
2.5 kW	300	115 000	58°	8°	1 700 000	22.8
4 kW	300	170 000	58°	8°	2 000 000	22.8
6 kW	500	275 000	64°	6°	4 300 000	50
12 kW	500	365 000	64°	6°	5 800 000	50

- Adjusting the top barndoor until it is just above the **hot spot** of the luminaire.
- Box side doors to the small doors to avoid unwanted spill.

If, however, there is a requirement to have a broad coverage horizontally, the barndoors will have to be used with large doors top and bottom. If the side doors are not needed, one can simply adjust the top door as before, i.e. until it is just 'sitting' on top of the hot spot. However, if the side doors need to be tucked inside the large doors (to control sideways spill) there could be a problem keeping the light off the background. Tipping down the luminaire is not recommended because the beam centre is no longer set on the centre of interest. Control can be achieved by using:

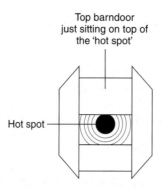

Top barndoor
just sitting on top of
the 'hot spot'

Hot spot

Figure 9.8 Barndoored Fresnel spotlight

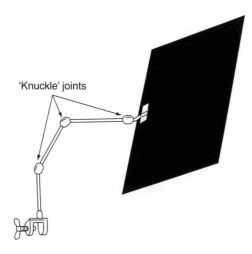

'Knuckle' joints

Figure 9.9 French flag (250 mm × 400 mm)

- A French flag – this is effectively an extra barndoor on the end of a 'knuckle-jointed' arm, which can be clamped to the luminaire (Figure 9.9).
- A black wrap – a matt black tin foil, which can be fastened with crocodile clips to the top barndoor, and shaped to provide the appropriate barndooring action (Figure 9.10).

Note that barndoors have a limitation on their effectiveness, namely that when they are closed in to the point where they cut across the 'hot spot', their action becomes one of dimming! Hence the barndoors have little effect on a full-spotted Fresnel spotlight except to control the light scattered by the lens.

The large barndoors should ideally be large enough to cover the complete light beam. If this is not the case, **black wrap** can again be used to prevent 'pig's ears' (Figure 9.11). Where 'sharper' or 'crisper' control of the beam shape is required this can be achieved with

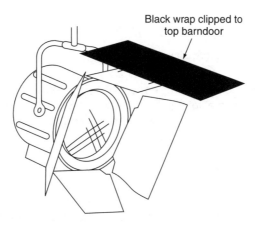

Black wrap clipped to
top barndoor

Figure 9.10 Use of black wrap

Figure 9.11 'Pig's ears' caused by barndoors which are too small

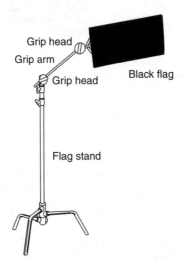

Figure 9.12 Flag stand and black flag

a **black flag**, a four-sided wire frame with a black serge covering. It is rigged in front of the luminaire on flag-arms to give flexible positioning (Figure 9.12).

The further the flag is from the luminaire, the 'harder' is the shadow created. Flags are usually rectangular in shape (4:3). When they are long and narrow they are called **cutters**.

9.5   Control of light intensity on location

The use of dimmers on location is an added complication to any set-up. However, they provide flexibility in achieving a lighting balance very rapidly provided, of course, the colour temperature variations are not excessive (see p. 139 on the use of dimmers). Alternatives to using a dimmer are:

- Use of inverse square law – moving luminaire position to be closer or further away as necessary
- Use of spot/flood on the luminaire – usually luminaires are used in their full-flood condition; an increase in illuminance can be made by 'spotting' but, of course, the beam angle is reduced

- Use of neutral density filters – these can be used to reduce light by $\frac{1}{2}$ stop, 1 stop, 2 stops, 3 stops or 4 stops (see later section on ND filters, Chapter 6)
- Use of wire scrims – discussed below
- Use of veils, nets or yashmaks – discussed below.

A wire **scrim**, fitted between the Fresnel lens and the barndoors (Figure 9.13) can be used to reduce the light intensity, with no change in colour temperature. Scrims are available as:

Full single with a transmission of 70% ($\frac{1}{2}$ stop loss) (green)
Full double with a transmission of 50% (1 stop loss) (red)
Half single with a transmission of 70% ($\frac{1}{2}$ stop loss) (green)
Half double with a transmission of 50% (1 stop loss) (red)

Full-scrims are useful for simply reducing the overall level. Half-scrims are useful for providing a reduction in lighting level for one half of the light beam (see later section on Interview lighting), for equalising illuminance when the artiste walks towards the luminaire (see later section on Artiste movement), or to equalise the illuminance on backgrounds.

Often it is necessary to have more precise control than that offered by a half-scrim. This can be achieved using a **veil**, **net** or **yashmak**, an open-ended wire frame fitted with black nets to give light loss of $\frac{1}{2}$ stop, 1 stop and $1\frac{1}{2}$ stops. Veils are available in a wide range of sizes to accommodate the beam angles of most Fresnel spotlights (Figure 9.14).

Veils are rigged on flag-arms similar to black flags. Like flags, they can be set a little in front of the luminaire to give precise control of the area to be reduced in intensity, e.g. reducing the illuminance on the down-stage area of a demonstration area, i.e. the front of a demonstration desk, when the keylight is used to light the artiste behind the desk as well as the desk front.

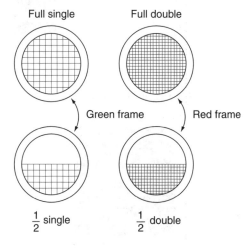

Figure 9.13 Scrim set

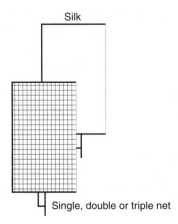

Figure 9.14 Veil, net or yashmak, and silk

Finger and dot kits provide the facility to modify a light beam in a localised way. Usually a kit has a range of dots from 3 inches diameter to 10 inches diameter and 2-inch × 12-inch fingers to 4-inch × 14-inch fingers, and fitted with nets, silks and black serge (Figure 9.15).

Cookie or **cucoloris** is the name given to a dapple plate placed in front of a Fresnel spotlight to provide 'break-up' of the light beam. Again, the further it is placed from the luminaire, the harder is the resulting shadow. Cookies are rigged on flag-arms similar to flags (Figure 9.16).

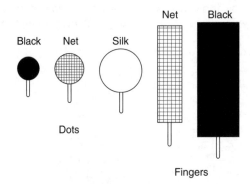

Figure 9.15 Fingers and dots

Figure 9.16 Cookie or cucoloris

9.6 Softlights – general principles

Softlights may be produced by:

(a) 'bouncing' **linear** lamps (strip lamps), tungsten halogen/HMI/MSR off a suitable reflector. The reflector may be matt white or dimpled polished metal (Figure 9.17(a))
(b) 'bouncing' a hard source off a suitable matt white reflector, e.g. polystyrene board (Figure 9.17(b))
(c) punching a hard source through diffusion material to create a second light source of large area (Figure 9.17(c))
(d) creating the effect of a large 'gas mantle' by diffusing several **linear** sources through a silk skirt (Figure 9.17(d))
(e) grouping together a number of light sources to produce a large area, e.g. fluorescent lights (Figure 9.17(e)).

Often, soft luminaires are grouped together to maintain a large effective area. A good soft source is one which:

(a) looks evenly bright over the complete area of the source
(b) does not change its effective area when some of the sources are switched off, to reduce light output without a change in colour temperature (rather than dimming excessively, resulting in a significant change in colour temperature)
(c) includes an egg-crate (louvre system) or honeycomb screen to give some degree of control of the sideways spill of light (Figure 9.27 on p. 105).

Note that barndoors have a limited effected on soft-sources (Figure 9.29 on p. 106).
Some manufacturers use the term 'Broad' source to indicate that it has a wide spread of light. Generally these are small area sources and produce hard-edged shadows.

Softlights are usually used:

(a) to provide the 'fill-light' to control the density of shadows
(b) as keylights where a softlight is appropriate
(c) to light audiences
(d) to provide a shadowless backlight when required.

The techniques which have evolved for deriving suitable softlight are often very ingenious, as is the application of the sources in providing the filler which does not intrude by:

● creating a second shadow – use of a large enough **area** source
● overlighting the foreground – use of egg-crate/honeycomb control screen plus **flag** or **veil**
● washing out the background – use of egg-crate/honeycomb plus **cutter**.

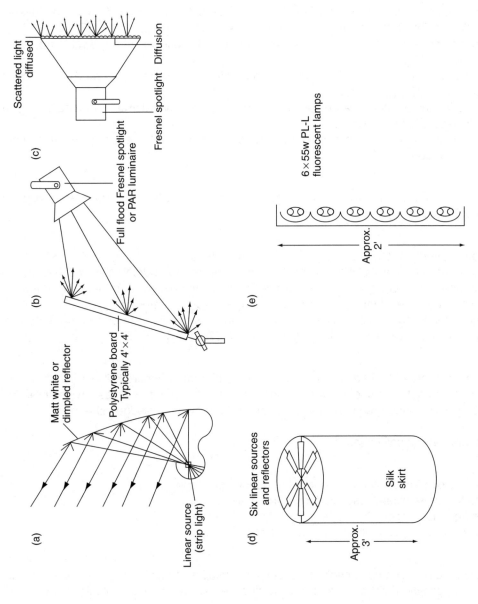

Figure 9.17 Methods of devising a softlight. (a) Linear source 'bounced' off a reflector; (b) use of a reflector board; (c) use of diffusion; (d) spacelight; (e) use of fluorescent lamps

(a)

Matt white or
dimpled reflector

Polystyrene board
Typically 4'×4'

Linear source
(strip light)

(b)

Full flood Fresnel spotlight
or PAR luminaire

(c)

Scattered light
diffused

Fresnel spotlight   Diffusion

(d)   Six linear sources
and reflectors

Approx.
3'

Silk
skirt

(e)

6×55w PL-L
fluorescent lamps

Approx.
2'

Soft sources and the inverse square law

The inverse square law is only strictly true for point sources. However, when considering soft sources this can still be used to estimate the illuminance. For large area sources the illuminance follows an inverse law up to the distances comparable with the size of the source. Thereafter it becomes an inverse square law. When making calculations at three times the largest dimension of the light source, the 'error' in using the inverse square law is 10%, at five times the distance it is approximately 2%.

9.7   Softlights – bounce

This is a very convenient way to derive a softlight from a point source:

1   By using a 4′ × 4′ or 4′ × 8′ white polystyrene reflector with a 'bounced' Fresnel spotlight, a large area softlight is created (Figure 9.18). Note that when using 'bounce' techniques:

   ● The effective candlepower is reduced to about one **fifth** of the original candlepower
   ● A Fresnel spotlight should **always** be used in its **full-flood** condition when 'bounced'. Recall the efficiency of this spotlight; about 32% of the generated light leaves the luminaire in the full flood mode but only 8% in the full spot mode!
   ● The need to control where the light goes using suitable size of 'flags' and 'cutters'
   ● Often PAR cans are used as bounce-lights because of their better efficiency, i.e. less power needed to achieve a particular lighting level
   ● The reflected light will be completely 'scattered' – no direct light (compare with use of diffusion).

2   By using a suitable polished reflector, i.e. one which has some form of dimple-type reflector. The nature of the reflection will be as though from many 'point' sources – one definition of a soft source. Many different textures of reflector are available which give different reflection directivity patterns to that of polystyrene (Figure 9.19).

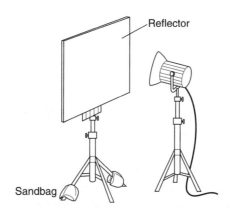

Figure 9.18 Reflector principle

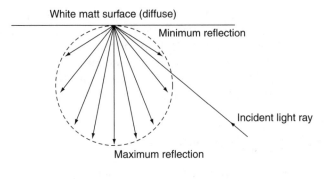

(a) Reflector characteristics – diffuse surface

White matt surface (diffuse)

Minimum reflection

Incident light ray

Maximum reflection

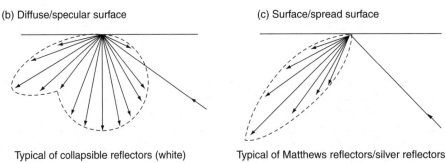

(b) Diffuse/specular surface

(c) Surface/spread surface

Typical of collapsible reflectors (white)

Typical of Matthews reflectors/silver reflectors

Figure 9.19 Reflector characteristics. (a) White matt diffuse surface; (b) diffuse/specular surface; (c) specular/spread surface

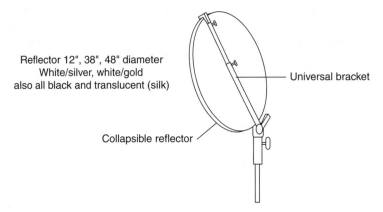

Reflector 12", 38", 48" diameter
White/silver, white/gold
also all black and translucent (silk)

Universal bracket

Collapsible reflector

Figure 9.20 Collapsible reflector

The collapsible reflector is an extremely useful and versatile form of reflector (Figure 9.20). Used with a universal bracket it enables a soft source to be created quickly from any point source or simply as a reflector – hard or soft. The reflector has two sides, one matt and one silver (or gold for a warmer reflected light).

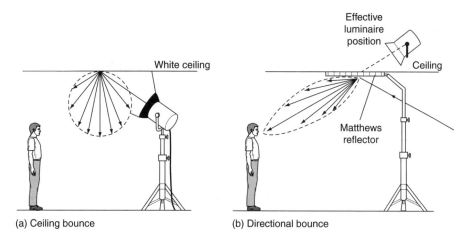

(a) Ceiling bounce   (b) Directional bounce

Figure 9.21 (a) Ceiling bounce; (b) directional bounce

Metallic-type reflectors will provide directional soft light and will be more efficient than a diffuse white reflector (more scatter of light). Consequently, they can be used at greater distances from the subject. Care needs to be taken in positioning the 'bounce' source to ensure that it does not obscure the reflected light.

One of the most common use of 'bounce' lighting is that of bouncing light sources off a white ceiling to raise the general lighting level. Use can be made of this technique to derive a soft keylight by choosing an appropriate part of the ceiling (Figure 9.21). This can be a useful technique, using a Matthews reflector material, to derive a directional soft keylight in rooms with low ceilings.

9.8   Use of diffusion

The use of diffusion clipped to the extreme edges of the barndoors on a Fresnel spotlight is a quick way of deriving a softlight. A quick browse through the filter swatch book will reveal many different varieties of diffusion, so which should we use? Diffusers fall into five categories:

- Spun
- White diffusion
- Frost
- Silks
- Silent diffusion.

Taking white diffusion, as an example, this is available as:

	WHITE DIFFUSION	$\frac{1}{4}$ WHITE DIFFUSION
$\frac{3}{4}$	WHITE DIFFUSION	$\frac{1}{8}$ WHITE DIFFUSION
$\frac{1}{2}$	WHITE DIFFUSION	$\frac{1}{16}$ WHITE DIFFUSION
$\frac{3}{8}$	WHITE DIFFUSION	

Each filter will provide a different degree of diffusion or scattering of the light, i.e. there will be reflection, absorption, direct transmission and diffuse transmission according to the properties of the filter.

The action of a diffuser on a light source is to create a 'new' light source – the diffuser. How well it does this depends on the nature of the diffuser. Figure 9.22 illustrates the principle.

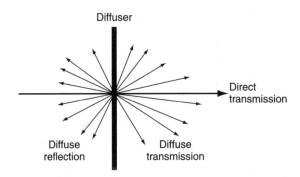

Figure 9.22 The action of a diffuser on a single light ray

A useful compromise is that of **half white diffusion**. This has a transmission of about 50% and provides a good level of diffusion. White diffusion has a transmission of less than 30%, but provides more diffusion.

To check which diffusion to use it is useful to set up a test using a luminaire on a stand as the test object, positioned about 0.15 m (6 inches) from a wall. Observe the quality of shadow achieved for the luminaire head, the cable and the lamp stand when the test object is illuminated with a Fresnel spotlight, plus the various diffusion media. This simple test will reveal quickly the amount of direct/diffuse transmission.

Whatever you decide to do with diffusion, remember that the **area** of diffusion filter used determines the maximum **softness** possible from a given luminaire position. Consequently, avoid 'strangling' diffused sources, i.e. not using maximum possible area of diffusion (Figure 9.23, page 103). Reducing the area of diffuser 'seen' will dim the source and result in it becoming a harder light source.

Where space is at a premium (small studio or small location), the space required for a large diffuser can be reduced by using a double diffusion technique (Figure 9.24, page 103).

Remember that the Fresnel spotlight is **most efficient in the flood mode**. If used with diffusion the light output from the diffuser is **reduced** when the light is spotted (Figure 9.25, page 104).

Often diffusion or silks are used on windows, and lit from behind to provide lighting for an interior. The difference achieved when using the diffuser/silk separated from the window as in Figure 9.26 (page 104) is worth noting, i.e. on the window the light spreads everywhere, clear of the window it is in the form of a soft-edged beam.

- **Spun** has the appearance of glass fibre. However, it is perfectly safe to use, is silent (no rustling noises) and is flame retardant.
- **Frosts** and diffusion are flame retardant and produce similar results except that some of the frosts are very subtle in their effects. For example:

(a) Diffusion clipped to 'boxed' doors

(b) Diffusion clipped to wide open barndoors

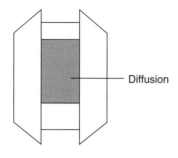

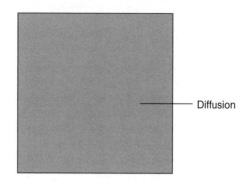

Figure 9.23 (a) 'Strangled' diffuse source; (b) using maximum possible area

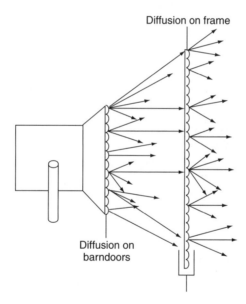

Figure 9.24 Double-diffusion technique

Hamburg Frost will soften the beam edge with little additional spread of the beam. **Tough Silk** (a plastic filter) has a textured surface and spreads the light at right angles to the 'line' structure.

- **Silks** are usually mounted on frames, not as flame retardant as Spun and Frosts, but silent.
- **Silent** diffusion or **Soft Frosts** are usually put on frames and should not be used directly on luminaires. They are silent, but not as flame retardant as Spun/Frosts.

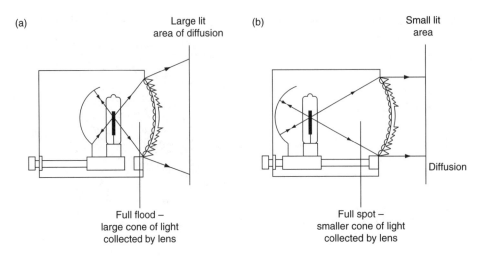

Figure 9.25 Flood/spot efficiency for a Fresnel spotlight. (a) Full flood – large cone of light collected by lens; (b) full spot – smaller cone of light collected by lens

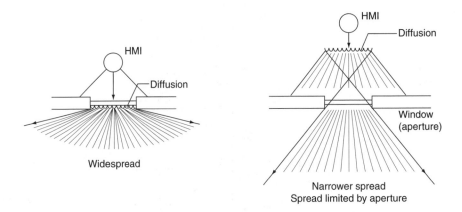

Figure 9.26 Beam spread with diffusion placement, at a window

Diffusion-related factors are:

- Noise factor – is the filter likely to cause noise problems in a windy environment, i.e. on location?
- Evenness of diffusion – some of the light 'spun' type of diffusers may give rise to a pattern of directly transmitted light. If this is a problem, consider using a double layer. This should help to even out the transmission as well as improving the diffusion.
- Space needed behind diffuser, whereas use of reflector required space in front of it. Depending on the nature of the shoot one of the two techniques may have an advantage.
- A projection screen material by Rosco, 'Light Transparent Screen', is particularly useful as a diffusion material with an element of directivity, i.e. less sideways spread of the light.

9.9 Softlights in practice

Conventional softlight

To be a good source of softlight a luminaire should be of a large area. This means that such a source will be bulky and to some extent impractical, especially when transporting these sources to location shoots. Hence the use of several softlights grouped together to produce a better 'softlight'.

Figure 9.27 illustrates a typical softlight complete with egg-crate or louvre to reduce sideways light spill from the unit. Usually these units have some form of lamp switching to half power, i.e. $2\frac{1}{2}$ to $1\frac{1}{4}$ kW or $1\frac{1}{4}$ kW to 625 W. This is to help achieve the correct intensity at the right colour temperature.

(a)

(b)

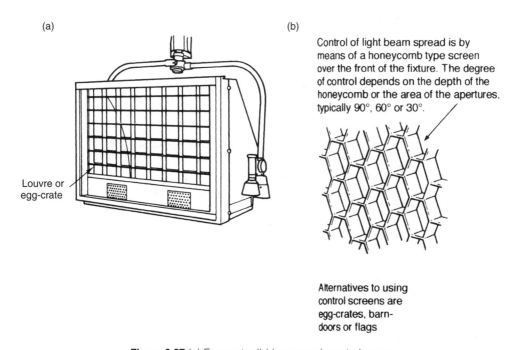

Control of light beam spread is by means of a honeycomb type screen over the front of the fixture. The degree of control depends on the depth of the honeycomb or the area of the apertures, typically 90°, 60° or 30°.

Louvre or egg-crate

Alternatives to using control screens are egg-crates, barn-doors or flags

Figure 9.27 (a) Egg-crate; (b) honeycomb control screen

The performance of a softlight can be shown in a similar way to the Fresnel spotlight (Figure 9.28). Note the following features:

- The beam angle is much larger than the Fresnel spotlight.
- Horizontal beam angle and vertical beam angle are different.
- Beam angle to field angle is much greater than the Fresnel spotlight. This is because the beam has a very soft edge, thus allowing several units to overlap easily when lighting a large set (see later note on cyclorama lighting, page 120).

The use of softlight as keylights as well as fill-lights is now part of recognised practice. The major problem is controlling the beam shape from such a large area source. Any flags

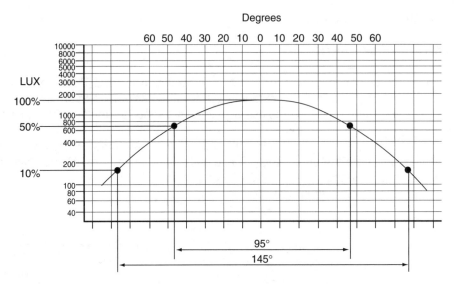

Figure 9.28 Polar diagram for a softlight

or barndoors must be comparable in size, or larger, than the luminaire if any degree of control is to be achieved.

A **fundamental** difference in controlling softlight to hardlight is shown in Figure 9.29. Basically **all** of the light source must be seen by the artiste for him to be lit fully. Any flag or barndoor, which masks part of the light source, as seen from the artiste's position, will

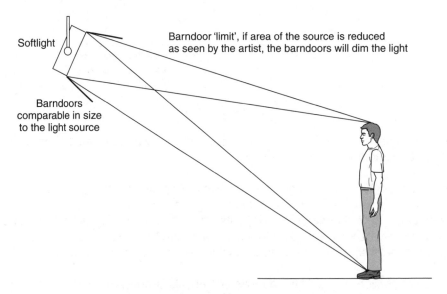

Figure 9.29 The limit for barndooring a softlight

result in a **reduction** in illuminance on the subject. Barndoors tend to be used to reduce sideways spill.

A better method for controlling the beam shape from a softlight is to use a form of honeycomb type screen (Figure 9.27). This can give very effective control with the degree of control depending on the depth of the honeycomb or the area of the apertures in the honeycomb, typically 90°, 60° or 30°.

Additional control of beam shape can be achieved by using a cutter as illustrated in Figure 9.30(a). Note how veils must be used so they do not obscure the light beam to the main subject (Figure 9.30(b)), unlike $^1/_2$ wires/scrims with Fresnel spotlights.

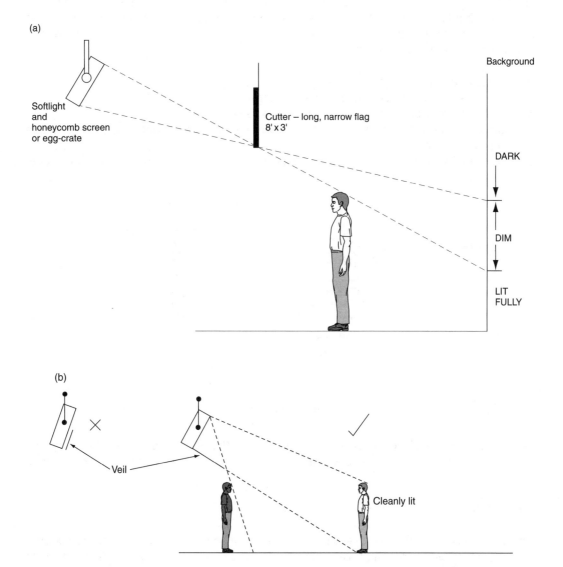

Figure 9.30 (a) The use of a cutter to keep light off the background; (b) use of a veil with coldlight/soft source to reduce foreground lighting

9.10   Softlights – specials

There are a number of special softlights/attachments, which have been especially developed for use in film/television lighting.

Chimera

This is a very popular diffuser which is basically a collapsible **snoot** that can be fitted to almost any light source using an appropriate speed-ring; the speed-ring is mounted on the luminaire after first removing the barndoors (Figure 9.31). The front of the chimera is made of diffusion material, and the inside of the 'snoot' has a metal-based reflective coating. The major benefits in using the chimera are:

- Simple and quick to use
- Collapses into an easily transportable package
- Enables large area softlight to be achieved easily
- Little or no spill light emitted from the rear of the chimera, unlike when using simple diffusion on a frame
- Collapsible egg-crate also available, which can be velcroed on the front of the 'snoot'.

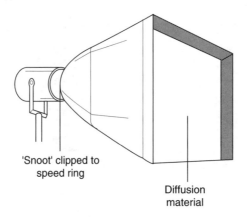

'Snoot' clipped to
speed ring

Diffusion
material

Figure 9.31 Chimera

Large chimeras should be used on suitably robust stands to ensure that the luminaire plus chimera does not overbalance. Use sandbags on the base of stands to give extra weight.

Rifa-light

The rifa-light is a very simple collapsible softlight, but it contains its own light source (Figure 9.32). It operates on the umbrella principle to produce a snoot with a diffuser; the light source (1 kW lamp) is suitably protected from coming into contact with the snoot when closed.

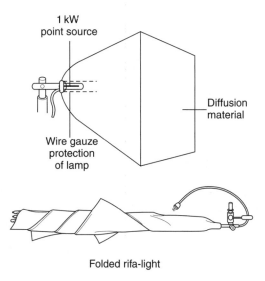

Folded rifa-light

Figure 9.32 Rifa-light

Aurosoft

This is an innovative development, which converts point sources into a softlight (Figure 9.33). Based on the principle that a softlight, i.e. shadowless lighting, can be obtained by using many point sources, the Aurosoft has a special reflector consisting basically of **many** polished hemispheres. Each hemisphere reflects the light source to produce an excellent softsource. This light source is unique in that it can operate with either tungsten sources or discharge sources by changing the light source unit.

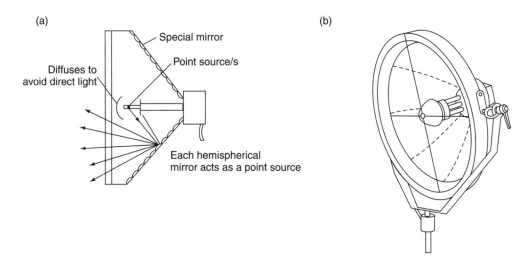

Figure 9.33 Aurosoft spotlight

Two versions exist:

Approx. diameter 0.7m $\begin{cases} \text{1kW/2kW/3kWtungsten} \\ \text{575W/1200W HMI/MSR} \end{cases}$

Approx. diameter 1.0 m $\begin{cases} \text{2 kW/4 kW tungsten} \\ \text{1.2 kW/2.5 kW HMI/MSR} \end{cases}$

The deep egg-crate has an asymmetric construction, so by rotating the egg-crate the sideways spread/upstage spread can be varied.

Spacelight

This is yet another way of deriving a softlight, this time using linear sources to illuminate a large silk 'skirt'. Figure 9.34 illustrates the principle. The bottom of the spacelight may be left open or fitted with suitable diffusion. An additional black 'skirt' on the outside of the white skirt may be lowered to give control to the sideways spread of the light. The spacelight is particularly effective for large sets, when it is used to simulate sky-light or for large chroma key set-ups when shadowless lighting is required.

Space lights are available in many sizes, from the original 6000 W to 12 kW. Table 9.2 shows the typical performance figures. The balloon lights (p. 111) are basically a self-supporting form of space light.

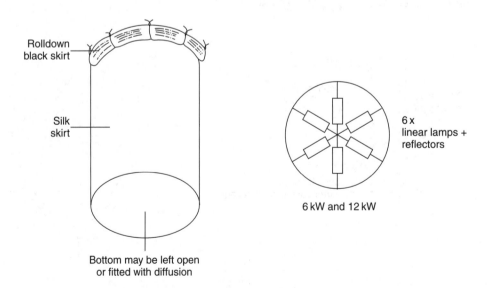

Figure 9.34 Spacelight

Table 9.2 Spacelight, typical performance data

Wattage	Dimensions diam. × height	Weight (kg)	Horizontal illuminance (lux)				Approx candlepower (cd)
			2 m	3 m	6 m	9 m	
12 000	1.1 m × 1 m	25		1550	387	172	14 000
6 000	0.7 m × 0.76 m	15		700	175	75	6 300
2 000	0.42 m × 0.42 m	8.6	820	366	96	60	3 400
1 000	0.34 m × 0.4 m	4.1	250	120	70		1 100

Novelight – folding light

This is a lightweight (6.5 kg) hybrid luminaire, capable of operating as tungsten, HMI or tungsten plus HMI. A solution to the problem of being able to use a really 'soft' light source on location has been achieved with the development of a novel 'folding' softlight. This unit, shown in Figure 9.35 folds up to a 500 mm × 400 mm × 120 mm package, but provides a **controllable** light source of 1000 mm × 1000 m dimensions when open. The front diffuser is lit with 3 × 1000 W linear tungsten sources; with one of the sources fed through an integral dimmer, the unit has variable control, in three steps:

> 0–1000 W
> 1000–2000 W
> 2000–3000 W

Colour temperature correction is achieved using filters fitted just in front of the light sources, i.e. not external to unit. Connection of an external ballast to the unit allows a 400 W HMI to be powered. The HMI source can be dimmed to 200 W or boosted to 500 W. It can be used in isolation or simultaneously with the tungsten sources. Egg-crate accessories are available to give some control of sideways spread. Table 9.3 (page 113) illustrates the performance of the Novelight.

Balloon lights/inflatable lights

Another recent innovation has been the development of Balloon lights and Inflatable lights. These both have application on location and can provide a unique solution to certain lighting problems, e.g. providing an elevated light source where luminaires cannot be suspended or supported on stands.

Balloon lights use a light-source suspended inside a helium-filled balloon. The balloon 'envelope' is made of a white translucent material, which diffuses the light source. They may be fitted with tungsten halogen or discharge sources (HMI/MSR), or a combination of both. In the latter application the ballast units are kept external to the balloon, on the ground. Figure 9.36 (page 113) shows the basic principle and Table 9.4 (page 113) gives an indication of the range of units available and basic photometric data.

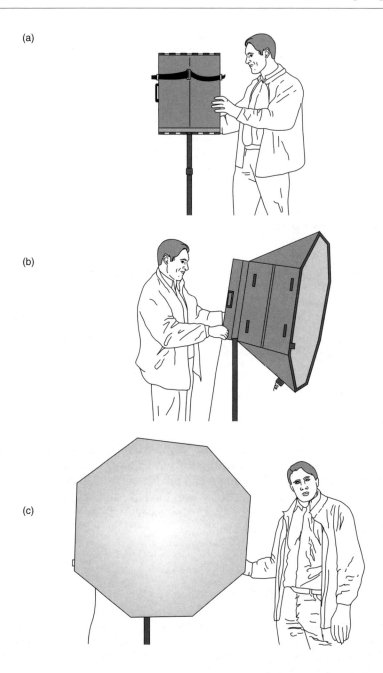

(a)

(b)

(c)

Figure 9.35 Novelight (assembled in less than 1 minute!)

The balloons may be spherical, elliptical or oblong in shape to suite particular applications (i.e. churches – oblong). Internal reflectors may be included to reflect the light as required. Similarly it is possible to use flags to help to control the beam shape. When used externally, balloon lights need to be 'guyed' to stabilise their position on windy occasions.

Table 9.3 Novelight performance

	Illuminance (lux)				
	1 m	2 m	3 m	4 m	5 m
Tungsten at 3000 W	8300	3000	1300	800	565
HMI/MSR 400 W boosted to 500 W	7250	2700	1150	700	490

Note: Max power at 120 V is 2400 W.

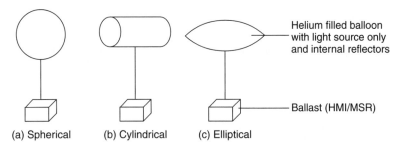

(a) Spherical (b) Cylindrical (c) Elliptical

Helium filled balloon with light source only and internal reflectors

Ballast (HMI/MSR)

Figure 9.36 Basic balloon light principle

Table 9.4 Typical balloon light performance

Name	Shape	Light source	Dimensions	Performance
Lumix 160	Spherical	2 000 W tungsten	1.6 m diam	
Lumix 200	Spherical	4 000 W tungsten	2 m diam	
Lumix 370	Spherical	8 000 W tungsten	3.7 m diam	267 lux @ 7 m (≈13 000 cd)
Lumix 500	Spherical	16 000 W tungsten	5 m diam	
Tube 320	Tubular	4 000 W tungsten	1.6 m diam × 3.2 m	
Tube 400	Tubular	8 000 W tungsten	2 m diam × 4 m	
Tube 700	Tubular	16 000 W tungsten	3.7 m diam × 7 m	
Tube 320	Tubular	2 400 W HMI	1.6 m diam × 3.2 m	
Tube 500	Tubular	4 800 W HMI	2.5 m diam × 5 m	400 lux @ (≈78 000 cd)
Tube 700	Tubular	9 600 W HMI	3.7 m diam × 7 m	
Solarc 500	Elliptical	18 000 W HMI	5.9 m × 4.37 m	165 lux @ 25 m (≈100 000 cd)
Solarc 250/300	Spherical	2 400 W HMI	2.5 m diam/3 m diam	
Solarc 370	Spherical	4 800 W HMI	3.7 m diam	
Solarc 420	Spherical	8 000 W HMI	4.2 diam	
Solarc 500	Spherical	1 600 W HMI	5 m diam	150 lux @ 25 m (≈90 000 cd)
Solarc 700	Spherical	32 000 W HMI	7 × 5.5 m	
Tube 400 HA	Tubular	4 000 W tungsten	1.2 diam × 3.5 m	
Tube 440 HH	Tubular	2 000 W tungsten	1.7 m diam × 4.9 m	880 lux @ 6 m (≈31 000 cd)
Tube 800 HA	Tubular	8 000 W tungsten	1.7 m diam × 4.9 m	
Tube 880 HH	Tubular	4 000 W tungsten 4 800 W HMI	2.5 m diam × 7.2 m	
Tube 2400 HH	Tubular	8 000 W tungsten 16 000 W HMI	4 m diam × 9.5 m	

Some systems allow for up to 35-knot winds (Force 7 – near gale!). The elliptical balloons have the best performance in windy situations.

Balloon lights are particularly useful for lighting the exterior of buildings at night without the need for a 'cherry-picker' or crane. These units have become extremely popular for situations requiring a fast solution to the problem of rigging a light source, literally 'in space'. Typical examples are inside 'protected' buildings where scaffolding cannot be rigged, e.g. courtrooms, stately homes, churches, cathedrals etc., or used very close over large dining tables (inverse square law can be used to ensure that the 'very near' artiste is lit to a much higher level than the background).

Inflatable lights

These are intended to be mounted on a stand, and the 'balloon' is either inflated by mouth or by a small compressor. The result is a soft light source. Figure 9.37 illustrates the principle.

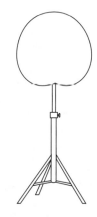

Figure 9.37 Inflatable light

The Tube O' Light and Bag O' Light use an inflatable 'tube' or 'bag' which may be rigged on large HMI/MSR PAR lights and then inflated (Figure 9.38, page 115). Tube O' Lights have been used very successfully with car commercials, avoiding the need for large 'butterflies' to be rigged over a car.

9.11 Open-faced luminaires

Open-faced luminaires were developed to provide an efficient lightweight wide-angle luminaire for location work. They consist simply of a mirror and lamp, no lens. The mirror is shaped to collect as much light as possible and project it forward. The original open-faced luminaires were the 'red-head' at 800 W and the 'blonde' at 2 kW (Figures 9.39 and 9.40, page 115). These luminaires were designed to be used with early colour cameras requiring 1600–2000 lux! Consequently, with modern camera sensitivity, they provide an abundance of light over a wide beam angle. Table 9.5 (page 116) illustrates the

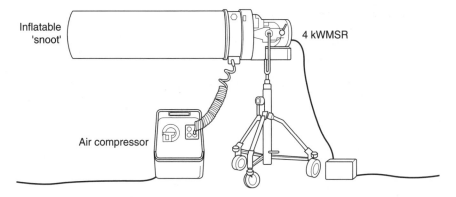

Inflatable 'snoot'

4 kWMSR

Air compressor

Figure 9.38 Tube O' light

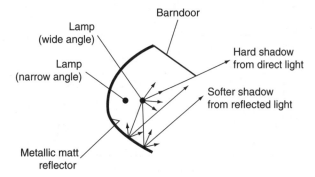

Barndoor

Lamp (wide angle)

Lamp (narrow angle)

Hard shadow from direct light

Softer shadow from reflected light

Metallic matt reflector

Figure 9.39 Basic open-faced luminaire principle

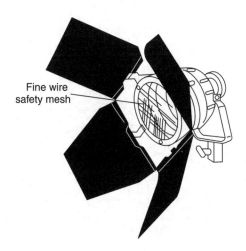

Fine wire safety mesh

Figure 9.40 800 W open-faced luminaire

Table 9.5 Open-faced luminaire performance

Luminaire	Beam (field) angle		Illuminance flood (spot lux)			Weight
	Flood	Spot	3 m	5 m	7 m	
800 W 'Redhead'	86° (132°)	42.5° (70°)	720 (4450)	230 (1490)	120 (690)	1.5 kg
2 kW 'Blonde'	70° (93°)	23° (54°)	3700 (2700)	1080 (7500)	450 (3400)	4 kg

(a)

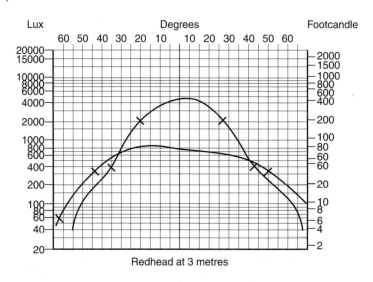

Redhead at 3 metres

(b)

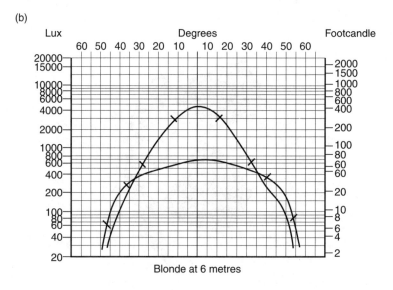

Blonde at 6 metres

Figure 9.41 Performance characteristics for the Redhead and Blonde

relative performance of these two luminaires and Figure 9.41 illustrates the performance characteristics. Many open-faced luminaires have been developed, based on the Redhead and the Blonde. There are several important aspects, which should be recognised when using them:

- **They must never be used without a fine safety mesh or safety glass** over the luminaire face as a safeguard to artistes/property should a lamp explode (and they do!).
- The simple optics results in a double shadow to the barndoors, thus effective barndooring, as with Fresnel spotlights, is not possible. The use of Hamburg Frost or Hampshire Frost over the barndoors is useful in reducing the visibility of one of the barndoor shadows. An alternative would be to use Half White Diffusion on the barndoors, then an appropriate flag to control the beam shape.
- The spot/flood mechanism is more of an intensity control (accompanied by a change in beam angle). Reference to Table 9.5 shows that the Redhead beam angle only halves in 'spot' mode, but intensity changes by a factor of approximately 6.
- Unlike the Fresnel spotlight, the open-faced luminaires become more efficient as the luminaire is 'spotted'. This is useful to remember when using the luminaire to 'bounce' off a suitable reflector or when 'punching' through a diffuser.
- Also, unlike the Fresnel spotlight, the open-faced luminaire in flood mode has a large difference between the beam angle and field angle, especially the Redhead.

To cater for the needs of news coverage, a lightweight compact 300 W luminaire has been developed. This can provide a similar performance to the 800 W Redhead, **but** (Table 9.6) without the very wide beam angle performance.

Table 9.6 Compact kit performance

	Beam angle		Illuminance flood (spot) (lux)			Weight (kg)
	Flood	Spot	2 m	3 m	5 m	
300 W open-faced	46°	30°	1250 (3750)	560 (1670)	200 (600)	0.8

9.12 Hard-edged projectors

This luminaire is known variously as an effect, profile, ellipsoidal or mirror spotlight, or gobo projector. It uses an ellipsoidal shaped mirror, which provides very efficient collection of the light (Figure 9.42). It has a lens system which can produce a sharply focused disc of light hence its name, or project the shape of a metal profile (gobo). The projector includes metal shutters within it to shape the beam with precision (Figure 9.43, page 119). They may have a single lens system or have twin lens optics. The latter has the advantage of providing a variable beam angle (zoom lens) usually over about a 2:1 ratio, i.e. variable image size, and also provide variable image focus at any image size, unlike the single lens projector with only have one focused size of image from a given position. An invaluable recent development has been the introduction of a rotatable gobo holder, which makes it very easy to correct gobo tilt errors.

Hard-edged projects are used:

(a)   To light artistes in complete isolation – the shaping shutters are more precise than barndoors on a Fresnel spotlight
(b)   Adding interest or effects to background or floors, usually using gobos, in combination or singly

It should be noted that the gobos get very hot, consequently (when changing hot gobos) it is recommended to use appropriate gloves.

Often the best results are obtained with defocused gobo images. However, if there is a need for a really sharp image with no flare, a 'doughnut' made from black wrap can be inserted on the front of the projector. This will dim the light to some extent. An alternative is to use projectors which have condenser optics. There are usually three ranges of zoom lens projectors providing a useful range of:

Wide angle   – 28° to 58°
Medium angle – 15° to 30°
Narrow angle –   7° to 17°

A recently developed single-lens projector offers six beam angles by using six interchangeable snoots (lens tubes), i.e. 5°, 10°, 19°, 26°, 36° and 50°. This projector incorporates a new axially mounted 575 W lamp which has resulted in on light output performance comparable with a 1 kW projector.

Another additional optional feature is the inclusion of a **dichroic** ellipsoidal mirror, which reflects the light but transmitting the heat. This results in a cool beam, hence longer life to any filters used on the luminaire, and a cooler lit area.

Although profile projectors use mainly tungsten halogen sources there is a range of projectors available that use HMI/MSR sources for long throw applications. Follow spotlights are a larger version of these lights, using tungsten HMI/MSR and xenon light sources.

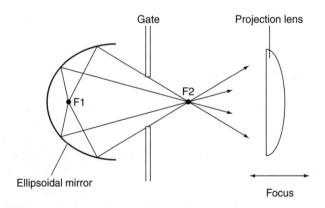

Figure 9.42 Optical principle of the ellipsoidal spotlight

The ellipsoidal projector is based on the optical principle that an ellipse has two focal points. A light source placed at one focal point results in all the reflected light passing

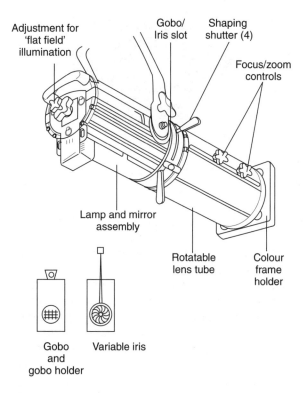

Figure 9.43 600 W profile projector with variable beam (angle 15°–32°)

through the second focal point. The second focal point is arranged to be near the projection lamp, i.e. the ellipsoidal mirror is a very efficient 'collector' of light resulting in typical efficiencies of 60% for these luminaires (Fresnel 32% in flood mode). The **gate**, a circular aperture, is therefore a brightly illuminated disc of light, which can be projected to give a sharply focused circular of light (hence hard-edged projector). A metal cut-out or pattern (gobo) placed in the gate results in projected image of the pattern. Four individually controlled shaping shutters are located near the gate.

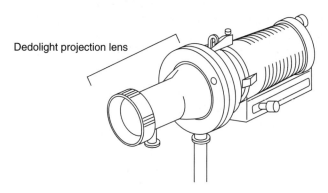

Figure 9.44 Converting a Dedolight to a gobo projector

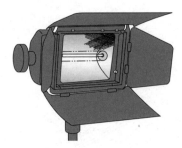

Figure 9.45 Typical 'Broad Source' (100 W/625 W/500 W)

9.13   Broad sources/cyclorama units and ground rows

Often the term 'Broad Source' is used to describe a luminaire which provides a broad light beam. These are usually linear tungsten sources, which are reasonably compact, i.e. they are **not** broad in themselves (Figure 9.45). They can be used to light backgrounds when a broad light source is needed or used with diffusion to create a soft source. Barndoors are usually fitted which give better control in the vertical direction than the horizontal direction when using the linear source horizontal. This is because the horizontal doors are operating on a small light source (lamp filament diameter plus reflection from reflector) giving better control of vertical light spread than the vertical doors operating on a long light source, resulting in less control to the sideways-spreading light.

Where there is a need to light a vertical surface uniformly, a **studio cyclorama light** is ideal. A normal Broad Source used at the top of a large wall area would give rise to shading from top to bottom due to the inverse square law and cosine law (Figure 9.46). Cyclorama lights are an especially designed Broad Source which uses an asymmetric reflector to light a vertical surface evenly. They are available as singles, doubles, triples and as a four-lamp luminaire (Figure 9.47). The multiple lamp units allow for colour mixing. Avoid overlighting the top of the vertical surfaces as highlights at the top of the picture frame will tend to lead the eye out of the picture.

Remember, the natural progression is for the horizon to be brightest with the darkest blue sky above us. Similarly, there is normally a darkening of walls as we reach the ceiling – if copied this helps to create the feeling of an out-of-shot ceiling (Figure 9.48).

Ground row units enable a vertical surface to be lit from floor level, available as single units and four-compartment units, the latter providing the facility for colour mixing (Figure 9.48). Typically the units use 500 W or 625 W lamps, spacing for even spread of

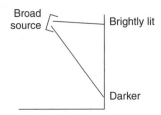

Figure 9.46 The problem of using a symmetrical reflector

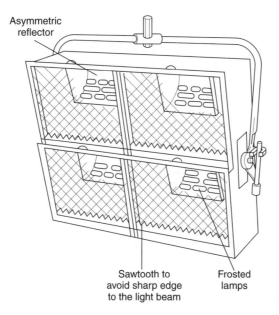

Figure 9.47 Four-unit top cyclorama lighting unit

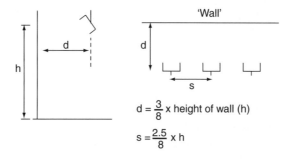

$$d = \frac{3}{8} \times \text{height of wall (h)}$$

$$s = \frac{2.5}{8} \times h$$

Figure 9.48 Plotting of top cyclorama units

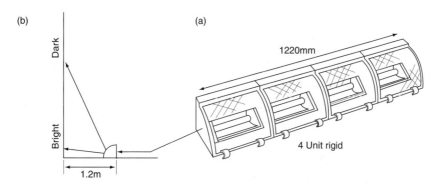

Figure 9.49 (a) Rigid four-unit ground row; (b) Spacing

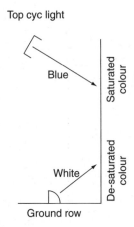

Figure 9.50 Production of graduated lighting

light between each compartment is shown in Figure 9.49. Use of ground row units will result in a gradual fall-off in illuminance vertically – a 'natural' effect. A hinged four-unit is available for corners.

With either top cyc lighting units in ground row the lighting effect will be a single colour. With both units the lighting can provide change in hue and saturation from top to bottom (Figure 9.50). When lighting surfaces, which involve corners, always start lighting in the corners and work outwards.

9.14   PAR lights

The parabolic aluminised reflector lights known as PAR lights or PAR cans were first introduced into the world of 'pop' before gaining popularity in television applications. The PAR can, as its name suggests, has a parabolic reflector to collect the light from the lamp into a very narrow beam (Figure 9.51).

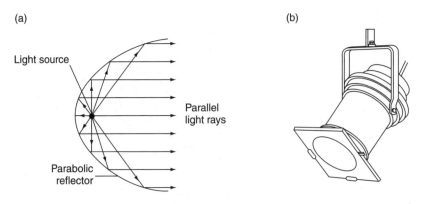

Figure 9.51 (a) Parabolic reflector action; (b) PAR can

The lamp, together with its reflector, are part of a sealed beam unit, the front element of which may be plain, diffused or in the form of a lens, similar to Fresnel lens, except that it is a diverging lens, i.e. concave. The merits of these luminaires are:

- Very intense and very narrow beam available which when used with smoke results in the production of dramatic shafts of light
- The short thermal capacity of the lamp filament which allows it to be switched on/off very rapidly, i.e. in time with music.

PAR cans are normally expressed PAR 64, PAR 56, PAR 16 etc. Dividing the number by 8 gives the luminaire diameter, i.e. PAR 64 is 8 inches in diameter. The performance of the 1000 W PAR cans is shown in Table 9.7.

The CP60 and CP61 sources have a long throw capability that makes them particularly useful for location work when lighting at a distance, i.e.

$$\text{CP61 at 15 m, illuminance} = \frac{\text{Candlepower}}{(\text{distance})^2}$$

$$\text{So illuminance} = \frac{270\,000}{15 \times 15} = 1200 \text{ lux!}$$

The 1 kW PAR can is rapidly being replaced by the 500 W version, following the development of more sensitive cameras (Table 9.8).

The ray light is similar to the PAR can, except that it uses a separate reflector and lamp, i.e. no sealed-beam unit, with the reflector providing the appropriate beam angle. This has the advantage of only needing to change the lamp, not a complete sealed beam when the lamp fails.

Table 9.7 1 kW PAR can data

		Beam angle	Effective candlepower (cd)
CP60	Narrow spot	9° × 12°	320 000
CP61	Spot	10° × 14°	270 000
CP62	Flood	11° × 24°	125 000
CP63	Extra wide	70° × 70°	15 000

Table 9.8 500 W PAR can data

		Beam angle	Effective candlepower (cd)
CP86	0.5 kW	7° × 10°	240 000
CP87	0.5 kW	9° × 11°	140 000
CP88	0.5 kW	10° × 21°	65 000
HX115	0.5 kW	66° × 66°	7 000

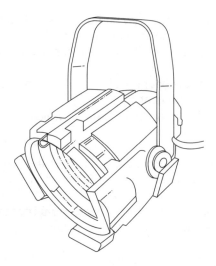

Figure 9.52 575 W PAR luminaire with axial lamp and interchangeable lenses

A further evolution has been the development of a unit, which has a fixed reflector, a special **axially** mounted 575 W lamp and a selection of five **interchangeable** lenses. The axially mounted lamp is a more efficient system resulting in almost the same light output as a 1000 W PAR can! See Figure 9.52. An option is available to use a dichroic mirror as a reflector. This reflects light but transmits heat, consequently, any filters mounted on the lamp have a significant increase in life, and the stage is cooler!

Discharge PAR lights

The advantages observed in using an axially mounted lamp have been developed for use in a range of PAR lamps with HMI and MSR light sources (single-ended). These use a fixed parabolic reflector with interchangeable lenses. They have the advantage of being more efficient than a Fresnel spotlight with a similar light source and provide a very 'punchy' light, very useful for 'bouncing'. It should be noted that the interchangeable lenses do not give quite the smooth beam enjoyed with a Fresnel spotlight, i.e. in wide angle conditions the beam is not so uniform. Discharge PAR lights are available from 125 W to 12 kW (Figure 9.53, page 125).

9.15   Scrollers and dowsers

Scrollers

When there is a need for colour changing but the number of luminaires and the budget are limited, scrollers can provide a useful solution (Figure 9.54). A scroller is an add-on attachment to the front of a luminaire. It enables any one of a 'string' of 11, 16 or 32 colours to be selected from a filter roll made up of the appropriate number of filter segments. Although originally designed for PAR cans it is now possible to obtain scrollers for most luminaires. Scrollers are normally controlled via a DMX 512 signal.

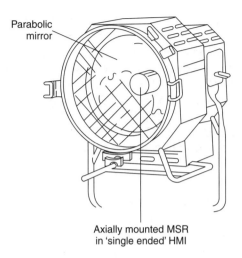

Parabolic
mirror

Axially mounted MSR
in 'single ended' HMI

Figure 9.53 Open-faced PAR 2.5/4 kW HMI with five different interchangeable lenses

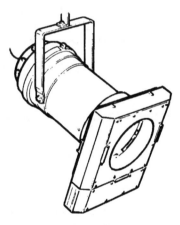

Figure 9.54 PAR can with scroller

A wide range of scrollers is available, covering 15 inch, 12 inch, 8 inch, 6 inch and 4 inch diameter units as well as 15 inches square (for 4-lite luminaires) and 27 inches $\times$ 15$\frac{1}{2}$ inches (for 8-lite luminaires). These two units have either 11, 16 or 25 colours to a 'string'.

A major problem when using any form of colour filter is that of heat absorption by the filter. This is especially so with the more saturated colours, i.e. dense filters. Two basic types of colour filter exist:

- Polyester – surface-coated filters.
- Polycarbonate – dyed filters, with ability to withstand exposure to heat.

Polycarbonate filters are obviously recommended for any types of scroller work or anywhere where the filters may become excessively hot (e.g. dense filter).

A further aid in running the filter cool is to use luminaires which have dichroic reflectors, as they reflect only the visible light and allow transmission of heat. This has a significant effect on the temperature of the light beam, e.g. Source 4 PAR and Source 4 Profile projectors. With dense filters it is also useful to assign the same colour to two adjacent colour positions in the colour 'string'. When using that particular colour it is easy to arrange a continuous slow 'scroll' between the two identical colours, thus running the filter cooler.

Scrollers operate on a 24 V DC supply. Usually suitable power supplies are available to provide supplies for up to 24 scrollers. The 24 V DC supply is distributed on cables using 4-pin XLR connections, typically connected as a ring main (Figure 9.55).

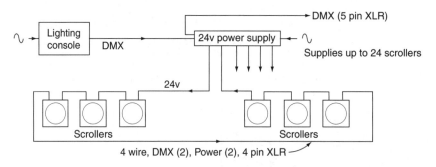

Figure 9.55 Scrollers – colour control system. 24 V connected in a ring

Control of scrollers is by means of DMX, and two control channels are required for each scroller.

1   Colour selection
2   Speed of colour scroll

Remember – scrollers have cooling fans, there will an element of noise when operating in a non-scrolling mode. Naturally when scrollers operate, especially many in synchronism, there is much more noise!

Important note – when choosing colours for colour strings (or any other purpose) be aware that when looking at a colour swatch you see a deeper colour than the filter if you are viewing the filter against the swatch white paper background! The reason for this is that the light reaching your eye will have travelled through the filter twice, once onto the filter then reflected off the white paper through the filter again! To judge a colour filter, hold it up to a light source you are using, i.e. tungsten/MSR.

Dowsers

A dowser is a similar unit to a scroller but fitted with a mechanical shutter. It can be used with HMI/MSR luminaires to provide dimming control from 100% to 0%. It is operated by a DMX control signal.

9.16 Special lights – Dedolight

The Dedolight system is both innovative and unique. Developed by Cinematographer Dedo Weigert to satisfy a need for an efficient, compact, low-wattage spotlight, the Dedolight has become an industry standard (Table 9.9).

Table 9.9 Dedolight performance

Transformer position	Colour temperature (K)	Effective candlepower full flood 40° (cd)	Effective candlepower half flood 23° (cd)	Effective candlepower spot 3.4° (cd)
Low	3000	970	2400	24 200
Medium	3200	1700	4800	41 800
High	3400	3000	7200	66 000

The principle of this luminaire is shown in Figure 9.56. The design features which make this different to the Fresnel spotlight are:

- use of two lenses, neither of which is a Fresnel lens
- use of low-voltage (12 V and 24 V) tungsten lamps.

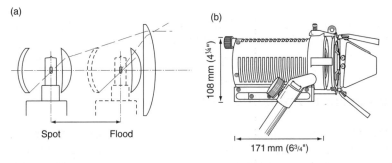

Figure 9.56 Dedolight. (a) Optical principle; (b) dimensions

The first lens (meniscus) close to the lamp acts as a collector of light, converging the light towards the second lens. This arrangement results in a spotlight, which has:

- a very flat field of illuminance over its beam width in flood mode (46°), no striations
- excellent transmission characteristics, thus avoiding the need for large lenses as with Fresnel spotlights
- an effective candlepower in flood mode for 100 W version comparable to that of a 300 W Fresnel spotlight
- no stray light due to scatter in the lens, as with the Fresnel spotlight.

This performance is even more impressive in the spot mode, where the special optical system provides a spot/flood ratio of approximately 10:1 on beam angle and a ratio of 25:1

on centre beam intensity! Usually a Fresnel spotlight will have a spot/flood ratio of about 7:1 on beam angle and about 8:1 on intensity.

The transformer used to provide the 24 V or 12 V supplies for a four-lamp kit includes voltage 'tap' adjustments to provide 'normal' operation at 3200 K, 'boosted' operation at 3400 K and 'dim' operation at 3000 K for each lamp. Alternatively, each luminaire may be supplied with an in-line dimmer/transformer (12 V/100 W version). In addition to the normal barndoors a 'super' barndoor is available which provides movement in **two axes** for each barn door – thus allowing barndooring of irregular shapes.

The system also provides:

- a scrim set, which also includes a graduated scrim, i.e. zero, single and then double
- a projection attachment to enable gobos (M size) to be projected; with a range of projection lenses (50 mm, 85 mm, 150 mm, 185 mm, 70–120 mm and 85–150 mm)
- lightweight stands
- lightweight grip items – shown in Figure 9.57.

The merit of its compact size and light weight (1.2 lb/0.6 kg) make this an ideal luminaire for rigging in places that would be inaccessible for a conventional spotlight. A wide range of lamps is available:

12 V: 20 W, 35 W, 50 W, 75 W, 100 W
24 V: 100 W, 150 W

Recent developments have seen the introduction of a 400 series 400 W MSR; 400 W/36 V tungsten and 650 W/500 W/300 W mains-operated tungsten.

9.17   Fluorescent luminaires (coldlights)

Most fluorescent luminaires consist of several lamps to make a suitable luminaire, i.e. sufficient light output. Although they can never be regarded as point sources they are of finite area, not infinite area. Consequently, they can be controlled to some extent by using suitable honeycomb control screens, 'egg-crates', barndoors or flags/cutters. The honeycomb control screen is particularly effective and is usually available in wide, medium and narrow angle (90°, 60° and 30°) (Figure 9.27 p. 105).

There are two basic types of fluorescent luminaire. One uses the conventional tubular lamps (TL-D) the other uses the compact fluorescent lamps (PL-L and PL-C). Like all discharge lights the fluorescent luminaire includes a current-limiting ballast in addition to auxiliary electronics for starting. The ballast also includes the necessary electronics to drive the lamps at high frequency (>40 kHz). Luminaires using the TL-D lamps are designed for use mainly on location. They are made with a separate ballast, usually dimmable, to provide an extremely lightweight and thin softlight, ideal for use in cramped conditions (Figure 9.58).

Luminaires using the PL-L lamps were initially designed for studio use, but derivatives of the designs are available for location use. These are especially useful on location where a compact source is needed (Figure 9.59).

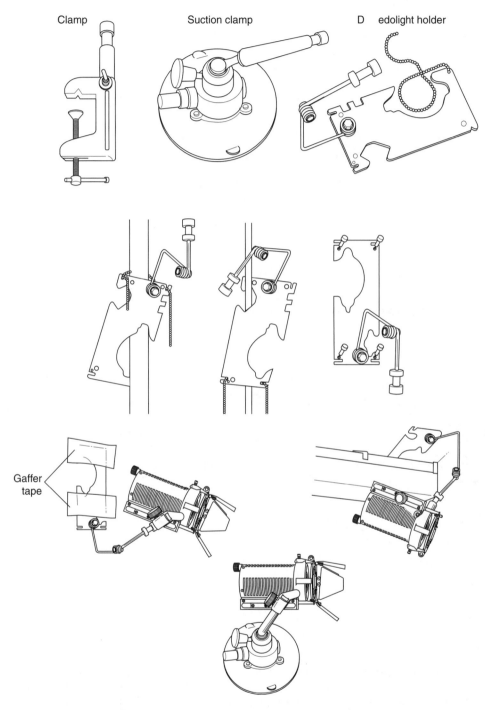

Figure 9.57 Dedolight grip items and examples of uses

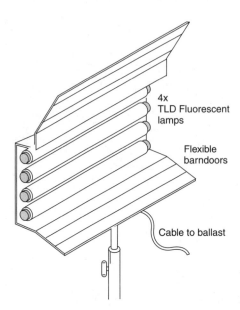

4x
TLD Fluorescent
lamps

Flexible
barndoors

Cable to ballast

Figure 9.58 Example of a lightweight fluorescent luminaire with external ballast

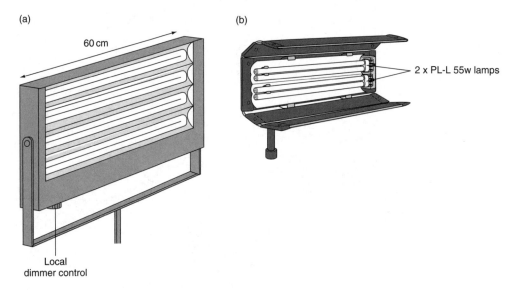

(a)

60 cm

Local
dimmer control

(b)

2 x PL-L 55w lamps

Figure 9.59 Compact location luminaire

The **Baselight** type of construction results in a luminaire with a very wide beam angle. Consequently, when a control screen is used the sideways spreading light is lost. An **intensifier**, basically mirrored barndoors, can be fitted to these luminaires which redirects the sideways-spreading light onto the main acting area. Use of an intensifier can double the on-axis illuminance for most luminaires. Control screens are available for use with intensifiers (Figure 9.60).

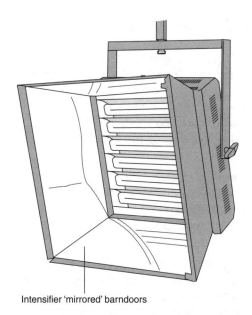

Intensifier 'mirrored' barndoors

Figure 9.60 6 × 55 W fluorescent luminaire and intensifier

Individual fluorescent lights (6 W) are available for use in car kits, i.e. for night lighting in cars. These are dimmable and can be powered from the car battery (cigarette lighter connection), or from mains (Figure 9.61).

(a)   (b)

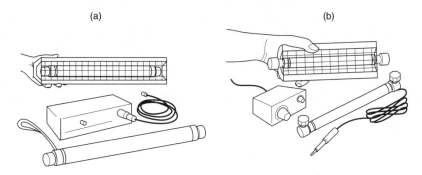

Figure 9.61 (a) 15-inch 12 V single system; (b) 9-inch 'mini-flo' system

Soft sources and the inverse square law

The inverse square law is strictly only true for **point** sources, but when considering soft sources this can still be used to estimate the illuminance. For large area sources the illuminance follows an inverse law up to lamp throw comparable with the size of the source. Thereafter, it follows an inverse square law. When making calculations at a distance of three times the largest dimension of the light source the 'error' in using the inverse square law is 10%, at five times the distance it is approximately 2%.

9.18   On-camera and battery lighting

The simplest form of supplementary lighting can be supplied by an on-camera light. Used correctly this light can be used to reduce the effect of 'natural' overhead lighting or simply to provide light where none, or very little, exists. These lights are normally 12 V, operated from the camera battery or from a separate battery belt. If used with the camera battery then clearly the battery power will be drained more quickly.

The four problems in using these lights are in providing:

- Sufficient illuminance **but** not overlighting
- Light which is colour matched to the local lighting
- Sufficient power to operate the light
- Light which does not 'blind' the reporter

Usually tungsten halogen lights are used for on camera work, so there is a need to correct this when operating in daylight situations. Its worth considering using $^3/_4$CTB as a compromise filter to reduce the loss of light through the correction filter, and adding some Half White Diffusion to reduce the glare for the reporter. A small Chimera is available for on-camera lights. Other alternatives are a small fluorescent light, including a circular 'around the lens' unit. The advantage of fluorescent lighting is the extra efficiency, compared with tungsten, and the ability to change lamps for a colour temperature change, i.e. no filtering.

A useful kit of on-camera lighting is available providing a selection of interchangeable lamps of different wattages (20 W, 35 W, 50 W, 75 W and 100 W) including a small 24 W HMI lamp. This allows the appropriate lamp to be used to match the local environment, i.e. it avoids the situation of the overlit 'frightened rabbit' look resulting from a night shoot when the on-camera lighting does not relate to the background lighting. Generally a lighting level about 400 lux will cater for most interviews in interior locations and this can be provided by a 25 W lamp, with the subject about 1–2 metres from the camera. It is useful to have some small pieces of 0.15 ND available to help balance the on-camera lighting with the local environment. Most tungsten halogen on-camera light, have a simple flip-over dichroic filter for matching to daylight.

Battery-operated lights

Many situations require the use of truly portable lighting kits to provide the cameraman the freedom to:

- follow moving actors, without the hindrance of a mains cable
- operate with lights in a crowded environment where 'on-stand' mains-operated lighting would be impractical and unsafe
- operate in remote areas where mains is not available
- operate in moving vehicles.

Table 9.10 Typical battery life/charging times for hire kits

Lamp wattage	Voltage	Life (min)	Charging time (hours)
125	30	75	4
200	30	40	4
400	30	15–20	4

Note: There will be variations in performance depending on manufacture. Battery capacity is indicated by its Ampere/Hour (A/H) rating. For example a 30 V 8 A/H battery would be capable of providing 8 Amperes at 30 V for one hour.

The prime concerns in using battery-operated lights are:

● Choosing the most appropriate battery lamp
● How long will the battery last?
● How long does the battery take to charge?
● Is the battery performance limited by the environment, i.e. temperature?

Battery-operated lamps are either 30 V or 12 V. Batteries are usually NiCad (nickel–cadium) and typically require about 4 hours to be fully charged. Table 9.10 illustrates the use expected from these batteries. However, if using a discharge source, the battery life will depend on the number of re-strikes as well as the 'lit' time. Clearly there is a need to have sufficient batteries for the anticipated duration of the shoot plus some reserve!

The range of battery-operate lighting includes:

Sungun: 250 W/30 V – the original battery-operated tungsten light
Pocket PAR: 125 W/30 V – MSR par with interchangeable lenses
Fresnel: 200 W/30 V – MSR
Open-faced: 200 W/30 V – MSR
Dedolight: 100 W/12 V – Tungsten
Dedolight: 150 W/24 V – Tungsten
Kinoflo: 6 W/12 V – Fluorescent
Macroflo
Microflo

9.19 Specials

The need for a large light source has resulted in a number of 'specials'. The **Wendy light**, produced at the request of David Watkins, a cinematographer, is a tungsten-based light using 192 individual wide angles 650 W PAR lamps! The 'light' is assembled in four sections and may be mounted on a crane or hydraulic 'cherry picker' which enables the source to be used at heights in excess of 120–150 feet. Some versions of the Wendy light feature a remotely controlled pan and tilt head, making it very flexible to use.

Each section ($\frac{1}{4}$ Wendy), approximately 5 feet × 3 feet, has 48 light sources arranged on eight vertical rows of the 650 W sources with six lamps/row. Each vertical row may be panned manually to allow the coverage to be modified as required. The lamps used are 120 V, and for 240 V operation they are wired in pairs. Power to the Wendy light is normally switched on in vertical rows, i.e. a gradual application of the total load. Dimming is achieved by switching off vertical rows as necessary. The total power of the Wendy light is a staggering 124 800 W (192 × 650 W), approximately 125 kW.

Any coloured filters must be mounted on 'stand-off' frames to avoid the filter melting. Unfortunately the Wendy light is vulnerable when used in the rain as the lamps 'blow'. This can make it expensive to use. One of the main uses for the Wendy light is on night shoots – it can backlight over 4 acres. A $\frac{1}{4}$ **Wendy** is an individual section of the Wendy light and may be used on a heavy-duty stand. It consumes 32 kW of power.

Musco light is a crane-mounted light using 16 × 6 kW HMI Fresnel spotlights rigged on a special frame to give remote pan/tilt of the complete unit. Performance depends on the spot/flood of each light source and individual setting. If all luminaires are set identically, the effective candlepower would be 4 million candelas! The Musco light is often used for sports lighting, individually setting each luminaire to cover large areas.

Movie Star is a vehicle which includes 190 kVA three-phase generator, 33-metre articulated arm plus light sources, namely 3 × 18 kW HMI, 3 × 12 kW HMI or 3 × 20 kW tungsten. The articulated arm has the advantage of 360° rotation of the lighting platform.

Dino or Maxi Brute uses 24 × 1 kW PAR lights. These may be very narrow, narrow or wide angle giving flexibility in providing a long throw 'punchy' source (narrow angle) to a wide angle short throw source.

Mini Brute or 9 light uses 9 × 650 W as in the Wendy light and consumes approximately 6 kW.

Lightning units using xenon lamps provide the facility of large bursts of light to simulate lightning and are available as wide angle and narrow angle (PAR) for windows.

Soft Sun units use the xenon-based ESL lamps to provide a soft source of light which matches daylight. They are useful for fill-lit or extending the day.

When using these sources, consideration should be given to:

- Rigging – how long does it take to rig and how many electricians?
- Weight – can it be supported, safely?
- Physical dimensions – will it fit available space?
- Power requirements – starting current?
  - – running current?
  - – electrical connections required?
  - – generator required?
- Cost to hire/run?

Clearly, the Gaffer will be able to provide answers to all these questions – they are his concern. However, as a Lighting Director or Director of Photography you should have an awareness of the implications of using these special sources (see Table 9.11).

Table 9.11 Performance data on 'Specials'

Luminaire	Luminous intensity (cd)	Beam angle
Wendy light (192 × 650 W) –125 kW	Flood 2 000 000	Flood/spot 80°/45°
¼ Wendy (48 × 650 W) – 32 kW	500 000	80°/45°
Musco 16 × 6 kW HMI	4 000 000	56°/6°
Movie Star 3 × 18 kW HMI	2 700 000	60°/9°
3 × 12 kW HMI	1 875 000	53°/9°
3 × 20 kW tungsten	1 200 000	60°/14°
Dino (Maxi Brute) (24 × 1 kW) – 24 kW	V.N 6 500 000	11°
	N 5 200 00	16°
	M 1 800 000	30°
	W 600 000	50°
Mini Brute (9 × 650 W) – 6 kW	80 000	80°/45°
20 kW tungsten Fresnel spotlight	400 000	60°/14°
15 kW HMI Fresnel spotlight	900 000	60°/9°
12 kW HMI	625 000	53°/7°
6 kW HMI	250 000	56°/7°

Lightning units (5600 K) wide beam angle	**Luminous intensity (candlepower)**
40 kW	800 000 cd
70 kW	1 000 000 cd
250 kW	4 500 000 cd
Lightning units (5600 K) PAR narrow angle	**Luminous intensity (candlepower)**
12 kW	2 000 000 cd
40 kW	4 000 000 cd
200 kW	8 000 000 cd

Soft sun

Wattage		Beam angle vertical	Beam angle horizontal	Candlepower (cd)
3.3 kW	S	15°	120°	45 000
	F	53°	120°	22 000
10 kW	S	14°	108°	580 000
	F	28°	108°	320 000
15 kW Circular		80°	80°	70 000
25 kW Circular		30°	30°	800 000
25 kW	S	13°	100°	1 000 000
	F	36°	100°	440 000
50 kW	S	11°	100°	2 267 000
	F	35°	100°	1 000 000
100 kW	S	11°	100°	6 300 000
	F	35°	100°	3 000 000

9.20   Moving lights – intelligent lights

Although very much a 'special light' compared with the normal location lighting requirements, the moving lights are becoming more readily available and easier to use. They can
enhance the lighting treatment used in groups or singularly as a special effect. Any 'pop'
shoot generally demands these lights as a 'normal' requirement. Moving lights fall into two
basic categories:

- Effects lights
- Colour wash lights.

Effects lights provide a wide range of effects in addition to being able to move the light beam. They break down into two further subcategories:

- Luminaires, where the beam is moved by movement of the complete luminaire (Figure 9.62)
- Luminaires, in which a mirror is used to move the beam (Figure 9.63).

Luminaires in the first subcategory have the advantage of smaller size and greater angles of rotation and tilt (360° and 270° respectively), but are slower moving than the moving mirror category. The 'moving light' category look more attractive 'in-shot' than the 'moving mirror' lights. Moving mirror lights have the advantage of a lightweight, low-inertia mirror, which can move much faster, but have restricted rotation and tilt angles of 170° and 110° respectively. They are also physically larger and heavier. Intelligent lights usually use a compact version of the HMI source (HTI) of 1200 W or 575 W rating.

(a)   (b)

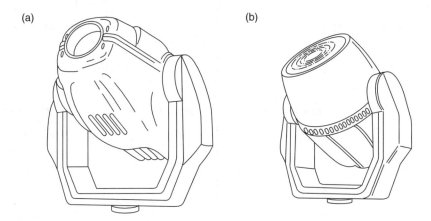

Figure 9.62 (a) Moving effects light; (b) moving colour washlight

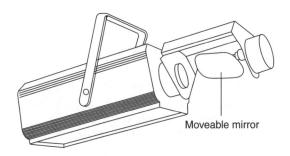

Moveable mirror

Figure 9.63 Moving mirror light

All moving lights offer a variety of effects. For example:

- Pan and tilt
- Colour change of light beam (infinite or limited colour wheel)
- Beam angle change
- Beam focus change
- Gobo wheel
- Rotating gobo effects
- Diffusion
- Colour correction
- Mechanical dimmer.

Generally, moving lights are used upstage of the artiste, from above, at ground level or side lighting positions. They have to be used with suitable haze machines to make the light beams visible.

Colour wash lights use 575 W HTI or 1000 W tungsten light sources and are based on the first subcategory of moving lights. They provide a variable colour 'wash' and variable beam angle, but no gobo effects. This pan/tilt range is typically 370°/240° (Figure 9.62(b)). All moving light systems generate some noise, either from the cooling fans or motors.

Control of intelligent lights is usually via a DMX 512 system for transmission of the control signals to the luminaire (see p. 140).

An intelligent light can require in excess of 20 control channels and it is recommended to use a dedicated moving light console for any set-up using many moving lights. This has the advantage of enabling the moving light operator to set up the moving light sequences independently from any other control requirements. The programming of moving lights can be very time consuming. Use of a computer and a WYSIWYG program can enable an operator to pre-plan the lighting treatment/changes, thereby saving time on the actual shoot day.

10
Dimmers on location

Dimmers can be used on location to enable:

- swift balance of light sources without the need for scrim/ND filters
- on-cue lighting changes to be affected.

Tungsten sources change their colour when dimmed (refer to p. 76 for a discussion on this topic). **Fluorescent sources** may have a dimmer integral with the lamp ballast. When dimmed the fluorescent light does not change its colour significantly.

Dimming control may be by:

- local control on the luminaire
- 0–10 V
- DMX signal.

HMI/MSR sources using flicker-free ballasts have an integral dimmer with a local dimming control 100–50%. However, the change in colour with dimming may not be tolerable. Consequently, these sources should be fitted with a mechanical dimmer (shutter) which will enable them to be dimmed 100–0%. This shutter may be manually operated or motorised with remote control using a DMX control signal.

Dimmers on location may fall into one of several categories:

- In-line dimmers, where a simple locally controlled dimmer is inserted into the mains feed to the luminaire.
- Simple four-way dimmer packs with local faders which can be plugged into a 13 Amp socket (providing the total load is less than 13 Amp).
- Centralised dimmer pack requiring a large mains feed. This needs to be a tied-in connection to the mains supply or generator.
- Distributed dimmer packs around the location. These may be 4/6/12/24 way packs according to requirements, again needing an appropriate mains feed or generator.

10.1 Dimmers

There are three categories of dimmers:

- Thyristor or Silicon Controlled Rectifiers (SCR) – Forward Phase Control (1960)
- Transistor Dimmers – Reverse Phase Control (late 1990s)
- Transistor Dimmers – Sine Wave Dimming (2000).

The principle of each dimmer is shown in Figure 10.1.

Dimmer interference problems have always been associated with the thyristor dimmer, caused by the rapid **switch-on** of current. This is minimised by including a choke in the circuit to slow down the rate of rise of the current. Microphone circuits using a special star quad cable have helped to minimise this problem.

The relatively new transistor dimmer switches **off** the mains during each half cycle at a controlled rate. It is silent in operation and consequently does not require a choke. As a result the transistor dimmer may be operated alongside the 'action' on location.

The latest dimmer, the transistor sine wave dimmer, uses fast switching to maintain the normal mains sine wave shape. Consequently there are no interference problems and the mains shape is preserved. This latter point is very important to those concerned with the 'pollution' of the mains waveform. Eventually all dimmers will be of the Sine Wave type!

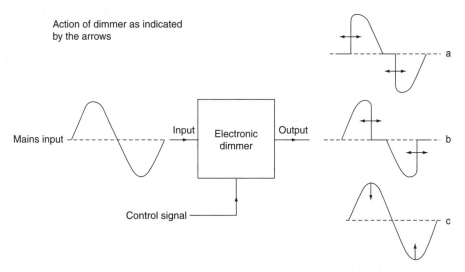

Figure 10.1 Basic dimmer principles. (a) Thyristor, silicon-controlled rectifier (SRC) or triac dimmer; (b) transistor dimmer (reverse phase control); (c) transistor dimmer – sine wave dimming

10.2 Dimmer law

The dimmer law is approximately square law, and this is almost a complementary law to the 'log' law of the eye/brain. This means that the perceived law is approximately linear (Figure 10.2).

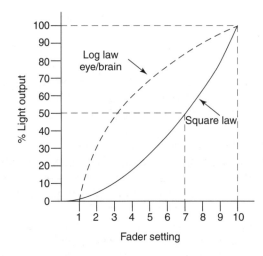

Figure 10.2 Basic dimmer law

10.3 Control of dimmers – DMX/512 (Digital Multiplex/512)

The basic control of dimmers is by means of a 0–10 V signal derived from a fader, 0 V = OFF, 10 V = FULL ON. Simple dimmer packs with local control incorporate this form of control. Most dimmer packs are controlled via a feed of a DMX signal derived from the lighting console. Instead of feeding 0–10 V individually to each dimmer, the fader setting (0–10 V) is converted to an 8-bit digital number. This provides 255 discrete signal levels plus ON/OFF information. This 'packet' of information is then sent sequentially, with all the other dimmer information, along one pair of wires to the dimmer pack. Up to 512 dimmers may be controlled in this way (Figure 10.3). This simplifies the distribution of control information to dimmers. At the dimmer pack the digital number may be:

- Converted to a 0–10 V signal to control conventional analogue dimmers.
- Used in its digital form to **directly** control the dimmers – these are known as digital dimmers.

Digital dimmers are more accurate, more reliable and provide many additional monitoring facilities compared with analogue dimmers.

The advantage of DMX control, apart from that of simplicity of connecting up a system, is that the signal received at the dimmer is **exactly** the same as the transmitted signal irrespective of the path length between the lighting console and the dimmer. This is particularly useful for other systems using DMX such as scrollers, 'intelligent' lights and fog machines.

The DMX signal may be 'daisy-chained' to up to 32 units using the DMX control signal. Each unit will have an 'address' which is set to the first channel in that particular unit, say '13' for a 12-way dimmer pack. DMX-controlled units therefore have a DMX 'in' and a DMX 'out'. The final unit in a 'daisy-chain' should be terminated in 120 Ω, similar to terminating monitors (Figure 10.4). The DMX signal operates at 250 kHz. If the DMX line is not

Channels are addressed sequentially as frames of data:

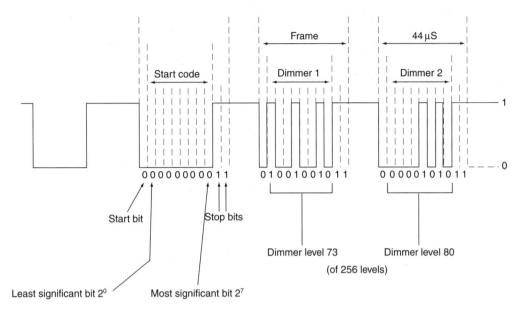

Figure 10.3 DMX 512 signal

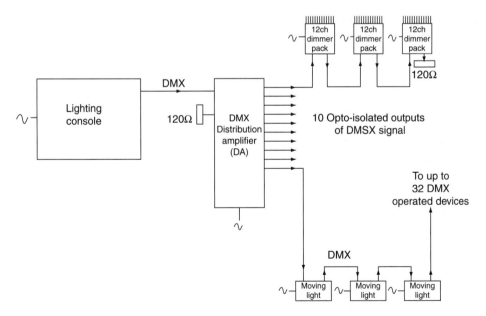

Figure 10.4 Basic DMX distribution

terminated **reflection** of signal will occur when the signal reaches the end of the line. This, depending on distances involved, could cause absolute chaos with the digital information.

With anything other than a simple control set-up it is useful to have a distribution of DMX via a DMX distribution amplifier. This provides up to 10 **opto-isolated** outputs ensuring complete electrical isolation between the outputs and the input. This prevents any mains electrical fault which may accidentally appear on the DMX control lines reaching the lighting console or affecting other DMX outputs.

11
Lighting grip equipment

11.1 Basics

Lighting grip refers to any equipment used in lighting which is not electrical. This can mean anything used to support lighting equipment or equipment used to modify the light beam in any way.

Lighting stands

The basic item of lighting 'grip' equipment is the lighting stand. These are available in a variety of sizes and specifications. The important parameters are:

Universal socket 28 mm/16 mm and 16 mm spigot
Extended height
Minimum height
Closed length
Required base diameter
Maximum safe working load (SWL)
Weight of stand
Complete with braked wheels?
Lazy leg (extendable leg)

Stands must always be rigged so that the stand 'column' is vertical. An extendable leg is a useful asset which enables a stand to be used on uneven ground or on steps/stairs (Figure 11.1).

Sandbags should be used on the base of the stand to give greater stability, if judged necessary, depending on load and environment, e.g. large luminaires used out of doors. Table 11.1 gives an indication of the parameters typical of available lighting stands. Light-weight stands with 16 mm studs/sockets are made from aluminium, heavier duty stands are

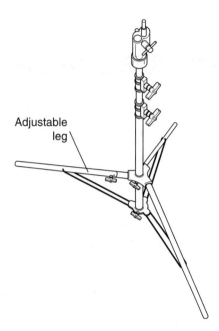

Figure 11.1 Lightweight three-section stand with lazy leg (adjustable leg)

Table 11.1 The range of stands available

Name	W/U	28 mm/ 16 mm	Weight	Sections	Lazy leg	Folded (cm)	Base (cm)	Min-max height cm	Max load (kg)
Super Crank	✓	28	71	5	X	225	213	190–610	70
Baby Crank	✓	28	30	2	X	122	139	97–165	100
Super Wind Up	✓	28	34	2	✓	176	160	152–366	80
Wind Up (3 sec)	✓	✓	21.4	3	✓	181	128	167–370	30
Wind Up (2 sec)	✓	✓	16	2	✓	153	128	139–247	45
A1. Combo	X	✓	6.9	3	✓	143	135	167–408	30
Ultra Low Combo	X	✓	3.6	2	✓	56	56	45–68	35
Junior Roller	X	✓	15.4	3	X	142	129	146–428	40
Rolling Base	X	✓	5.8	0	X	52	100	35	40
Baby Roller	X	16	6.3	3	X	105	75	115–330	12
Junior Universal	X	✓	7.5	2	✓	116	118	118–220	30
High Super Alu	X	✓	10	5	✓	173	174	190–730	10
Heavy Duty	X	✓	8.3	2	✓	131	126	153–330	40
Small Stacker	X	16	1.1	3	X	64	79	66–217	4
Large Stacker	X	16	2.3	3	X	110	107	223–385	9
Mighty Baby	X	16	3.3	1	✓	47	44	51–106	15
Compact Kit	X	16	1.03	3	X	76	106	89–260	5
Backlite	X	16	1.3	0	X	48	60	9	3

W/U = Wind Up.

made from steel and ideally should have a universal 28 mm socket/16 mm socket plus pop-up 16 mm stud (Figure 11.1). Other types of stands are (see also Table 11.1):

- **Turtle** – very low level stand enabling a luminaire to be rigged safely at floor level, instead of simply propping up the luminaire on the floor. Using an appropriate turtle allows the full range of pan and tilt adjustments on the luminaire and avoids possible heat damage to floor coverings. Once set, the luminaire should remain set and not vulnerable to being disturbed as with the propped luminaire.
- **High lift extension** – these are extra sections (28 mm spigot) which can be used to gain extra height. They need to be used with caution to ensure that the stand, plus extension, is safe.
- **Boom stand** – allows a luminaire to be used at the end of an extendable boom. This is ideal for rigging a luminaire upstage of the action without getting the stand in shot. Extreme care has to be exercised to ensure that the boom arm is correctly counterbalanced and that the stand has extra stability of sandbags (Figure 11.2).

Figure 11.2 'Boom' stand used with counterweights and sandbags

11.2 Stand accessories

Lighting stand accessories include a number of attachments designed to increase the facilities provided by the stand (Figure 11.3):

(a) Junior triple header (28 mm) – allows extra luminaires to be rigged on steel stands.
(b) Baby triple header (16 mm) – allows extra luminaires to be rigged on aluminium and steel stands.
(c) Junior offset arm (28 mm) – allows a 50 cm offset to the luminaire from the stand, must be used with sandbags.
(d) Baby offset arm (16 mm) – allows a 38 cm offset for a luminaire.

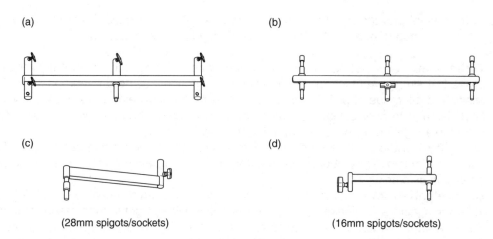

(a)

(b)

(c)   (d)

(28mm spigots/sockets)   (16mm spigots/sockets)

Figure 11.3 (a) Junior triple header 100 cm long; (b) baby triple header 100 cm long; (c) junior offset 50 cm long; (d) baby offset 38 mm long

Century stands (C stands) are designed to be used with flags and scrims, but may be used with lightweight luminaires having a 16 mm socket. Century stands have a narrower 'base' than luminaire stands and should be used with sandbags when using all but the smallest flags and scrims. The component parts of a Century stand rigged for grip work are shown in Figure 11.4.

Normally two extension grip arms are provided to give maximum flexibility in the placing of the flag or scrim. It is best to find the optimum position for the flag/scrim, then connect the grip arm to it. Always rig flags and grip arms so that the downward torque of the flag weight **tightens** the grip arms. The 40-inch extension arms can provide a useful offset for small lightweight luminaires, again with suitable sandbagging of the stand base.

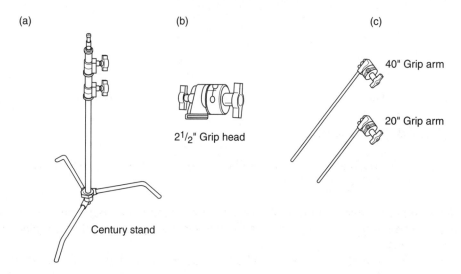

(a)   (b)   (c)

40" Grip arm

$2^1/_2$" Grip head

20" Grip arm

Century stand

Figure 11.4 Basic Century stands – 20 inches, 30 inches, 40 inches and 60 inches extending to 482 cm for loads up to 10 kg

Flags stop light completely. When using flags remember:

- The shadow of the flag becomes 'harder' when the flag is moved away from the light source.
- With hard sources the flag must be large enough to cover the required beam width.
- With soft-diffused sources, to be effective, the flag must be larger than the light source.

Scrims are available as single, double and triple in black and white net. The black scrims reduce illuminance, white scrims also provide a degree of light scatter, i.e. diffusion. **Silks** provide diffusion, with a $\frac{1}{4}$-stop scrim providing a more subtle effect. Collapsible scrims and flags are available in sizes 12 inches $\times$ 18 inches, 18 inches $\times$ 24 inches and 24 inches $\times$ 36 inches. Larger Black flags with a more rectangular than square shape are called **Cutters**, e.g. 10 inches $\times$ 42 inches, 18 inches $\times$ 48 inches, 24 inches $\times$ 72 inches.

11.3 Super-clamps and telescopic poles

Rigging a luminaire in a required position usually relies on the ingenuity of the gaffer. However, it is useful to be aware of the attachments and 'gadgets' available to solve rigging problems. Many simple grip items can be carried to increase the flexibility of the short-handed crew.

One of the most useful grip items is the **super-clamp** (Figures 11.5 and 11.7). This has a 16 mm socket/16 mm spud with an adjustable jaw that can clamp to tubes 13 mm to 55 mm

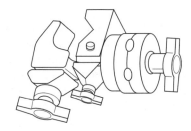

Figure 11.5 Super-clamp grip head allows grip arms on pipes/Auto-poles

(a)   (b)

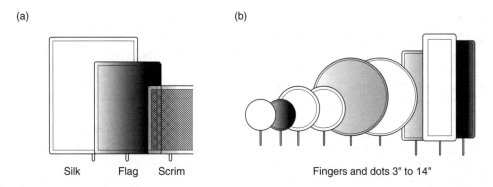

Silk   Flag   Scrim   Fingers and dots 3" to 14"

Figure 11.6 (a) Silks, flags and scrims; (b) fingers and dots 3–14 inches: gold, silk, solid, white net, black net

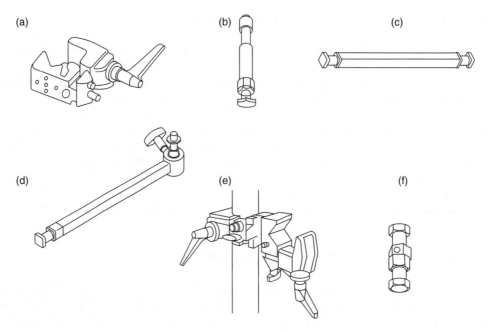

Figure 11.7 (a) Super-clamp with 16 mm socket, jaws open to clamp lines 13–55 mm; (b) 16 mm stud for super-clamp; (c) extension bar for super-clamp (16.5 cm); (d) offset arm for super-clamp (19.5 cm); (e) use of two super-clamps; (f) joining stud for two super-clamps

diameter. It forms the basic element in the adjustable lighting pole system, often referred to as Pole-cats or Auto-pole system. These provide a selection of telescopic poles, which can be used vertically or horizontally (Figure 11.8). When extended between floor and ceiling the lever is operated to firmly jam the pole, and super-clamps with appropriate attachments can be used to suspend small lightweight luminaires. Two super-clamps may be used together to provide the necessary right-angle fixing to make a 'goal-post' arrangement with three Auto-poles (Figure 11.7(e)). The shorter Auto-poles can be used to provide a useful facility across windows, doorways and for car interiors.

When using Auto-poles:

- **Check that the ceiling is strong enough** to take the tensioned pole.
- Always use a piece of card between the top rubber pad and the ceiling (an unused beer mat is ideal!) to avoid leaving a black mark on the ceiling! Alternatively, use the white protective cap – provided they are clean.
- Because of the small 'base' required, Auto-poles may be hidden within a set, or easily disguised to hide the pole.

A particularly useful item is the **magic arm** (Figure 11.9). This has three flexible joints that can be locked with a single movement of the locking arm. Typically, using a super-clamp on one end, a lightweight luminaire may be rigged in difficult situations and provide the facility of the luminaire hanging properly, so that the pan/tilt mechanism operates correctly.

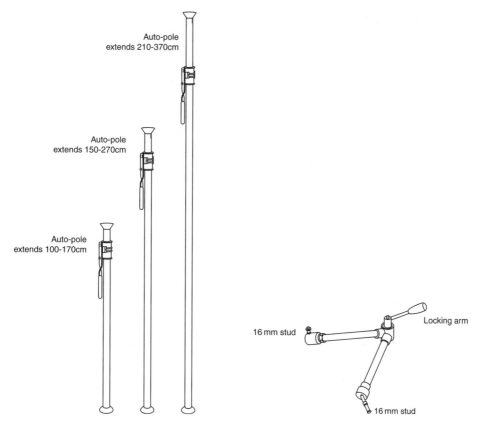

Figure 11.8 Telescopic poles; pole diameters 45 and 40 mm

Figure 11.9 Magic arm (length 53 cm)

11.4 Clamps

A wide range of clamps exist to aid the rigging of luminaires and the more common ones are featured below. For a description of the full range, the reader is recommended to consult the Doughty, Manfrotto or MSE (Matthews) catalogues (Figure 11.10).

(a) **G-clamp** – basically a carpenter's clamp with spigots/sockets, very useful where there are ceiling beams. Available in various sizes and 16 mm or 28 mm sockets/ spigots.

(b) **Beam clamp** – a lightweight fitting that can be clamped to concrete ceiling beams/ pillars. Used with lightweight luminaires.

(c) **Pillar clamp** – used to provide a rigging position for a luminaire on a circular pillar (or any irregular shaped pillar). It can be 16 mm or 28 mm depending on the model used.

(d) **Light beam** – heavy-duty aluminium beam, adjustable in length to fit a particular opening, say a window, then expanded to jam securely between any two parallel walls.

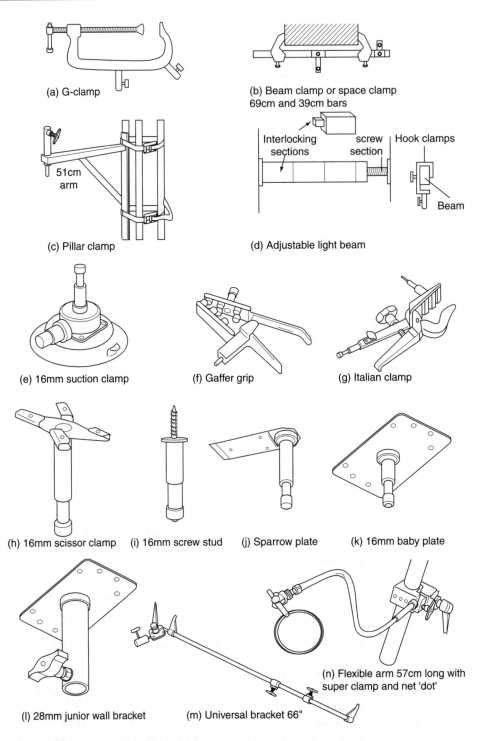

(a) G-clamp

(b) Beam clamp or space clamp
69cm and 39cm bars

(c) Pillar clamp
51cm arm

(d) Adjustable light beam
Interlocking sections   screw section   Hook clamps
Beam

(e) 16mm suction clamp

(f) Gaffer grip

(g) Italian clamp

(h) 16mm scissor clamp

(i) 16mm screw stud

(j) Sparrow plate

(k) 16mm baby plate

(l) 28mm junior wall bracket

(m) Universal bracket 66"

(n) Flexible arm 57cm long with super clamp and net 'dot'

Figure 11.10 Lighting grip – clamps

(e) **Suction clamp** – a useful clamp, which has to be used on surfaces that are absolutely smooth, i.e. glass or metal.

(f) **Gaffer grip** – spring-loaded clamp with 16 mm stud.

(g) **Italian clamp** – heavy-duty version of gaffer grip, but with adjustable jaws, has a 16 mm stud and 16 mm socket.

(h) **Scissor clamp** – used with suspended ceilings to provide an anchorage for a 16 mm spud.

(i) **Screw stud (16 mm)** – easily screwed into wood to provide a secure anchorage. Obviously can only be used with the site owner's permission!

(j) **Sparrow plate** – lightweight mounting that may be jammed into a suitable crevice or fixed into wood.

(k) **Baby plates and Junior wall plates** – a selection of 16 mm and 28 mm studs and spigots mounted on metal plates, which can be screwed to suitable positions on location (again, with permission). Alternatively, may be screwed to a wooden/metal base to make a Turtle.

(l) **Universal bracket** – adjustable bracket for holding collapsible reflectors.

(m) **Flexible arm** – 55 cm flexible arm, either 18 mm or 12 mm diameter, useful for attaching small flags/veils to lighting stands (when no C-stands are available) or for mounting small lightweight luminaires such as the Dedolight (18 mm).

11.5 Scaffolding, trussing and scissor lifts

Getting the luminaire in the right place and without the suspension system 'in shot' often requires some ingenuity. Thankfully, when stands are not practical there are several alternatives, e.g. scaffolding, trussing or scissor lifts.

Scaffolding uses tubing 48.3 mm diameter steel or aluminium. The inclusion of a scaffold bar or a scaffold tower is a simple way of deriving a suitable lighting suspension facility. Care should be exercised to ensure that any scaffolding used is safe, i.e.

● Correctly designed for the particular load.
● Correctly assembled.
● Correctly earthed.

Use of a professional rigging company is essential to ensure that these criteria are met, within any complex structure. Hired 'Zip-up' towers in aluminium tubing offer a quick and easy way to derive a lighting/camera platform. Due note should be made of the weight loading and height restrictions. As a general principle any tower should not be **taller** than four times the minimum base dimension unless outrigger supports are included.

Trussing (Figure 11.11) may consist of two, three or four aluminium bars (of various standard diameters) 'tied together' to make a very strong lightweight building component. Trussing has the advantage of being easy to assemble and de-rig. It may be used in two basic ways:

● Self-supported structure, which may incorporate a facility to raise and lower the lighting suspension system. This enables all the rigging of luminaires and cables to be completed at ground level – a faster and safer method than at high level, off ladders.

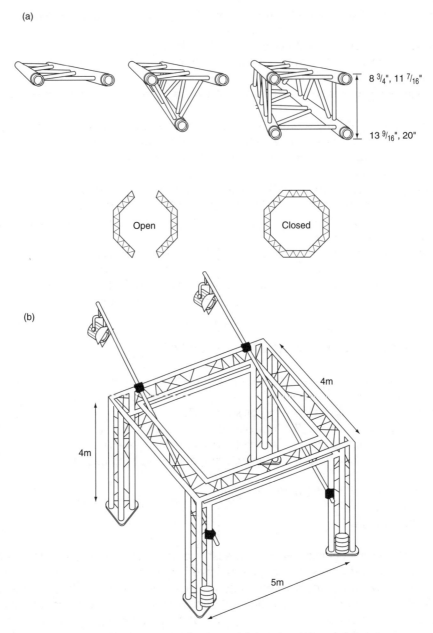

(a)

8 3/4", 11 7/16"

13 9/16", 20"

Open   Closed

(b)

4m

4m

5m

Figure 11.11 (a) Typical truss elements; (b) truss structures

Usually these structures are a complete shape, i.e. no open ends, thus making a strong rigid structure (Figure 11.1(b)).

● Supported from the ceiling on temporary electric chain winches. Ideally the structure should be a 'complete' shape to give it extra rigidity and extra strength. This also enables rigging at floor level.

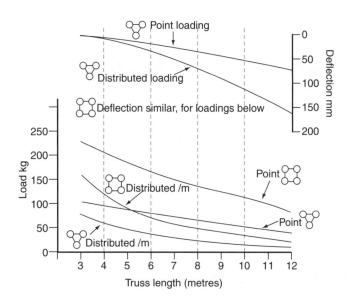

Figure 11.12 Typical performance loadings for 8-inch truss

Pop concerts are good examples in the use of trussing, but lightweight trussing can be very useful for many smaller scale requirements. For example, if there is a need to construct a small lighting 'grid' over a location, a simple four-sided trussing box could be erected, supplemented with aluminium bars to create a 'grid'. The upstage 'legs' could be disguised by suitable drapes or an extra 'return' designed by the designer. The basic rectangular structure may be used to derive a lighting position upstage using cantilever bars, e.g. stately home, expensive wall coverings, coverage required for piano recital with string accompaniment. Nothing can be attached to the walls. If the director wants it shot multi-camera close-up, then repeat to the sound track in wide-angle. The use of the wide truss plus cantilever plus stage weights saved the day (Figure 11.11(b)).

Figure 11.12 illustrates typical loading for the 8-inch lightweight aluminium truss. Always double check truss diameters and required fixing clamp size for luminaires!

Scissors lift, an electronically operated lift, is an alternative way to achieve a lighting platform, extremely quick, capable of siting several luminaires including a follow spot plus operator. Scissor lifts are an excellent way to rig suspended luminaires fast and in complete safety, being mobile they can be moved rapidly between lighting suspension points. Usually, they must be operated by a certified operator.

Genie towers, although primarily used as access equipment, may also be used to provide a suitable lighting 'platform'.

Cherry pickers or hydraulic platforms are the ultimate high-level lighting platforms, often used when large areas have to be lit at night, e.g. to provide a lighting platform for the 'moon'. They must be operated by a certified operator.

12
Electrical essentials

12.1 Electrical mains supplies – basics

Anyone using mains-operated luminaires should have an awareness of how to use mains supplies safely. This chapter discuss the important features of electrical mains supplies, safety and installation.

Domestic premises

The normal mains supply to domestic premises is a single phase alternating voltage (Figure 12.1 and Table 12.1). The quoted mains supply is normally the **r.m.s value** (root. mean. square value). This is based on calculating the average heating effect over one half-cycle of the mains waveform. The r.m.s value is the equivalent direct voltage to give the same heating effect and is sometimes referred to as the **effective** value. For a sine wave, the r.m.s value is 0.7 × peak value. The same principle applies to the alternating current, i.e. the r.m.s value of the current is 0.7 × peak value.

In a circuit that is made up of a **resistive** load, Ohm's law applies:

$$R = \frac{V}{I}$$

where

$R =$ circuit resistance in ohms
$V =$ r.m.s voltage (Vr.m.s) in volts
$I =$ r.m.s current (Ir.m.s) in amperes

Note: it is usual to omit the **r.m.s** suffixes.

Power in the AC circuit is measured in watts:

$$\text{Power} = I \times V \text{ or } \frac{V^2}{R} \text{ or } I^2 R \text{ watts (resistive load)}$$

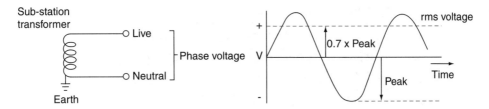

Figure 12.1 Single-phase

Table 12.1 Mains voltage (single phase)

	Main frequency (Hz)	Mains voltage (r.m.s voltage)
Europe	50	230
USA	60	120

Note: UK mains used to be quoted as 240 V ± 6% but is now 230 V + 10−6%.

The heating effect of the current is therefore proportional to the **square** of the current. This illustrates one of the dangers of excessive current, i.e. a **doubling** of the current results in a **four-fold** increase in the heating effect, a **tripling** of the current results in a **nine-fold** increase in the heating effect!

Commercial premises

Commercial premises are usually supplied with three phases of alternating voltage, each 'phase' being out of step with each other by 120° (Figure 12.2). This arrangement has significant advantages over single-phase generation and distribution. However, one should be aware of the dangers associated with three phase supplies, namely:

Voltage between any phase and neutral is normal single-phase voltage.
But voltage between any two phases is $\sqrt{3} \times$ phase voltage (Table 12.2).

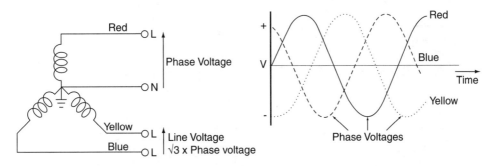

Figure 12.2 Three-phase

Table 12.2 Mains voltage (three phase)

	Phase voltage	Line voltage
Europe	230 V (240 V)	400 V (415 V)
USA	120 V	208 V

Note: Original voltage shown in parenthesis.

The 208 V/120 V system has the major advantage of a 120 V single-phase voltage which is safer from an electric shock viewpoint than the 230 V single-phase voltage. However, for a given load the 120 V system will require twice the current, hence larger cables. With a three-phase system supplying identical power loads on each phase, the neutral current is zero! Usually there is a need to 'balance' the loads on a three-phase system to minimise the neutral current.

Three-phase supplies must always be operated by qualified electricians. Similarly, any connections to single-phase supplies, other than by installed power sockets, must be made by a qualified electrician.

12.2 Installations

Domestic installation – UK (230 V)

Domestic installations normally are protected at the consumer unit, which is a main breaker and fuse panel (or miniature circuit breaker, mcb) fitted immediately after the supply company's meter. All modern premises should be wired in flat pvc insulated cable. If the cable is round and rubber insulated, beware – this is very old! Old rubber-insulated cables may not have the desired insulating properties due to ageing of the rubber, and as a consequence they represent a potential danger.

The modern practice is to have three basic circuits wired from the consumer unit:

- **Lighting circuits**, wired in cable with conductors of 1 mm^2 cross-sectional areas and fused at 5 A.
- **Ring main, power circuits**, wired in cable with conductors of 2.5 mm^2 cross-sectional area and fused at 30 A. These feed 13 A socket outlets rated at 3 kW (3000 W) (Figure 12.3).

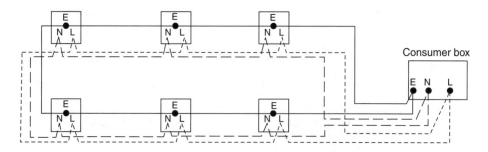

Figure 12.3 30 A ring main of power sockets (UK)

Each ring main may cover $100\,m^2$. A typical two-storey house would have two ring mains, one for each floor.

- **Special power circuits**, rated above 3 kW, e.g. cookers, immersion heaters, electrical shower units etc.

Obviously, on location, the main use will be of 13 A sockets. Although the ring main is fused at 30 A, each plug top is individually fused at 13 A, brown; 5 A, black; or 3 A, red. Three-Amp fuses should be used in equipment taking less than 720 W; 5 A for equipment up to 1150 W; and the 13 A fuse on equipment up to 3 kW.

Domestic installation – Europe (230 V)

Power circuits are protected at the consumer unit with an mcb. Each power circuit is rated at 16 A and typically may have up to ten outlets on one circuit. Each outlet has a maximum capacity of 16 A. However, the total capacity for each circuit is also 16 A, i.e. one may use as many outlets as possible until the total load is 16 A (3680 W).

Domestic installation – USA (120 V)

This is similar to Europe, except that in domestic installations the power outlets are rated at 16 A (1920 W). Offices have power outlets rated at 20 A (4600 W).

Calculation of current/wattage

As we have seen, the safety aspects of an installation are current operated, so there is a need to be able to determine the current for a given wattage of a lamp. Current (I), voltage (V) and power in watts are related by the formula:

Power (P) = Voltage $(V) \times$ Current (I) watts $\qquad P = I \times V$ watts

Rearranging:

$$I = \frac{P}{V} \text{ amps}$$

e.g. What is the current when using a 1000 W tungsten light source with a 230 V supply?

$$I = \frac{1000}{230} = 4.3\,A$$

(Often an approximation of 4 A/kW is used, but do remember that this gives a **lower** answer than reality.)

e.g.   5 kW $\cong$ 20 A, in reality is 21.7 A

Example 1   How many 800 W Redheads can you safely operate from a 13 A socket?

Max power to be taken from a 13 A socket $= 3000\,\text{W}$

No. of 800 W Redheads $= \dfrac{3000}{800} = 3.75$

Answer: $3 \times$ Redheads is maximum number

Example 2   How many 2000 W Blondes can you safely operate from a 13 A socket and in total on a 13 A ring main?

A 13 A socket can supply 3000 W, so only one 2000 W Blonde. A ring main can supply a maximum of 7 kW, so three Blondes can be plugged in to one ring main, i.e. a total of 6000 W.

   Normally an installation would have several ring mains, each one covering a maximum of $100\,\text{m}^2$. For a two-storey house this would mean a ring main for each floor.

12.3   Electrical safety

The main safety hazards associated with any electrical installation are fire and electric shock. Working on location usually means that the electrical installation is unknown. However, in properly protected installations protective devices such as fuses and miniature circuit breakers (mcb's) should operate before such a catastrophe as a fire occurs.

Fuses and mcb's – protection against fire

It is normal to earth one 'leg' of the mains supply, thereby creating a LIVE and NEUTRAL connection. This, together with the EARTH connection, provides the necessary safety protection should a LIVE to EARTH connection occur. The fuse is designed to protect the installation from the consequences of an excessive current caused by a circuit overload or an earth fault by 'blowing', i.e. breaking the circuit (Figure 12.4).

   Fuses are designed to handle their rated current continuously, i.e. a 13 A fuse will handle 13 amps without 'blowing'. Typically, wire-wound fuses blow at about $\times 2$ the fuse rating and cartridge fuses (as in a 13 A plug) at $1.5 \times$ the fuse rating. It should be noted that fuses can be weakened by repeatedly running them above their rated value. This makes them unpredictable in their performance. Miniature circuit breakers are **current-operated** trips, which can have a well-defined performance and normally trip once their current rated value has been exceeded. Miniature circuit breakers have the advantage over fuses in that they can be reset. However, if they continue to trip after being reset twice the circuit should be investigated for faults before further attempts at resetting the mcb.

   Note that circuits using a large amount of electronic equipment will have a large surge current on 'switch-on'. A special slow-blow mcb (Type C) should be used in these installations to avoid nuisance tripping at switch-on of the main circuit breaker.

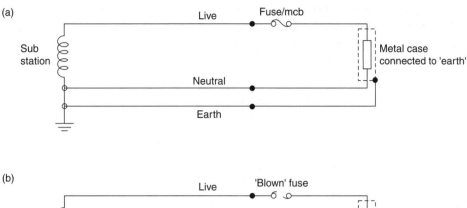

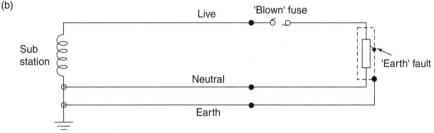

Figure 12.4 (a) Basic electrical protection; (b) fuse protection

ELCB/RCD – protection against electrical shock

Unfortunately, fuses and mcb's do not operate fast enough to provide protection against electrical shock. Most electrical installations include an **earth leakage circuit breaker** (elcb) or **residual current device** (rcd), which can detect a small imbalance in the current flowing in the neutral conductor compared with that in the live conductor. The missing current will have taken an **earth-leakage** path such as through a person accidentally touching a line conductor. Elcb's or rcd's can be set to trip at a predetermined value of leakage current, typically 30 mA (a current greater than 30 mA, through the heart, can be fatal!) or sometimes 100 mA (Figure 12.5).

Note that rcd's will not give protection if you have contact with Live and Neutral! Not all installations have rcd's. It is recommended to use an rcd with all portable lighting equipment when connected to mains power sockets of unknown specification, i.e. no rcd.

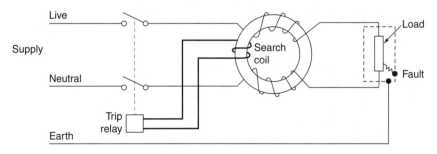

Figure 12.5 Residual current device (rcd) – basic principle

Under normal no-fault conditions equal but opposite magnetic fields are induced in the soft iron ring, i.e. cancel each other. When a fault occurs (earth leakage fault) the live and neutral currents are not the same, the magnetic fields do not cancel. The induced voltage in the search coil operates the trip relay.

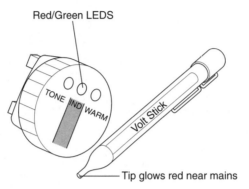

Figure 12.6 Simple mains testers

A simple tester (Figure 12.6) is available to check power sockets, which gives an indication of the status of Live, Neutral, Earth (except on Earth/Neutral reversal). A 'Volt stick' is another simple tester (Figure 12.6), which will safely detect the presence of mains voltage within about 4 mm from its tip. It is useful to identify quickly the loss of mains to the lamp, fuse, cable, switch etc. (will not help with neutral faults!).

Three phase installations (3Ø)

Ideally equipment should be more than 2 m apart if on different phases. This is not always practical, however, clear notices of 3Ø must be displayed. The danger associated with accidentally simultaneously touching two phases is illustrated in Figure 12.7.

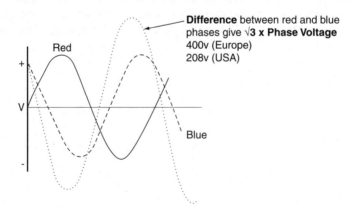

Figure 12.7 Three-phase danger!

12.4   Use of generator

There may be a need to use a generator on location to provide the AC mains supply for the following reasons:

- No suitable mains supply available – insufficient power
  - unreliable supply
  - low voltage
  - no mains available
- Back-up supply to the National Grid for actuality coverage of an important event
- Operational convenience, when needing to cover many areas to avoid having to make a special mains connection. Plus convenience of standard plugs and sockets, no need for adaptors to domestic mains.

Generators may be:

- Portable – providing just a few kVA of power.
- Static – delivered to site by a separate vehicle and left.
- Mobile – generator complete with its distribution system on its own vehicle.
- Carrier – in which space is provided on the generator vehicle for carrying lighting equipment.
- Trailer – generator complete with its distribution system on a trailer.

Generators must be operated by a skilled electrician and must always be earthed to provide the appropriate electrical safety features.

Generators may be silenced or unsilenced (noisy!). Clearly a generator used to power the lighting on a distant background at night does not need to be silent. However, generally the generators should be silent so that they may be used as close as possible to the action, i.e. keep cable runs short.

Generator rating

Generators are rated in kVA (kilo Volt-Amps) not in kW, i.e. the product of the voltage and current. It is important that the load presented to the generator is a resistive one – current and voltage in phase with each other. If the load is not resistive, i.e. not totally tungsten lighting, the generator should be **down-rated** to accommodate the fact that the current and voltage are out of phase. For example, when the load is of a significant number of discharge sources (HMI/MSR) there is a need to down-rate the generator by a factor of 0.7, a 100 kVA generator then becomes 70 kVA.

HMI/MSR ballasts are available which operate with a **Unity Power Factor** (UPF). These present a resistive load to the generator, consequently there is no need to down-rate the generator if using UPF ballasts. However, always allow some 'headroom' with generators, that is, choose a generator capacity that allows for some latitude on loading, e.g. for an 80 kVA load use a 100 kVA generator. Equally, diesel generators should not be run lightly loaded as this may cause the exhaust system to soot up resulting in an exhaust fire!

Three-phase/single-phase

Many hire companies quote generator ratings in kW, assuming a resistive load kW = kVA. It is therefore easy to calculate required generator loading. A three-phase generator is more efficient and lighter than an equivalent rated single-phase generator. The complications in using a three-phase generator are:

● the need to provide a balanced load to all three phases, i.e. to within 20%
● the need for a triple distribution of power
● safety aspects of three-phase (400 V).

Typically, generators up to about 50 kVA are single-phase. Above 50 kVA they will probably be three-phase, but with the facility to operate at single-phase if required.

Siting of generators

● As close as possible to the location to minimise cable runs.
● On firm ground, generators are heavy! Steel plates may be needed to spread the load.
● On level ground so that the generator's diesel engine is properly lubricated. There may be a need to block-up the generator wheels to achieve a level 'platform'.

13
Safety

The main safety hazards associated with lighting on location are:

electrical fire
electric shock
tripping accidents
falling objects/contact with lighting equipment
equipment falling over
lamp explosion
ultraviolet radiation
lifting incorrectly.

Electrical safety

- Total electric load must be within the capacity of the mains supply/generator.
- All lighting equipment must be properly fused and the correct rating of cable used, as appropriate.
- All lighting equipment should be properly maintained with regular checks of cable and connections and have PAT tested certification (Portable Appliance Test).
- All luminaires should be rigged such that the heat generated cannot do any danger or cause the risk of fire.
- Residual current devices (rcd's) should be used to protect against electric shock.
- rcd's should be checked for correct operation before use.
- All scaffolding and trussing should be earthed.
- Generator must be earthed to ensure the normal safety conditions.

Tripping accidents

- Lighting cables should be rigged to avoid public thoroughfares. If this is not possible, cable ramps or rubber matting should be used on the cables to minimise tripping accidents. Special hazard tape, black/yellow striped, can be used on cables.

Falling objects, contact with lighting equipment

- **All suspended lighting equipment must be securely safety bonded to the suspension system, i.e. scaffolding/trussing, and barndoors to the luminaire.**
- All suspended lighting equipment must be at an appropriate height to avoid head contact. Human awareness of luminaires on stands is generally good. However, we are not good at avoiding items hanging down from the ceiling!
- When adjusting the height of a stand, especially when lowering it, be aware of which section you are undoing. Many accidents, resulting in trapped fingers, occur through loss of attention to this detail! Take care with wind-up stands!

Equipment falling over

- All lighting stands should be rigged correctly with the stand vertical. A useful feature on many stands is a lazy leg or adjustable leg. This enables the stand to be rigged on uneven ground or on stairs.
- Cables from luminaires or stands should be rigged through two of the legs of the stand. This avoids the possibility of the stand falling over should anyone trip over the cable (Figure 13.1).
- All stands with diffuser frames, reflector boards and butterflies should be sandbagged to ensure maximum stability. This is especially so when rigged out of doors.
- Luminaires must be rigged at an appropriate height to be safe. Special note should be made, not just of the maximum height of the stand but also of the maximum safe working load.
- Free-standing luminaires, in public places, must be manned by an electrician.

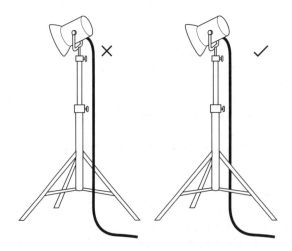

Figure 13.1 Correct rigging of stands/cables

Explosion

- All lamps, except low pressure lamps, have a history of exploding. All luminaires fitted with these lamps must have a suitable wire safety mesh or safety glass to ensure that any flying glass from an exploding lamp is contained within the luminaire.
- High Pressure lamps (HMI, MSR, CID, CSI and Xenon) should **not** be moved when **hot**, they should be allowed to cool before moving.
- Xenon lamps must only be handled with special safety equipment (see p. 81).

Ultraviolet (UV) radiation

- All high pressure discharge sources emit **harmful** UV. Luminaires using these sources **must** be fitted with a suitable UV filter (glass filter). The safety interlock which prevents these sources igniting should the glass UV filter become damaged must **never** be bypassed.

Lifting

- Lifting incorrectly over a long period of time can result in damage to the spine. All personnel engaged in any lighting operations should be trained in correct lifting procedures to reduce the risk of a very painful condition.

Note: Rough handling of a lit tungsten lamp can lead to filament failure, e.g.

- wheeling a luminaire/stand over rough ground
- accidentally dropping a section of the stand
- stand falling following a tripping accident.

On exterior shoots, rain can be a problem. Usually, once a luminaire is switched on the heat it generates will evaporate any rain. Some degree of protection can be gained by making a simple 'hood' over the luminaire with clear filter and crocodile clips/gaffer tape. Driving rain onto a lens of a lit lamp may cause the lens to crack due to cooling on the inside of the lens. The lamps used on the Wendy light are particularly vulnerable in the rain – they explode!

14
Basic lighting on location

14.1 Basic lighting kit

The 'basic three-lamp kit' is a term often used to describe the kit of luminaires carried by most cameramen engaged in single-camera operations. In many instances the cameraman may be working alone, sometimes with a sound recordist, and sometimes with the luxury of an electrician! The early portable lighting kits often meant three Redheads plus stands in a lightweight case, often supplemented with a 2 kW Blonde for any special requirement. The three Redheads at 800 W each can be safely connected to a 13 A socket ($\cong$3 kW maximum power) without the need for a special supply. It has to be remembered that light sources such as the open-faced Redhead were required to light for cameras needing in excess of 1000 lux.

Often, because of the need for speed of working, the cameramen only had time for one trip from the car. Consequently, on many occasions only one Redhead ever reached the 'action' unless an electrician was present. Many situations, however, only required one luminaire plus a reflector, to supplement daylight. Nevertheless, the concept of having three luminaires as a basic kit still prevails and of course is useful in situations of no natural lighting.

The Redhead provides a wide beam angle (86°) with a candlepower of approximately 6500 candelas in the **flood** mode. At 2.5 m this produces 1040 lux which can be increased to approximately 6000 lux by **spotting** the luminaire. This is more than adequate for modern cameras. Consequently, other luminaires may be considered in identifying the 'ideal' three-lamp kit, e.g.

1 × 800 W Redhead

- for providing wide coverage, especially in confined spaces
- a good source for 'bouncing'
- excellent for use with a Chimera.

1 × 650 W Fresnel spotlight (with 500 W lamp)

- for providing a controllable keylight (good barndooring)
- with correction filter/diffusion still provides enough illuminance for most applications.

1 × 300 W Fresnel spotlight

- for providing a controllable backlight.

The 650 W spotlight has the obvious advantage of being used with a 650 W lamp to provide extra light when required. One could consider using two 300 W spotlights (+Redhead), using a 500 W lamp in the 300 W spotlight when required. Unfortunately, the smaller lens diameter of the 300 W spotlight results in an inferior performance, hence the recommendation of the above 'kit' to give a flexible lighting system with minimum weight and size.

A useful addition to this kit would be a single Dedolight (see p. 127) with a projection lens attachment. This would provide the facility to project gobos on backgrounds, that is, break-up patterns, window patterns etc.

Many news cameramen use a lightweight kit of 3 × 300 W open-faced luminaires, which can provide an absolute essential lighting facility combined with being lightweight. Another alternative is to use a Dedolight kit, supplemented with a Redhead or similar, for wide-angle lighting requirements or when needing to 'bounce' light.

The following list is suggested as a basic lighting kit and accessories to enable a cameraman to cope with many basic lighting set-ups (all lights to include stands):

1 × 800 W open-faced luminaire, plus Chimera
1 × 650 W Fresnel spotlight, fitted with 500 W lamp
1 × either 300 W Fresnel spotlight or 650 W Fresnel spotlight fitted with 300 W lamp
1 × 100 W Dedolight plus gobo projection attachment and in-line dimmer
1 × 38-inch silver/white collapsible reflector plus universal arm
1 × 24-inch × 36-inch black flag
1 × 24-inch × 36-inch single black veil
2 × flexible arms to support flag/veil plus clamps to stands
1 × magic arm plus super-clamps
Pre-cut correction filters full CTB, ¾CTB, ½CTB, and ¼CTB. Full CTO, ¾CTO, ½CTO and ¼CTO.
Pre-cut ND filter 0.15 ND, 0.3 ND for lights
Rolls/Part rolls 0.6 ND and 0.9 ND
Pre-cut White Diffusion, ½ White Diffusion, Hamburg Frost, Tough Silk, Tough Spun
16 crocodile clips
Scissors clamp
3 × RCDs
1 × Mains tester
Spare fuses (for 13 A plug tops and equipment)
1 × small torch
Roll of gaffer tape
Spare lamps

3 × 4-way mains distribution box
Extension mains leads

Many set-ups require only one luminaire and reflector. It is worth having these plus filters etc. available as a lightweight kit, in a rucksack, ready for immediate use.

14.2   Effect of light – not just illumination!

Before discussing the basic principles of lighting, it is valuable to discuss the effect of light – illumination is only one aspect of light. We need to have illumination of the scene in order to see it, but illumination is not alone. Consider the following (see Figure 14.1, pages 169–170):

- Light creates **shadows**, unless lighting a flat surface. Shadows reveal the form of the subject. The nature of the shadows will depend on the light source, that is, hard or soft source (Figure 14.1(a)).
- Light creates **contrast** between different planes, depending on how much light reaches each plane and the reflectance of the plane. Shadow density also introduces contrast on the subject.
- Light reveals **texture**, the nature of a surface. For similar lighting angles to a subject a hard source will reveal more texture than a soft source (Figure 14.1(b)).
- Light can reveal the **shape** of a subject by silhouetting the subject, i.e. by lighting the background (Figure 14.1(c)).
- Light can **separate** planes by rim lighting from up-stage (Figure 14.1(d)).
- Light can create **depth** in scene by lighting the planes in a scene such that 'light' is against 'dark' and 'dark' is against 'light'.
- Light can be used to create **mood** by appropriate use of **shadows** and **contrast**, and distribution of tones. The term 'key' is often used to describe mood (this has nothing to do with key or keylight), i.e.

  Low key – predominance of dark tones and heavy shadows – dramatic pictures
  Medium key – normal tonal distribution, shadow, contrast approx. 2:1
  High key – predominance of light tones and 'thin' shadows – almost two-dimensional.

- The **colour** of lighting can be used to create **mood**. We associate the longer wavelength colours, reds/oranges/yellows with feelings of warmth, friendly and inviting. The shorter wavelengths, blues/lavenders we associate with coldness and being unfriendly. Green is a strange colour. However, when used desaturated it can convey a cool feeling. Often, used in a limited way, the more saturated greens can suggest 'evil'.
- The **saturation** of the colour can be used to help in the creation of **depth**. In Nature the shorter wavelength colours (blues) recede – thus appear further away, and the longer wavelengths (reds) advance. Distant colours are seen desaturated with little contrast, often as a blue haze. Close colours are seen at full saturation and, compared with the distant scene, warmer, with maximum contrast.
- Light can be used in creating **clarity** of subject or **ambiguity**. There are two extremes; for news/current affairs situation there is a need for the portraiture to have an 'open and honest' look with no dramatic lighting of the presenter. On the other hand, a drama

script may call for a strong element of mystery to be created by using selective lighting of the subject and background.

Armed with these observations about light, we can now consider basic lighting principles.

14.3 Basic portraiture – 'creating a good likeness'

Good portraiture is an essential part of television lighting and is an obvious aim for anyone engaged in lighting. This means creating a good likeness of the subject; in drama lighting, the portraiture is often more dramatic, using the visual clues in the location to determine how the person should be lit. As a basic principle on location, observe the lighting occurring naturally and add whatever is required to make the lighting 'look right'.

(a)

(b)

Figure 14.1 The effect of light: (a) Shadows revealing form; (b) texture

(c)

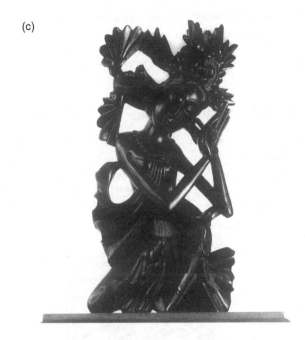

(d)

Figure 14.1 *Continued* (c) use of silhouette to reveal shape; (d) rim lighting to separate planes

However, it is useful to review the basics of portraiture to establish a solid base of awareness of light on faces and to give a starting point in the lighting process. Ideally, the aim is to light artistes separately from their backgrounds enabling separate control over subject and background. Three lights are used to establish basic portraiture:

- Keylight
- Fill-light or filler
- Backlight.

Keylight – basics

As its name suggests, this is the main light in any lighting set-up:

- It is usually a hard source such as a Fresnel spotlight, providing crisp shadows and good control of the lit area. Note that it could also be a softlight, if the situation so required.
- It establishes the direction of light within a set, e.g. from a window or practical light.
- It creates shadows (modelling) on the subject to reveal form and texture.
- The effect seen on camera is determined by the angle between the keylight and the camera.

This latter point is a **fundamental** statement about lighting. By experimenting with a small Fresnel spotlight on a floor stand together with a television camera and monitor, you can quickly establish some important principles of portraiture, for example; the larger the angle between keylight and camera, the greater the degree of modelling (shadows) and texture revealed. This is true in both the vertical direction and horizontal direction.

Much stress is often made of the effects of horizontal angle in portraiture. In most instances it is the vertical keying angle that can change the look of a subject from acceptable to unacceptable, e.g. too steep a keying angle.

- The need to keep 'catchlights' in the eyes is also important to give the eyes 'life'. Without 'catchlights' the eyes will look dull. If there is no light in the eyes at all, the subject will tend to look 'shifty', even 'menacing' (Figure 14.2).
- The subject's shadow should be kept out of shot (Figure 14.3). In any formal set-up, e.g. news presentation, it is essential to avoid an in-shot shadow of the artiste on the background – it will be a distraction for the viewer. If, however, it is unavoidable, the shadow can be made less of a distraction by using diffusion on the keylight to 'soften' the shadow (Figure 14.4). Similarly, use this approach with subjects in high-backed chairs.
- Any light source below the artiste's eyeline will result in underlighting, an unnatural way to light people, especially if taken to extreme angles (Figure 14.5). This is a technique usually used for 'horror' lighting; or with less extreme angles together with a 'flicker' pole to create a fire-flicker effect.
- An 'open and honest' look is achieved with minimum shadows on the face (Figure 14.6). However, it will look very flat if the light is literally just above the camera lens. A typical set-up would be to use a keylight with an elevation of about 25° and offset about 15° from the camera axis.

Figure 14.2 Too steep a keying angle – pack of catchlights in the eyes

Figure 14.3 Hard shadow on background – distracting

Figure 14.4 Use of diffusion on keylight to soften shadow on background

Figure 14.5 Under-lit subject

Figure 14.6 Typical 'open and honest' keylight position, with key localised to subject – barndoored or 'flagged' off the background

- For dramatic lighting, it can be useful to join the nose shadow to the cheek shadow to produce a triangle of light on the shadow side of the face (Figure 14.7). This is often referred to as **Rembrandt** lighting, after the famous painter, who incorporated this lighting feature into many of his portraits (Figure 14.8).

14.4 Keylight – practicalities

Very few faces are truly symmetrical and often actors will talk about their 'better side'. This is perfectly true – they may look better if lit from one side. A simple test with two lamps set up symmetrically to the camera will help to identify the 'better side'. Switching between lamp A and lamp B will show if one side produces the better portraiture. Often there is no

Figure 14.7 Semi-profile shot, framed to use modelling side of the face

Figure 14.8 Semi-profile shot, illustrating Rembrandt lighting

need to analyse the picture – the differences are obvious. The features which affect the portraiture, or portrayal of likeness, include:

- shape of the face – round, oval, egg-shaped
- shape of the jawline – square or rounded
- asymmetry of the face about the centre-line. The modelling will make the shadowed side of the face appear to be narrower. Clearly one needs to avoid making the naturally narrow side even narrower
- line of the eyes
- line of the mouth
- bent nose – if the subject is keyed the same way as the bend of the nose this will exaggerate the nose bend. If keyed in the opposite direction it will tend to straighten out the bend
- hairline – this may be higher on one side, so if keyed from that side will tend to make the face look longer than if keyed on the opposite side

- protruding ears – try to avoid lighting the ear which stands out the most
- scars, bumps etc. – the principle here is to avoid revealing texture in the area of the blemish, i.e. 'key' into the blemish.

Watch out for artistes with deep-set eyes or artistes using their eyebrows to shade the keylight from their eyes. It used to be said that 'if the keylight doesn't hurt it isn't right!' With the high sensitivity of modern cameras this does not have to be so. Many location situations involve lighting and shooting people in their own home. Aim to make the experience as 'painless' as possible by making the lighting unobtrusive, i.e.

- Use half-white diffusion on the keylight, which will reduce the glare from it. The light will no longer be a dazzling point source but a larger area source. The barndoors no longer work, so there may be a need to use a flag to keep the light off the background. Note that a small area of diffusion will not transform the lighting into a softly lit scene like on an overcast day! The modelling from, say, a 0.25 m × 0.25 m light source will still look crisp, but you will have made the subjects' life more bearable.
- Use a Chimera on the keylight (typically an open-faced luminaire).
- Use a Rifa-lite as the keylight.
- Consider using fluorescent lights as a source of keylight to provide a large area light source – again less glare for the subject.
- Ensure that the area behind the camera is lit so that the subject is not looking into a single light source against a dark background.

Using any of these techniques to 'soften' the keylight means that barndoors are no longer effective in keeping the light off the background. This is where a simple black flag, of dimensions greater than the light source, can be used to provide some 'shading' to the background. The further from the light source is the flag, the harder will be the shadow edge created (and the larger will the flag need to be to cover the complete light 'beam').

When shooting interviews there is a need to light a semi-profile shot. Generally, light these to give the shadows towards the camera. This will allow more modelling to be seen on camera and allow more dramatic modeling, e.g. Rembrandt lighting, to be seen to best advantage.

How much keylight? With the camera aperture set to $f2.4$, say, adjust the keylight intensity until the facetones look correctly exposed (typically about 0.5 V of video or about one stop below peak white if the Knee facility is not operational).

The keylight reveals the form of the subject but generally results in shadows, which are too dark. There is, therefore, a need to fill-in the shadows with an additional light – the **fill-light**, **fill** or **filler**.

14.5 Fill-light, fill or filler

The fill-light, fill or filler is used to add light to the shadow areas to reduce the density of the shadows, i.e. make the shadows transparent. Ideally the fill-light should not introduce additional modelling or result in a second shadow being created which is visible on-camera. A soft light source will generally be used as a fill-light, but it does suffer from the disadvantage of the light going everywhere, unless it can be controlled in some way, i.e. flooding the background with light! In a dramatic situation it may therefore be more appropriate to use a 'hard' fill-light to contain the light only to the artiste.

How much fill-light? Fill-light is very much like medicine – to be used as necessary! The illuminance provided by the fill-light will depend on a number of factors, i.e.

- Nature of the programme and the requirement or otherwise for dramatic looking pictures – drama, documentary, comedy.
- Nature of the subject's skin tone, i.e. fair or dark.
- Nature of the subject's costume. A very dark costume will reflect very little light onto the subject's face, whereas a light costume will reflect some light into the shadow areas on the subject's face.
- Nature of the set – dark floor and dark scenery will reflect very little light into shadow areas of the subject; light-toned floors and scenery will give rise to some light being reflected into the subject's face.

The exact amount of fill-light to be used will be down to the **judgement** of the lighting operator (based on satisfying the director's requirements) (see Figures 14.9 and 14.10).

Fill-light placement

There are two major schools of thought about where to place the fill-light (Figure 14.11):

- Alongside the camera at lens height.
- On the opposite side of the camera to the keylight, located approximately 90° from the keylight.

The first positioning is based on filling in the shadows 'seen' by the camera. It is usually placed on the opposite side to the keylight, although there are some practitioners who use the same side as the keylight. The latter practice is based on avoiding conflicting second shadows. The disadvantage of the fill-light at the camera is that, for normal keylight angles,

Figure 14.9 Keylight and filler

Figure 14.10 Semi-profile shot with keylight and filler

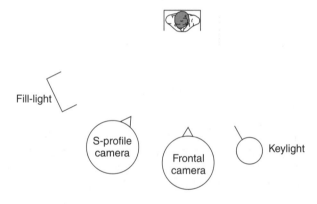

Figure 14.11 Basic plot

it will add to the exposure achieved by the keylight, i.e. it is difficult to balance the fill-light and keylight independently. It also may not satisfy the needs of multi-camera shooting.

● Can give rise to 'muddy' in-shot shadows on the background.

The second approach of placing the fill-light at 90° to the keylight results in:

● Ability to balance lighting levels of the keylight and fill-light independently.
● No 'muddy' in-shot shadows behind the artiste.
● No second shadows if the fill-light is of a large area.
● Multi-camera shooting (on shadow-side of subject) being catered for.

An important point to remember is that the fill-light should be of as low an elevation as possible to ensure that the light reaches all shadow areas, e.g. into the eye-sockets, under the chin.

The main practical points about the fill-light are:

- Ideally a soft light.
- Placed to minimise shadows – approximately 90° to keylight.
- Low elevation.
- Double shadows should be avoided if possible.
- Minimise amount of fill-light reaching the background by using soft-light close to the subject (inverse square law).

Flags can be used to prevent the fill-light reaching the background, or a veil used to **reduce** the level of fill-light on the background. Remember, flags and veils have to be of a larger area than the fill-light to be effective.

14.6   Control of light – use of inverse square law

The inverse square law is a fundamental 'fact of light', i.e.

$$\text{Illuminance} \propto \frac{1}{(\text{distance})^2}$$

$$\textbf{Illuminance} = \frac{\text{Candlepower}}{(\text{distance})^2} \text{ lux (if using metres)}$$

(Units of **illuminance** are foot-candles if measuring distance in feet.)

It has been seen earlier that use can be made of this law in estimating illuminance at a given distance for a particular luminaire of known candlepower (candelas). Strictly speaking the inverse square law is only applicable to point sources such as the Fresnel spotlight. However, it can be used with soft sources provided it is remembered that a soft source will behave as an **inverse law** of illuminance until the distance from the source is comparable with the dimensions of the light source, it then becomes inverse square law. What this means in practice is that of using the inverse square law for a soft source, the error at three times the dimension of the source from the source is only 10%!

Inverse square law in practice

The inverse square law may be used to best advantage in:

- Predicting illuminance from a light source at a given distance.
- Calculating luminous intensity of luminaire to achieve a particular illuminance at a given distance – and hence determine a suitable luminaire to be used.
- Reducing the change in relative illuminance on the lit scene by increasing the subject to luminaire distance.
- Increasing the change in relative illuminance on a lit scene by reducing the subject to luminaire distance.

The first two points have been covered elsewhere in this book (pp. 17–18).

The third point is probably the most commonly encountered, i.e. lighting a set-up so that the subjects can move around without significant changes in illuminance. Generally the aim is to keep the lighting simple by using as few luminaires as possible, that is, using a luminaire to cover as large an area as possible and at the longest practical distance. This will minimise the effects of the inverse square law. If is not practicable to use luminaires in this way due to small locations, nets/veils can be used to minimise the effects of the inverse square law *provided* there is a significant angle change at the luminaire between the upstage and downstage acting areas (Figure 14.12).

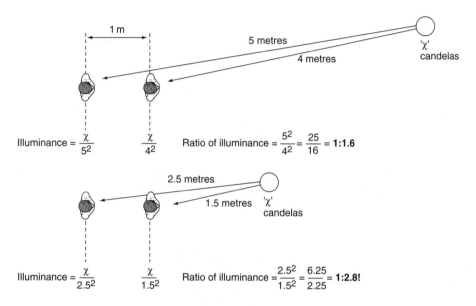

Figure 14.12 Reducing change in illumination with subject movement

The fourth point may, at first, not be obvious. It seems wrong to say 'reduce the exposure on the background by moving the luminaire **towards** the subject'! However, it is the **relative illuminance** between subject and background which will increase as the luminaire is moved closer to the subject. Figure 14.13 illustrates the principle.

It is often required to reduce background illuminance levels to gain good tonal separation between the foreground subject and the background. Many modern offices, for example, have light-toned walls. With shallow keying angles it is more difficult to use flags/veils to reduce the background illuminance then with excessive keying angles (usually less flattering). Consequently using the Inverse Square Law is a useful technique to obtain improved tonal separation.

14.7 The backlight

This light is variously known as backlight, rim-light or hair-light. 'Backlight' tends to be the preferred term. The backlight, normally a hard source of light, is used to light the subject from upstage to provide:

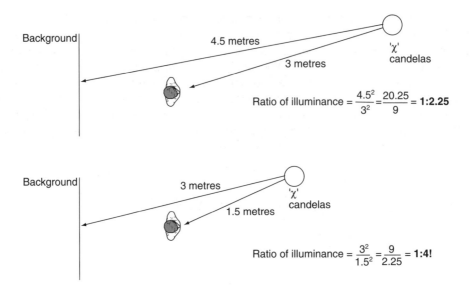

Figure 14.13 Increasing relative illuminances between subject and background

- Separation of the artiste from the background by putting a rim of light around the artiste
- Depth to the head by lighting the hair
- Roundness to the shoulders and arms
- 'Life' to the hair.

A single backlight is normally used so that it is backlight with reference to the camera position. Clearly on location this may not be possible because of the lighting stand appearing in shot. Normal practice is to place the backlight 'counter' to the keylight, that is, on the opposite side to the keylight (Figure 14.14).

Figure 14.14 Keylight, filter and backlight

- Because of the dramatic effect of the backlight in providing separation, great care needs to be exercised to ensure that it is not too bright, i.e. a distraction!
- The backlight is excellent as a glamorising light for female subjects. The single back-light aimed at the hair parting can be particularly effective for females. Beware of excess backlight with male presenters!
- Normally the backlight is a hard source, giving good control of beam shape and revealing texture to a maximum.
- Typically the backlight is at least 50% down on the keylight power. If the keylight has half-white diffusion fitted it reduces the power to 50%, i.e. a 500 W Fresnel spotlight becomes effectively 250 W!

Problems in using a backlight are:

- Avoiding camera lens flare

    - use barndoors to control beam shape
    - avoid too shallow a vertical angle for backlight
    - use an on-camera flag on a flexible arm

- Over-lighting of bald-headed/silver-headed subjects

    - diffuse backlight to make a large area instead of a point source. This 'spreads' the reflection of the light source over a larger area, resulting in a less bright reflection.
    - Use a half scrim or Neutral Density filter to reduce the intensity of the light beam in the region of the subject's head.
    - Use spot/flood mechanism to 'spot' the light onto the shoulders, thus minimising the amount of light on the top of the head.
    - If all else fails switch off the backlight to avoid a **distracting** highlight on a bald head **but** make sure that the subject is separated from the background by lighting the background (see Background light below).

- High-backed chairs – these can make it difficult to utilise an effective backlight (as well as producing a 'close' shadow of the subject's head from the keylight).

Subjects in easy chairs tend to 'slump'. This can sometimes result in the backlight lighting the front of the subject, often giving rise to a head shadow on the subject's chest (Figure 14.15). A shallow angle of elevation backlight is required to overcome this problem. In many instances it is more appropriate and more practical to use a 'kicker' – see p. 185.

14.8 Background light

Unless requiring the artiste against black there is a need to provide lighting for the background. Ideally this should be lit separately to enable individual control of lighting level. The background light:

- Reveals the nature of the background, background shape and texture.
- Adds depth to the picture by separating the artiste from the background.
- Reveals the **shape** of the artiste by silhouetting.

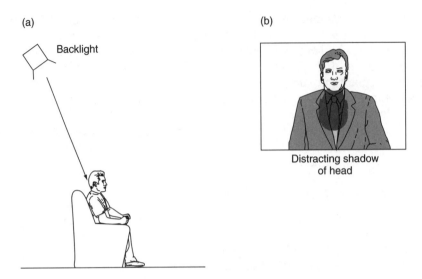

(a)

Backlight

(b)

Distracting shadow
of head

Figure 14.15 The problem of 'slumping' subjects and backlights

The background light has to be one which will reveal texture, and model the form of the background, it must be capable of being **directed** to the area to be lit and provide control of beam-shape – a hard source, i.e. Fresnel spotlight, is ideal. A softlight would light the nearest part of the background to be the brightest. If this is at the top of the picture it will tend to draw the eye out of the picture. A softlight could, however, be used to suggest light from a window (skylight only) if placed to one side of the background, and provided there was some means of controlling the lit area.

Plain backgrounds should be avoided. Always remember to shade the top of the background to maintain the feeling of a ceiling out of shot; add shadows from a suitable plant, or even from a step-ladder. The most important factors in lighting backgrounds are (see Figures 14.16–14.21):

- Plain backgrounds can be made more interesting by the addition of coloured light, shafts of light or simple gobo patterns using profile projectors. Alternatively, use cookies in front of a hard light source to create a break-up pattern or window pattern on the background. Note that any projected window pattern **must** be set so that the vertical lines on the pattern **remain vertical** on a vertical wall!
- A window with glazing bars or a venetian blind could be used with a suitable hard source (HMI) outside the window to create an appropriate effect on the background.
- Backgrounds which include drapes should be side-lit to reveal textures, i.e. the folds in the drapes.
- Avoiding an overlit background or one which has a distracting feature on it.
- Ensuring that the background colour and tonal value are significantly different to the facetone. The background tonal value should be at least $1\frac{1}{2}$ stops away from the facetone.

Normally aim for background tone to be less than facetone. This makes faces stand out. If the facetone is less than background it will, subjectively, look darker. When using 'limbo'

Figure 14.16 Natural window

Figure 14.17 Highlight at top of picture

avoid significant overload – flare correctors will not work properly, resulting in an incorrect black level!

When the background is made up of several **planes** aim to put light against dark, and dark against light to gain maximum depth and separation. Backlight any translucent backgrounds for best effect.

Figure 14.18 Correct window pattern

Figure 14.19 Drapes, side-lit

Figure 14.20 Dark background

Figure 14.21 Light against dark background

14.9 Kicker

Without doubt the kicker or kickerlight is one of the most effective lights to use when able to depart from a basic three-point lighting set-up. The **kicker** is an extra modelling light which is used upstage from the artiste to 'kick' the side of the head. It is distinct from a backlight in that it is rigged at head height and aimed towards the temple of the subject (Figure 14.22).

The kicker can be a hard or soft source positioned to 'kick', i.e. cause a **glare** reflection which models the shape of the face and reveals texture. A useful exercise is illustrated in Figure 14.23 in which a kicker light is set onto a subject and viewed from different angles. Initially the side of the face will simply look illuminated until a point is reached where the glare reflection (kick) can be observed. **Recognising this effect and using it can make a tremendous difference to any location lighting**.

The 'kicker' light is an naturally occurring light source! Observe people in bars and restaurants, buses and trains, offices and public places and you will quickly realise the significance and the value in using a kicker in your lighting.

When motivated, a kicker can make pictures look more three-dimensional by lighting an extra plane to the keylight, revealing texture and modelling by:

- Reinforcing the direction of sunlight when used on the same side as the keylight.
- Reinforcing the multi-light aspect of night-lighting when used on the opposite side to the keylight.

A useful concept is indicated in Figure 14.24. Imagine the subject in plan view, divided into four segments. When lit to give lit/dark/lit/dark as shown will result in a good three-dimensional subject. 'Dark' means 'darker' than the lit segments, how dark will depend on the required mood. Best results are obtained when symmetry is avoided, i.e. lit segments to be of unequal lighting levels and of unequal areas.

Figure 14.22 Basic three-point lighting plus 'kicker' light

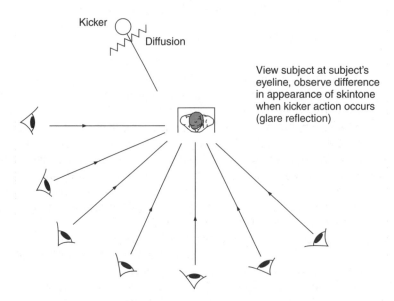

Figure 14.23 Examination of 'kicker' action

Often coloured light can be used to reinforce/create a particular mood, for example nightlighting, light from practicals etc.

Maximum texture is revealed when using a hard kicker, but this can be less than kind on females. As a general principle, always use a 'soft' kicker unless a hard kicker is motivated.

Remember, also, that the kicker is a 'glare' reflection, and an on-camera polarising filter may be used to give variable control of the intensity of the kicker seen on-camera. Correct use of 'glare' reflection in your lighting can have a significant effect on the quality of your results!

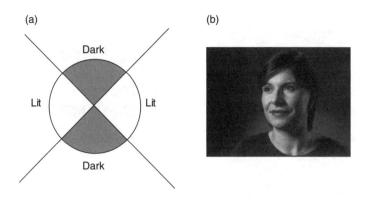

Figure 14.24 (a) Lit/dark/lit/dark scenario; (b) example

14.10   Lighting the offset presenter

In formal presentations to camera with a single presenter there is no preferred keying direction. The decision to key from left or right side of the camera will be made on the observation and skill of the lighting person to light for best portraiture, consistent with no distracting shadow on the background.

When there is a need to offset the presenter to include some background interest or logo, the presenter 'looks right' if lit from 'within the picture'. Figures 14.25 and 14.26 illustrate this principle. In Figure 14.25 the presenter is lit from camera left, with the presenter framed on the right-hand side of the picture the shadows fall outside the picture. The subject is said to be lit 'from within the picture' and it looks correct, the lighting of the subject 'belongs' to the picture.

In Figure 14.26 the presenter is lit from camera right, and the presenter is framed on the right-hand side of the picture. The shadows of the subject fall within the frame – the subject is said to be lit 'from outside the picture' (this does not look so correct as Figure 14.25). The lighting no longer looks to belong to the picture.

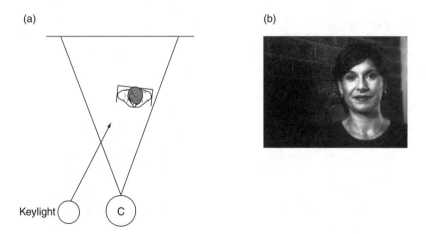

Figure 14.25 Subject lit 'from within the picture'

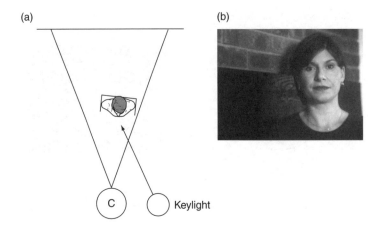

(a)   (b)

C   Keylight

Figure 14.26 Subject lit 'from outside the picture'

Apart from not looking right, lighting from outside the picture can give problems of the subject shadow being in shot.

The principle of lighting from within the picture is a useful concept to adopt in many applications, although there will be occasions when the opposite approach has to be adopted:

- When a presenter has to be lit from outside the picture to avoid bad portraiture due to facial defects. One way around this problem would be to reverse the framing, if possible.
- In a drama situation where a source of light has been established 'outside' the picture.

14.11   Interview lighting – single camera

This has to be one of the most common set-ups to be encountered. Typically the initial set-up is with the interviewee. After completing the interview, the interviewee is released and the 'reverses' from the interviewer are completed.

Shooting single camera does give a certain amount of freedom to the lighting set-up. One does not have to be concerned about keylight stands in shot! Figure 14.27 illustrates the

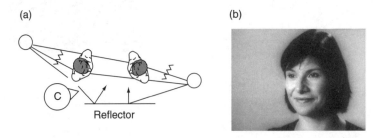

(a)   (b)

C

Reflector

Figure 14.27 Over-the-shoulder key, from upstage veils/scrims used to balance key/backlight levels

set-up. Generally key the interviewee so that the modelling falls towards the camera. This has the advantage of providing:

- good portraiture, with the 'form' of the subject well modelled, with the modelling seen on-camera
- the illusion of being lit from 'within the picture', i.e. the lighting looks quite natural
- 'shadow-free' sound pick-up if a fishpole or gun-mic is used as indicated.

To avoid any mutual shadowing the keylight should be placed so that the keylight is seen by the interviewee, just upstage of the interviewer's shoulder (Figure 14.27). One short-coming of this arrangement is the rather severe modelling if the subject turns to address the camera. This eventuality can be catered for by moving the keylight a little downstage (Figure 14.28).

The biggest problem here is mutual shadowing. This can be reduced by separating the artistes a little or if consistent with good portraiture, raising the height of the keylight.

A second solution would be to move the keylight to be such that it lights from downstage of the interviewer (Figure 14.29). This has the advantage of:

- avoiding mutual shadowing
- providing flattering modelling (although more 'flat')
- minimising shadows from spectacles if worn by interviewee
- ensuring clarity of the eyes of spectacle wearers.

Having decided a strategy for placing the keylight, decide on the appropriate luminaire and whether diffusion is required. It should be remembered that the more comfortable you can make the interviewee in the lighting environment, the more relaxed he is likely to be;

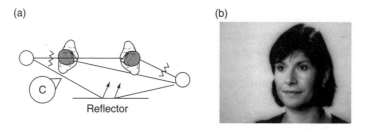

Figure 14.28 Keylight directly on the eyeline

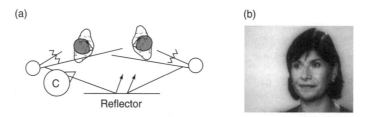

Figure 14.29 Downstage key

use of diffusion, although it immediately results in the loss of control of beam shape, is to be recommended. Use of a simple flag can restore some degree of control to the beam shape, i.e. to darken off the top part of the 'picture'. If a third luminaire is available, the reflector can be lit separately, giving better control and more flexibility in its position.

14.12   Two-handed interview – multi-camera

When shooting a two-handed interview with multi-cameras the principles are the same as when lighting for single camera, except that the use of upstage lighting stands is not possible unless only shooting close-ups. Using luminaires upstage of the action will require some form of suspension which does not appear in shot.

Basic approach

The basic approach is illustrated in Figure 14.30(a) with the luminaires used on lighting stands, the furthest upstage one can use these stands is on a line joining the two artistes. The two keylights can also be used as backlights, provided care is taken to reduce the backlight illuminance to an appropriate value – they are very close to the subject and, without using some form of scrim, will provide an excessive amount of backlight!

Alternatives

1   A very quick arrangement is shown in Figure 14.30(b). In this the luminaires, Redheads, are fitted with white diffusion with a central circular hole, approx. 50 mm diameter (2 inches). The aim is that each subject sees the lamp filament through the hole (keylight). The diffused light provides backlight and a measure of fill-light. The level of the backlight provided in this way can easily be adjusted by using a neutral density filter on the keylights, also with a 50 mm diameter central hole, e.g. 0.6 ND will reduce backlight by 2 stops.

2   Using fluorescent lights, plus control screens instead of Redheads, can provide a useful lighting set-up. In this arrangement, the control screen is used to give the reduction in illuminance for backlighting the nearer subject. If further reduction is required, this can be achieved with scrims, set as shown in Figure 9.30 (p. 107).

3   Using two Century stands with 40-inch extension arms (plus sandbags) it is possible to rig the keylights/backlights a little upstage (Figure 14.30(c)). This provides more modelling to the subjects. Care needs to be taken to ensure that there is no flare on the camera lens. This can be minimised by:

- barndooring of keylight
- using a flag on the keylight
- using a flag on the camera.

The last option is usually the simplest and quickest solution.

4   Using a boom-arm on a heavy-duty stand (plus suitable counterweights/sandbags) (Figure 14.30(d)) can be an alternative way of rigging luminaires upstage. It also provides a means of using separate backlights. The compromise of using combined

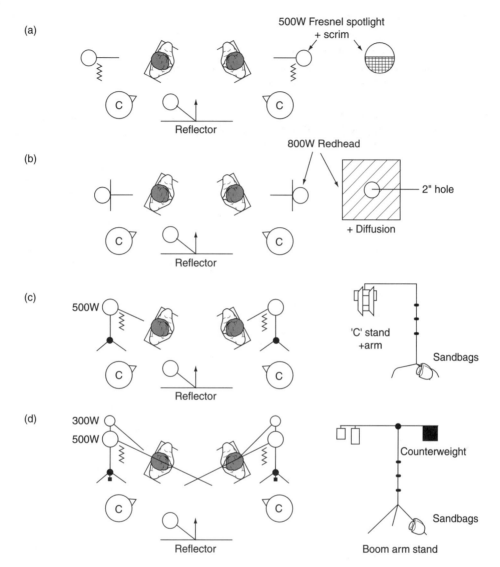

Figure 14.30 (a) Combined key/backlights and scrim; (b) combined key/backlights and diffusion; (c) use of Century stand (40-inch arm): (d) use of boom arm and separate key/backlights

keys/backlights can result in over-exposure problems if the subject is bald-headed or has silver/fair hair. Separate backlights give greater control of backlight illuminance. Whenever it is possible, the use of separate backlights is to be recommended.

5 Using telescopic poles with crossbars also provides the facility to use upstage lumin-aires, but restricts any square-on two shots unless the upstage poles can be hidden or disguised.

6 A variation of 5 would be to use lightweight trussing or scaffolding to make a suitable 'grid'. Clearly this is not a quick fix but one which could be adopted if budget/time allowed and there was a need to not work off stands from some particular safety aspect.

The lighting balance in a two-handed interview is best achieved by:

- Using identical keylights at the same luminaire 'throw'.
- If using separate backlights, use identical luminaires and 'throw'.
- Light backgrounds to identical illuminance.

Cameras should be operating on similar f-stops, i.e. f 2.8. It is useful to use an incident light meter or spot meter to check that the lighting levels match between the two shots.

15
Lighting in the real world

15.1 Basic observations

So far we have considered formal presentations, with the lighting aim to produce pictures with an open and honest look. In the real world the need is to light in a given environment or perhaps to create a particular environment. Generally, the aim is to create the *illusion* of reality, not necessarily reality. For example, a domestic interior may be lit with a single central overhead light. If one used only this lighting treatment or created the same effect it would be less than satisfactory, resulting in very steep 'toppy' lighting.

In the real world, in an interior most people are lit by softlight not hard light. Every window provides a source of light from natural lighting during the day, e.g. sunlight (hard source) and skylight (soft source) (Figures 15.1–15.4). Generally people do not sit in direct sunlight when working or relaxing (unless seeking a sun-tan!). Note fall-off in illuminance at a window in Figure 15.5.

During daylight, natural lighting in a room will be from the skylight, as a direct light source, plus this skylight bouncing off the walls, floor and ceiling. This will be supplemented by sunlight, if entering the room, bouncing off the walls and floor. It's interesting to note how many natural light sources exist in a room to provide keylights, fill-lights and kickers – often not of sufficient level but good indicators of lighting possibilities. Observe people lit in public places and note the lighting, i.e. in a bar, café, train, bus etc.

Use should be made of natural lighting when possible, as this will simplify the lighting set-up **but**, as a general principle, avoid using direct sunlight on interior shots:

- very high lighting level
- usually uncomfortable for the subject to sit and work in direct sun, eyes will be half-closed
- the angle of the sun to the location will change during the day
- unless the location is blessed with cloudless skies the sun will disappear behind the clouds from time to time!
- the sun, for most countries, represents a totally uncontrollable and unpredictable light source.

Figure 15.1 Skylight only

Figure 15.2 Frontal lighting only (left of camera)

Figure 15.3 Skylight plus frontal lighting

Figure 15.4 Using glare reflection (kicker)

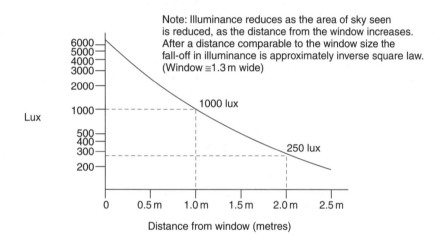

Note: Illuminance reduces as the area of sky seen is reduced, as the distance from the window increases. After a distance comparable to the window size the fall-off in illuminance is approximately inverse square law. (Window ≅1.3 m wide)

Lux

Distance from window (metres)

Figure 15.5 Fall-off in illuminance from a window – overcast day

Historically, because of the need for high lighting levels (1500–2000 lux) with the early colour cameras, hard sources were used as the main keylight. However, as explained above, subjects will generally be lit with softlight when lit naturally. Current techniques embrace the use of lighting with soft-light, when appropriate, on the basis of:

● vastly improved camera sensitivity
● skilful use of softlight, i.e. control of light 'beam'
● development of many new soft sources including the use of fluorescent lights.

Figure 15.6 reiterates a useful concept when considering lighting of a subject, namely that if the segments are lit as shown – dark, light, dark, light – they will look three-dimensional from any viewed angle. If the lighting looks good it will invariably have these properties. Generally, avoid symmetry both in lighting level and the lit areas for best results.

Figure 15.6 Lit/dark/lit/dark

15.2   Creating the illusion of reality

Emphasis has been placed on using natural lighting whenever it is suitable. However, there may be occasions when wishing to create a particular natural lighting environment to take advantage of the resulting picture quality. As an example, consider creating the **illusion** of the subject by a window (Figure 15.7).

The natural lighting in such a set-up would be skylight (soft source) through the window. This can be created by 'punching' a hard source – say 800 W Redhead – through a diffusion screen. The resulting effect will be to light one half of the subject, revealing texture in the clothing and on facetones. Using a flag, the diffused light can be masked off the background to create the illusion of light reaching the wall from a window. Remember that light from a window rarely reaches the corner of a room, it 'starts' some distance from the corner.

Using the light from the window as the keylight poses the question, how do we 'fill' the shadows to best advantage? The simplest solution would be to add a simple reflector or light source to add light to the shadow area. Although this may be a quick fix, it results in adding light to a previously 'all dark' area, i.e. no modelling! A better solution is to use a soft

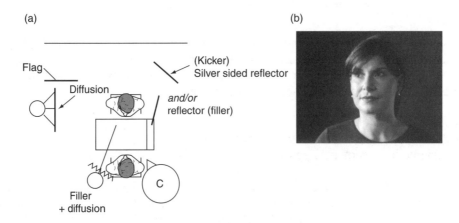

Figure 15.7 Simulating a window

source on the **same side** as the **keylight**, positioned as shown in Figure 15.7, just to the camera's left of the subject's eye-line. This:

- provides catchlights in the eyes from the correct side
- retains the shape of the nose
- gives shape to the subject's face on the camera's right-hand side of the face.

This fill-light can be adjusted in position/level to provide the appropriate fill level. Ideally, it should be flagged off the background to maintain separation of the subject and background. A simple low-level kicker can be added to good effect.

   This basic lighting set-up is well worth experimenting with to observe and identify the value of creating texture with the keylight used in the above. If the 'skylight' is switched off and the camera iris opened to compensate, the difference is very much between 'the illusion of reality' and 'an open and honest look'.

- the value of glare reflection in extending highlight values and revealing texture.
- how an effective lighting set-up can be created very simply.
- how comfortable the lighting is for the subject.

This is very much a step beyond simple three-point lighting, bending some of the rules – but it works well!

15.3   Coping with reality

Having established the basic principle above, it becomes a small step to cope with reality, i.e. subjects by a window, lit by skylight. In this example, the skylight is provided by nature, so we need to provide:

- fill-light
- kicker or backlight
- control of background lighting.

With the window as the keylight, we can use the lighting set-up in Figure 15.8. If using tungsten sources they need to be corrected to daylight (full CTB filter). However, one can use $\frac{3}{4}$ CTB to preserve a coolness to the daylight. Note that with Nature providing the keylight, the lighting levels required from the artificial lighting are minimal, i.e. easily achieved with low-wattage light sources.

15.4   Coping with excessive contrast

There are two basic objectives in lighting a subject at a window:

- Coping with excessive contrast introduced when shooting interiors which include exterior scenes
- Ensuring that the subject 'looks right' against the window

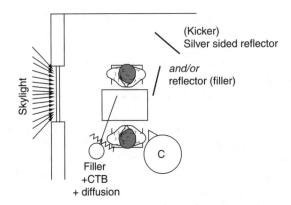

Figure 15.8 Coping with mixed lighting at a window

Satisfying only the first objective will result in the subject appearing almost as a chroma-keyed foreground subject! It is normally not practical to use similar lighting levels on interiors as those which exist on exteriors:

● Requires too large a light source needing impractical levels of power from a domestic source.
● Too much light and heat for the artiste to be comfortable!

The solution to this problem is to use a neutral density filter on the window to increase the exposure on the exterior so that it matches the exposure of the interior.

What value of ND filter?

The value of ND can be established very quickly by setting up the shot, exposing the camera correctly for the exterior scene, and noting the lens aperture. Assuming the desired aperture to the be f 2.8, if the exposure for the exterior is f 8.0 we have a difference of three f-stops between the interior and exterior; 0.9 ND is therefore required on the window.

An alternative method using a spot meter would be to check exposure values of outside highlight, e.g. blue sky or cloud. If EV9 is the exposure value for facetones, peak white should be about one stop above this, i.e. EV10, so if the highlight reads EV14 the required ND is 1.2 (four stops). Always err on undercorrecting – the exterior should always appear to be brighter than the interior!

How is ND fixed?

It is important to always use the ND filter **outside** the window unless shooting large plate-glass windows, otherwise the ND in front of a window with glazing bars will have the exposure reduced on the glazing bars! The ideal way of attaching the ND filter would be to staple it to undersized wooden frames, which can be wedged in place. This ensures that the filter is tightly stretched, minimising effects of wind and avoiding reflection of interior lights.

When impractical because of height of window above the ground, the required area of ND may be fastened to the inside window with double-sided tape, as applied to plate-glass windows, after slightly moistening the window with a 'squeegee', e.g. car windscreen wiper blade. Alternatives are:

- If the required value of ND is about two stops, 'Scrim' in the form of a perforated plastic reflector material may be used 'inside out' to present a 'black net' towards the camera. (This **must** be used outside the window, otherwise the silver side would reflect back on to the glass, producing an interference pattern. Similarly, this material cannot be used in multi-layers – interference patterns would result.)
- Use 3 mm, ND acrylic panels. These can easily be attached to windows, do not flap around in the wind and, being flat, the problem of reflected lights in 'crinkled' ND is overcome.

How much ND?

Only use the minimum area of ND consistent with not shooting off the ND material. This ensures that not all of the light through the window is reduced, i.e. it can have a natural effect on the subject.

The second objective can be met by ensuring that light from outside **appears** to hit the subject. A consequence of using too large an area of ND is that the subject lacks reality. This can be remedied using a small kicker as shown in Figure 15.9. This lighting plot illustrates a simple but effective way of tackling this particular problem. It is essential that the colour of the kicker is an exact match for the daylight. Similarly, unless trying to simulate sunlight, the kicker should be diffused.

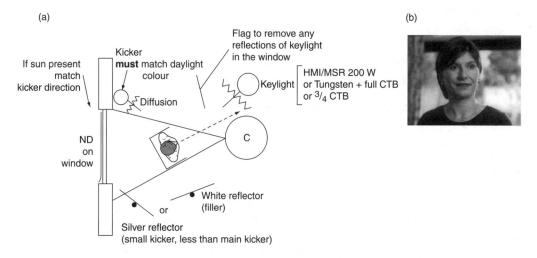

Figure 15.9 Subject against a window

15.5   Lighting continuity

A major problem of lighting for single-camera shooting on location is that of lighting continuity. The most commonly occurring problems are:

● matching the lighting between the first set-up shots and reverse shots in an interview or drama situation
● natural lighting conditions (also applicable to multi-camera shoots)

– continuous positional changing of the sun
– possible moment-to-moment changes of lighting condition due to clouds passing in front of the sun.

Matching lighting in an interview

The main lighting criteria for matching interviews are:

● common lighting level for subjects
● identical key/fill ratio
● common lighting level for background
● common f-number for both shots
● common colour temperature for keylight/fillers

These can be met by:

● using similar light sources and similar distances from luminaires to subject for each set-up
● using similar light sources and similar distance from luminaire to background for each set-up
● maintaining a fixed f-number checking that correct exposure is achieved at this lens aperture

A number of aids are available which, in addition to being useful for matching problems, can be of benefit generally:

● small exposure meter (incident light meter) such as the Sekonic meter
● spotmeter
● 'zebra' viewfinder facility
● Hamlet waveform monitor, e.g. picoscope
● Hamlet Vical

The regular use of an incident light meter will very quickly give an awareness and familiarisation of lighting levels. This is particularly useful in setting up **any** lighting situation as well as for the interview set-up. The Sekonic meter has direct reading of lens aperture as well as illuminance when working with Hyper HAD cameras (f 8.0 cameras), e.g. 40 foot-candles also indicated f 2.8.

The use of a spotmeter is invaluable in checking luminance values. Again, regular use will assist in making one aware of typical scene luminance values, and hence scene contrast. The viewfinder 'zebra' facility may be used to check facetone exposure, provided the zebra is set to facetone value, that is typically 75%.

When a video waveform monitor is not available, the use of a Hamlet picoscope (see p. 210) is to be recommended when consistent exposure and correct matching of backgrounds are essential. The variable cursor can be used to indicate facetone video level or background video level, or both variable cursor and voltage scale may be used to help in matching video levels.

The Hamlet Vical (see p. 211) is a very precise instrument, which can enable perfect matching of tones with a reference tone.

16
Vision control and measurements

16.1 Vision control – the essence of good picture quality

Good vision control is fundamental to picture quality and to lighting continuity. Basic vision control means:

- white balance
- exposure
- black level.

White balance

Cameras usually have three white balance options:

- Preset – Preset to tungsten (3000 K) or daylight (5500 K)
- Auto A ⎱ Programmable preset of White Balance.
- Auto B ⎰

Because of the wide range of lighting conditions to be found on location, it is recommended to white balance each set-up prior to recording/transmission. An alternative to this would be to use the 'preset' tungsten or daylight, as appropriate, then make any 'colour' adjustments in post-production.

Normal practice is to white balance to the colour temperature of the keylight so that any areas lit by the keylight appear in their 'natural' colour. Pictures can be made warmer or cooler by holding a ¼CTB or ¼CTO filter in front of the camera lens when completing the white balance. If, for example, a ¼CTB is used when white balancing to tungsten (3200 K) the camera **white point** would be 3600 K. Subjects lit with 3200 K sources would look slightly warm (orange).

Exposure

Although cameras have auto-iris control and manual iris control, it is recommended to use manual iris control whenever possible. The auto-iris facility is useful to indicate the 'ballpark' setting for the lens aperture. However, it operates on an average 'weighted' principle, so if the picture content changes, say panning across an area of sky, the iris will change. Clearly auto-iris is essential when following moving action, such as on a news story.

Correct exposure, and consistent exposure, is best achieved with:

1 Correctly set-up camera viewfinder – minimum facilities available.
2 Use of a correctly set 'Zebra' – 75% (facetones) or 95% and **know** which one is in use! Some cameras offer a dual Zebra facility.
3 Correctly set-up colour monitor.
4 Use of a waveform monitor or Hamlet device.

The reproduction of facetones is of prime importance, and these should be correctly exposed. Any overexposure will create a distraction, under exposure if severe will result in loss of clarity of the subject – again a distraction.

A preset Knee can be introduced which acts to 'compress' any video signal above the Knee value. This can extend the dynamic range of the camera, but it does mean that the tonal gradation above the knee is crushed. See pp. 31–3.

Black level

The importance of correct black level has already been stressed when discussing human perception. Colour cameras normally have a preset black level which is set when carrying out a black balance. It should be remembered that this black level value is modified by the camera flare correctors – these operate on the average picture content after 'clipping' – so a scene of excessive luminance, say sky, will produce in an incorrect flare correction resulting in 'lifted' black level!

Many shooting applications, other than very simple set-ups, for drama use a mobile vision control trolley (Figure 16.1), which enables the lighting director or lighting cameraman to monitor the picture and waveform and have adjustment of the parameters listed below.

Where a consistent particular 'look' is required to the productions, some cameras offer the facility of a **smart card**. This is a miniature 'credit card' which may be used to provide data for setting up a number of vision parameters, typically:

Gamma
Linear matrix settings
Black level
White balance
Knee setting
Detail
Electronic 'filter' effects.

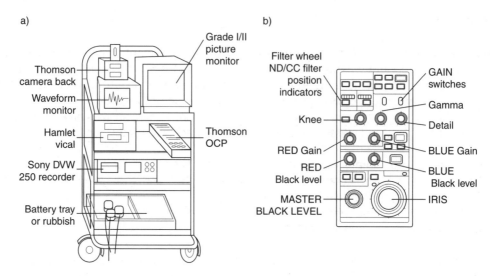

Figure 16.1 (a) Vision control trolley; (b) typical operational control panel (OCP)

16.2   Use of colour monitor

Except for the simplest of set-ups when time is limited, the use of a colour monitor on location is invaluable. A picture monitor is larger than the camera viewfinder and has the advantage of being in colour allowing:

● easy monitoring of action
● assessment of picture quality – on-site, not in editing room

  – colour – white balance correct
  – picture contrast
  – exposure – limiting or saturating on any areas
  – detail
  – composition of picture
  – special effects – effective?

● review of action to appraise artiste performance.

The colour monitor should be **at least Grade II**, capable of giving a good-quality picture in difficult surroundings. When working on exteriors it is impossible to judge picture quality on a monitor face that has daylight on it. There is a need to exclude the daylight by using a black cloth over the monitor and the person(s) viewing the monitor.
    It is essential that the colour monitor is used properly if the information is to be displayed correctly:

● Monitor should be in the **underscan** mode, **at all times**, so that the edges of the picture can be seen, i.e. all of the picture is monitored.
● Monitor must be correctly terminated in 75 Ω to prevent unwanted reflections of signal. Many monitors are 'self-terminating'. However, check that the video feed to the monitor

is plugged to INPUT, not OUTPUT, otherwise the monitor will not be self-terminating. Manual termination in 75 Ω is done with a switch alongside the INPUT socket.
● Video display to be correctly set up, i.e. Chroma, Contrast and Brightness.

The alignment of colour monitors has been 'the weakest link' in the picture-making process since the beginning of colour television. Ideally, these should be set up in 'base' so that the preset values ('indent' on each control) are correct.

A colour monitor line-procedure is described below, which can be used in the field as a quick alignment check, using colour bars:

1 Check that monitor is switched to UNDERSCAN.
2 Select camera to COLOUR BARS.
3 CHROMA – select BLUE ONLY and adjust Chroma so that the three right-hand bars look to be of the same brightness (Figure 16.2). This adjustment is more easily judged if the BRIGHTNESS is reduced to minimum. Release BLUE ONLY so that full colour bars are displayed, restore brightness control.
4 BRIGHTNESS. Observe the right-hand bar (BLACK bar) and adjust BRIGHTNESS so that the BLACK bar is visible, i.e. above black level. Reduce BRIGHTNESS so that the BLACK BAR just coincides with BLACK. It is important not to leave the video black level crushed below black level.
5 CONTRAST adjustment, adjust CONTRAST so that the Peak White bar does not defocus. Recheck BRIGHTNESS.

'Chroma' adjusted for equal brightness

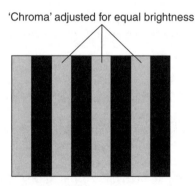

Figure 16.2 Colour monitor display with EBU bars, switched to 'Blue' only

Use of a PLUGE signal, if available, is an excellent way to set BRIGHTNESS and CONTRAST. Figure 16.3 illustrates PLUGE in which the BRIGHTNESS control is adjusted to make the **dark grey** bar visible and the black bar not visible. An analogue spotmeter is used to observe the peak white area of the display while adjusting the CONTRAST control to obtain a reading of EV 7.

(a)

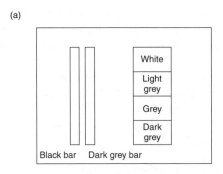

(b)

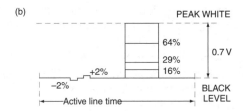

Figure 16.3 PLUGE signal. (a) Picture display; (b) waveform

16.3 Light measurement – incident light meters

Incident light meters measure illuminance (illumination) and are useful on location for:

- establishing existing lighting levels (illuminance)
- verifying lighting levels provided by artificial lighting and determining the need/amount of scrims/veils etc.
- checking lighting balance
- lighting continuity measurements
- checking illuminance values on action involving artiste movement, and determining the need/amount of scrim/veils required
- checking the illuminance values on the background to determine lighting balance to foreground and to help in determining any requirements for scrim/veils and their values.

Incident meters may be analogue or digital. Analogue meters (Figure 16.4) have the advantage of being:

- robust
- in many cases, operated on the photovoltaic principle, they generate an appropriate current when exposed to light – thus no batteries are required
- compact
- reliable
- relatively cheap
- 'continuous reading' – useful for measuring 'walks' and illuminance on scenery

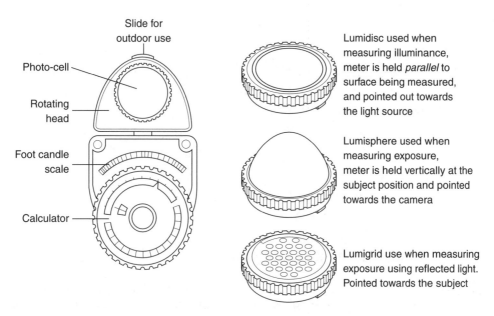

Photo-cell

Slide for outdoor use

Rotating head

Foot candle scale

Calculator

Lumidisc used when measuring illuminance, meter is held *parallel* to surface being measured, and pointed out towards the light source

Lumisphere used when measuring exposure, meter is held vertically at the subject position and pointed towards the camera

Lumigrid use when measuring exposure using reflected light. Pointed towards the subject

Figure 16.4 Analogue waveform (Sekonic)

- many have a non-linear scale which means that when measuring low values of illuminance; less than 400 lux, the scale becomes cramped
- calibrated with a logarithmic scale which can be made to give the camera-operating aperture when direct-reading slides are used (Sekonic). The Sekonic meter is, in fact, direct reading, without any direct-reading slides, for the '*f* 8.0' sensitivity cameras. The half-division calibrations represent half of one *f*-stop change – useful for determining value of scrims/veils
- because of the film background to incident light meters, the scales are normally marked in foot-candles. This can be converted to lux, approximately, by multiplying by 10 or precisely, by multiplying by 10.76.

Digital meters (Figure 16.5) are:

- more expensive
- more accurate – displaying exact illuminance in lux
- not 'continuous reading', but operate on the 'sample and hold' principle. As such they are not so useful for checking long walks etc.
- battery-operated – spare batteries **must** always be carried to ensure the meter will always be operational!
- robust
- reliable
- often available as multi-role meters, e.g. Minolta Colour Meter measures illuminance, colour temperature and chromaticity (colour) coordinates *x* and *y*. Similarly the Thoma TF5 meter.

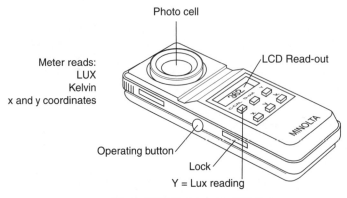

Photo cell

Meter reads:
LUX
Kelvin
x and y coordinates

LCD Read-out

Operating button

Lock

Y = Lux reading

Figure 16.5 Digital meter (Minolta)

16.4   Light measurement – spotmeter

A spotmeter is used to measure the **luminance** of a subject, that is, the **reflected light**. Typically, a spotmeter (Figure 16.6), has an acceptance measuring angle of 1°, which means that it can be used for accurate measurement of subject features, i.e. facetones, shadow areas etc. The spotmeter is calibrated to read in exposure values, its prime use being to determine correct exposure of film in photography and cinematography (see Table 16.1). It can, however, be used in television for:

- measuring the relative exposure values in a scene and hence determine the relative contrast ratio
- determining the neutral density required on in-shot windows
- taking luminance values (EV values) within a scene for lighting continuity purposes, especially inaccessible places
- setting the contrast on monitors (analogue version of spotmeter only).

(a)   (b)   (c)

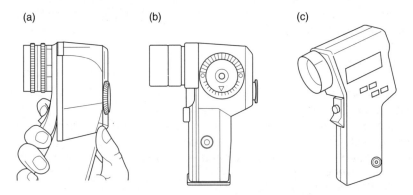

Figure 16.6 Selection of basic spotmeters. (a) Pentax digital spotmeter, simple to use, readings in one third EV values; (b) Pentax analogue spotmeter, simple to use, continuous scale from EV 1 to EV 19 – more bulky than (a); (c) Minolta digital spotmeter F, more complex facilities, readings in 0.1 EV steps, has external readout and memory facilities

Table 16.1 Exposure values/luminance

EV	Cd/m²	Cd/ft²	Apostilbs	Ft-l
1	0.28	0.026	0.88	0.082
2	0.56	0.052	1.76	0.164
3	1.1	0.1	3.22	0.3
4	2.2	0.2	7.53	0.7
5	4.5	0.4	14.00	1.3
6	9.0	0.8	28	2.6
7	17.9	1.7	56	5.2
8	35.8	3.3	112	10.4
9	71.6	6.7	225	20.9
10	143	13.3	450	41.7
11	286	26.6	900	83.5
12	573	53.2	1 800	167
13	1 150	107	3 600	336
14	2 290	213	7 200	668
15	4 580	425	14 400	1 340
16	9 170	852	28 800	2 680
17	18 300	1 700	57 600	5 340
18	36 700	3 410	115 200	10 700
19	73 400	6 820	230 400	21 400

Exposure in photography is based on a combination of **exposure time** and *f*-**number**. Cameras which operate with EV values automatically set the lens aperture when the shutter speed is set for a particular exposure value (or vice versa). The increment in exposure values represents a **doubling** of scene luminance. A change in EV from EV 8 to EV 9, therefore represents a contrast ratio of 1:2. Similarly, a difference of 2 EVs represents a contrast of 1:4.

Spotmeters may be analogue or digital, but analogue meters have the advantage of:

- continuous reading
- ability to be used for measurement of monitor luminance in setting the monitor contrast.

Digital spotmeters have the advantage of:

- being more compact than analogue meters
- providing greater range of calculations than analogue meters
- memory of EV readings

The analogue meter is more difficult to read in low-luminance areas (so uses an internal light source to illuminate scale). The digital spotmeter (LED/LCD display) is more difficult to read when measuring high luminance values, e.g. sky and clouds.

The 'sample and hold' system of measurement with the digital meter makes it unsuitable to measure monitor luminance or luminance of projected video images. Monitor scanning rate and the sample and hold rate interfere with each other.

Unless requiring the extra facilities of the more elaborate spotmeter, the simple 'point and measure' system with the Pentax meters is to be recommended – less room for errors! Note the need for spare batteries for all these meters!

16.5   Zebra/Picoscope/Vical – aids to exposure and continuity

Zebra has been long established with lightweight camera, whereby a visible diagonal 'zebra' pattern is superimposed in the viewfinder on picture information when a predetermined video level is present. Typically the zebra onset is preset to 75% for facetones or 95% just prior to reaching full exposure or 'saturation'. The 75% level corresponds to typical Caucasian skin tone signal level **after** gamma correction. Some debate exists among cameramen on which level to operate the zebra. Some prefer not to have the distracting zebra pattern all over facetones – the main centre of interest – preferring instead to have an indicator for just about to run out of 'head room'. The important factor is to be aware of which one is in use! Later cameras have a choice, of switching between the two preset zebra levels, or have two operating zebra levels, displaying a fine and coarse zebra pattern to discriminate between the two levels.

As well as indicating correct or ballpark exposure for facetones, the zebra facility can be used to indicate relative exposure values, e.g. facetone 'zebra' pattern at f 2.8. 'Zebra' pattern on the background occurs at f 2.0 indicating one f-stop difference in exposure between facetone and background. To check darker tones, use Gain, momentarily, to increase the range of iris control, i.e. switch to +12 dB gain. Iris now needs to be set to f 5.6, allowing at least a 3-stop adjustment to f 2.0 for checking relative exposure values.

Hamlet Picoscope is a compact portable device, which can be inserted into the video feed to a picture monitor to enable the monitor to be used as a waveform monitor. It provides a graticule (Figure 16.7) which may be adjusted in brightness, as well as a moveable 'cursor'. The display may be:

● solid – total replacement of picture with waveform
● superimposed on picture
● full screen
● reduced size in the top or bottom corner of monitor
● coded or bandwidth limited to luminance only.

The cursor provides a useful reference facility for lighting continuity.

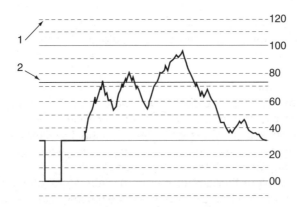

Figure 16.7 Hamlet Picoscope waveform. (1) Variable brightness graticule; (2) adjustable cursor

Figure 16.8 Hamlet Vical

Like Hamlet Picoscope, **Hamlet Vical** is inserted in the video feed to a monitor. It provides a facility to insert a moveable vertical video 'bar' of known calibration into the monitor picture. This allows for accurate side-by-side comparison between the reference level and a particular tone. It is very easy to match the video level to the reference signal when compared in this way – either by lighting level adjustment or iris adjustment. Similarly, the level of the VICAL signal may be easily adjusted to match a particular video level providing an instant calibration level and reference signal for matching purposes. Because the inserted Vical signal is a grey signal it can also be used to check the white balance of the camera when compared with the camera 'grey' (Figure 16.8).

17
Exterior lighting

17.1 Observing the day

It's probably stating the obvious but anyone engaged in lighting out of doors should be as familiar with the 'natural' light sources as with artificial sources used indoors. On a clear day the basic light source is of course the sun, plus skylight, with skylight being blue. Figure 17.1 illustrates the lighting levels typical of a fine sunny day. It is worth asking the question 'why is the sky blue?' Figure 17.2 shows that when direct sunlight enters the Earth's atmosphere the shorter wavelengths (blue light) are scattered by the particles in the Earth's atmosphere. Hence we see the 'sky' as blue.

Using this model of sunlight and skylight we can complete the picture of a day of natural lighting:

- **Dawn**: initially only the shorter wavelengths scattered by the atmosphere reach the observer – softlight, of a high colour temperature. The illuminance gradually increases until direct sunlight becomes visible (Figure 17.3) and horizontal.
- **Sunrise**: direct sunlight has to pass through a very thick layer of atmosphere leading to a scattering of all except the longer wavelengths (red light), hence we are see sunrise as a warm light-source. The period after sunrise is sometimes referred to as the 'Golden Hour' (although not an hour long!). As the sun rises the illuminance increases and the colour becomes less red/orange/yellow, the colour temperature changes from about 2000 K to the quoted 'Average Summer Sunlight' of 5500 K, as the day progresses.
- **Daylight**: the elevation and direction of the direct sunlight will change constantly. Charts exist which predict the position of the sun throughout the year. After mid-day the sun's vertical angle commences to decline and the process is repeated, in reverse.
- **Sunset**: as the sun's rays penetrate an increasing amount of atmosphere the direct sunlight is progressively scattered leaving the yellow, then orange and finally the red wavelengths before setting (Figure 17.3). The period before sunset is also often referred to as the 'Golden Hour'.
- **Dusk**: once the sun has 'set' the natural lighting process is the opposite to dawn with a softlight source of high colour temperatures.

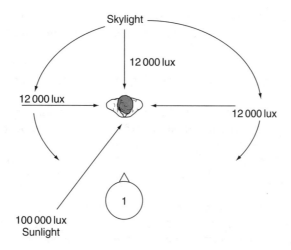

Figure 17.1 Typical lighting levels on a sunlit day

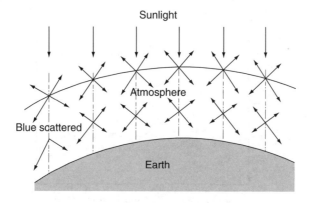

Figure 17.2 Illustrating why the sky is blue

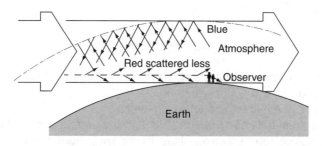

Figure 17.3 Illustrating sunset/sunrise colour

A question often asked is, what is the difference between dawn and dusk? The important point to remember is that you are dealing with a **dynamic** lighting condition – one that is continually changing!

- The obvious observation is that the lighting at dawn becomes brighter whereas dusk becomes darker.
- The colour temperature at sunset, in theory, should be the same as at sunrise. However, at sunset the colour temperature is often lower than at sunrise because of the effects of the extra dust particles in the Earth's atmosphere caused by the day's activities.
- Early morning will include dew on all surfaces due to the condensation when the surfaces cooled overnight and often include early morning fog.

Dawn and dusk are often used for creating night effects with the total location being lit to a low level, and additional lighting can be applied easily, as required. Car headlamps and 'practicals' can register on-camera. Because of the usefulness of these two periods they are often referred to as the 'Magic Hour' (Figure 17.4). Beware of the definition: it is not necessarily one hour long – it depends on global position and time of year! Use of the dawn requires the crew to be called very early to set up the lighting on the location, whereas use of the dusk allows normal daylight to prepare for the shoot.

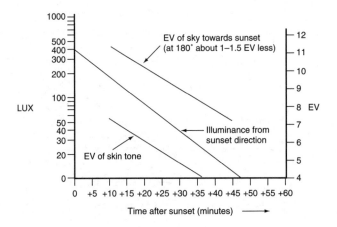

Figure 17.4 The Magic Hour (dusk)

Effect of clouds

Clouds passing in front of the sun will have four effects:

- Reduce the illumination: with dense clouds this can be as much as a 4 *f*-stop reduction and even as large as a 5 *f*-stop variation.
- Diffuse the sunlight making the light much 'softer'.
- Reduce the contrast between the shadows and the surface facing the sun's position.
- Increase the colour temperature – less illuminance from the direct sun and more influence from the skylight.

On heavily overcast days, the attenuation of light can be significant, e.g. on a winter's day in England the illuminance can be less than 500 lux! Yet on a bright sunny day illuminance levels in excess of 100 000 lux are normal in the UK, almost an 8 f-stop difference to the overcast situation!

17.2 Daylight exteriors

Sunlight

Generally, unless faced with the extremes of climates, the illuminance provided by natural lighting will be sufficient for most needs. However, it is a quality issue not one of quantity which confronts us when tackling exterior shots. Although there may be sufficient illuminance, the **direction, contrast** and **hardness** of the lighting may not be right. Daylight is a 'dynamic' light source, it is constantly changing, and on long shoots there may be a need to maintain a static lighting condition to preserve lighting continuity.

- It is possible to predict the exact location of the sun throughout the day and throughout the season. Unfortunately its extreme vertical elevations will result in less flattering portraiture.
- Although the position of the sun is predictable, the weather usually is not – unless living in a part of the world, which enjoys endless days of sunshine!

There is therefore a need to be prepared for a wide range of lighting conditions to cope with lighting exterior locations, i.e.

- Provide fill-light
- Overcome effects of steep sunlight angle (see Figure 17.7)
- Possible lighting continuity of a sunlit environment.

Fill-light can be provided in one of two ways:

1 Use a suitable reflector to reflect sunlight into the shadows (Figure 17.5). Usually some form of dimpled specular reflector is needed to allow some physical separation between

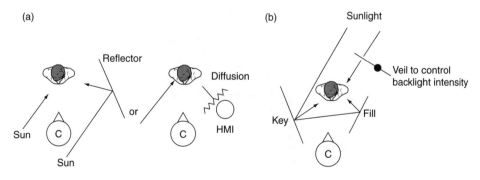

Figure 17.5 (a) Coping with excessive contrast; (b) using sunlight

the subject and the reflector. A diffused reflector (white surface) usually requires to be used very close to the subject unless it is of a large area.

The advantages of using a reflector are:

● Simple to apply, requiring no electricity
● If the sun fades the level of fill-light fades in proportion.

Disadvantages are:

● Requiring to be adjusted to follow the sun's movement
● Ideally requires an electrician to set it and adjust it
● Difficult to follow a moving subject – unless using a mobile diffused reflector close to the subject, i.e. for shots no wider than mid-shot (waist shot)
● Depending on the situation it may not be possible to put the reflector in a suitable place, e.g. shadow from a building in the ideal spot! Double reflectors may be required (Figure 17.6).

When using reflectors:

● Avoid blinding the artiste – keep reflector off the artiste's eyeline
● Avoid reflectors causing a problem for passing motorists!

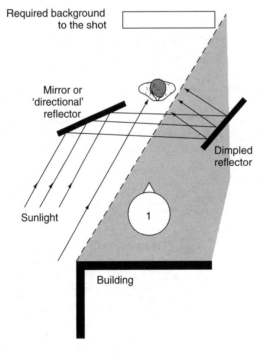

Figure 17.6 Use of two reflectors

2   An alternative to using a reflector is to use a diffused daylight source (HMI). This has the advantages of:

- Covering a large area
- Easily adjusted to achieve appropriate balance – spot/flood
                                                – ND filters

- Easy to follow moving subjects.

Disadvantages are:

- Requires a source of electricity. For large HMIs and in a remote locations this probably means using a generator
- If sun fades, the fill-light remains!

Overcast

A completely overcast day can generally make lighting easier with no direct sun to contended with:

- No steep keying angles
- No excessive contrast
- No 'dynamic' light source – the moving sun
- Artistes should not have a need to 'squint' – eyes will be wide open!

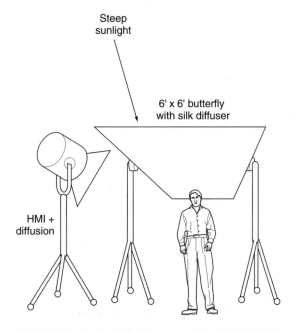

Figure 17.7 Use of a butterfly to cope with steep sunlight

Generally an overcast day will result in pictures which lack contrast. However, the vertical illuminance will probably be about twice that of the horizontal illuminance. Consequently, the eye sockets tend to look dark (Figure 17.8). The use of a diffused daylight source (HMI) will help to overcome this problem or simply use a reflector board, such as a Matthews reflector to add light into the eyes. Unless one is aiming to create an obviously lit effect (sunlight effect) this additional lighting should be subtle.

A battery-operated hand lamp (HMI or corrected tungsten source) can be useful in providing some form of kicker light. Remember that because this light is kicking the surface to give a **glare** reflection, very little light intensity is required to give an effect on-camera.

It is useful to remember that on an overcast day some modelling may be achieved simply by using appropriate positioning of the subject and using flags (stoppers) and reflectors. Figure 17.9 illustrates this principle where a black flag of suitable dimension is used to **remove** light from one side of the face thus introducing modelling. A refinement would be to use a specular reflector to reflect light into the eyes. If a flag or even a double veil is available this could be used to reduce the toplighting.

Alternatively, if a dark-sided building of neutral colour is nearby, place the subject near to the building. The reduction in reflected light from the building will again produce shadow on one side of the face (Figure 17.10).

The luminance of blue sky can be 1–2 stops below white clouds. Facetones normally stand out against blue sky, but on an overcast day facetones may be significantly below the overcast clouds. Avoid low-angle shots of subjects against overcast clouds (Figure 17.11).

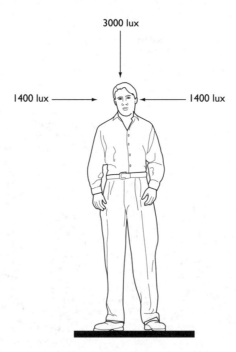

Figure 17.8 Overcast lighting, typical levels

Black flag
or black 'reflector'
(any form of light block)

Figure 17.9 Use of a black 'stopper' to create modelling

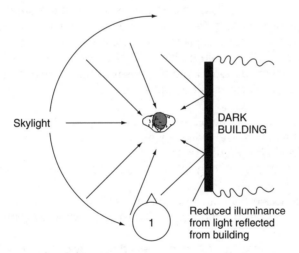

Skylight

DARK
BUILDING

1

Reduced illuminance
from light reflected
from building

Figure 17.10 Creating modelling on an overcast day

Overcast sky
15.5 EV

Overcast sky
>3 f_{stops}
above
face tone

Face tone
12 EV

Figure 17.11 Overcast sky and facetones

18
Expanding the basics

18.1 Lighting for subject movement – basics

There is often a need to light artistes moving in vision within the area of action. There are occasions when it is quite natural for artistes to go in and out of lit areas, for example in drama action at night, but many applications require the lighting levels to be maintained during an artiste's move. The main problem is, of course, the basic inverse square law, resulting in the artiste getting more illuminance as they move towards a keylight. There are a number of techniques, which may be applied to avoid noticeable illuminance changes:

- stopping down the lens as the artiste gets more brightly lit
- dim the keylight as the artiste walks towards it
- use a spotted luminaire (Figure 18.1)
- use a luminaire with a very long throw, so that the effects of inverse square law are minimised, i.e. follow spot
- avoid the artiste walking directly towards the keylight
- use half-scrims or veils to even out the illuminance when walking towards a keylight (Figure 18.2)
- use two identical luminaires to cover the artiste's two acting areas and arrange a suitable 'cross-over' or 'take-over' between the two luminaires (see p. 223)
- use the bounce technique to produce a 'graded' walk (see p. 225).

Dimming the keylight is fine if the keylight can be localised to the artiste, i.e. not lighting backgrounds or other artistes seen in shot, provided it is not a noticeable change in colour temperature. It must not cause problems for the next shot, with the keylight dimmed.
Stopping down the iris is a better option (no change in colour temperature), but the same principles apply, the artiste must be seen in isolation.
A **spotted** luminaire can sometimes solve the problem, where the artiste starts in the beam centre and as he/she walks towards the luminaire they move progressively into the edge

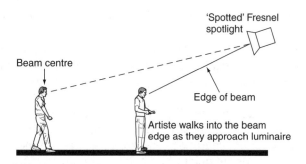

Figure 18.1 Subject movement – use of a spotted luminaire

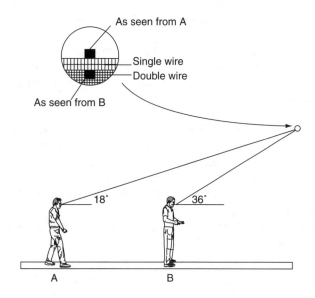

Figure 18.2 Subject movement – use of half-wires/scrims/yashmaks

of the beam. An alternative to this, often used on location work, would be to start with a spotted lamp and progressively flood it as the artiste walked towards the luminaire. Again, the luminaire must be localised on the artiste.

The use of **half-scrims**, **half-wires**, **veils** or **yashmaks** is the common technique for helping to provide even coverage. These have been introduced during earlier discussion. The essential requirement for these to work is that there must be a significant change in the angle between the keylight and the artiste (Figure 18.2).

The half-scrim provides a very soft edge to the start of the reduction in illuminance because it is very close to the lens. Veils and yashmaks have to be positioned close to the lens if they also are to give a smooth reduction in illuminance. A small incident light meter, e.g. Sekonic, is ideal for checking illuminance at position A and position B before deciding which scrim/veil to use. An alternative to using scrims or yashmaks would be to use half white diffusion in a colour frame close to the fresnel lens.

18.2   Lighting for subject movement – setting a crossover

Where a large distance separates the two acting areas, and it is not practical to use one keylight, two keylights with a suitable changeover between them is the solution. Before discussing this technique it is worth examining some salient points about barndooring:

- Barndoors are most effective when the luminaire is fully flooded.
- The barndoor produces the 'sharpest' cut of light when its edge is farthest from the lens.
- The degree of barndooring 'sharpness' increases as you get nearer to the luminaire. This is a particularly important point when setting a crossover, and can be checked by putting a luminaire on a floor stand at head height. Set it to, say, 6 m and put the large barndoor vertical and at 90° to the lens. Observe how much you have to move your head from seeing all the hot spot to seeing none of the hot spot. At 3 m it will probably be about 0.5 m, and at 6 m it will be about 1 m. Incidentally, note how the hot spot follows you as you move within the beam.
- The barndooring sharpness depends on the sharpness of the hot spot image. This is controlled by the particular Fresnel lens and the amount of diffusion introduced on the rear of the lens. A well-defined hot spot will give sharper barndooring than one with a diffused image (Figure 18.3).

Incidentally, if you see two hot spots, it means that the mirror/lamp base assembly is loose or bent in some way. Normally, the reflected image of the filaments should 'lie' over the actual image of the filaments, to produce one hot spot. Sometimes, 'saggy' filaments can give rise to one image being slightly displaced from the other.

Beware of trying to achieve 'sharp' barndooring from a luminaire which has got two hot spots, it will not be (Figure 18.4)!

Figure 18.5 illustrates the problem of lighting the artiste for position A and position B, with a walk between A and B.

'Crisp edged' hot-spot: Soft-edged hot-spot:
crisp barndooring   'Soft' barndooring

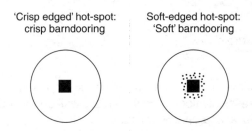

Figure 18.3 Hot spot 'sharpness' (Fresnel spotlight)

Figure 18.4 Double hot spot (Fresnel spotlight)

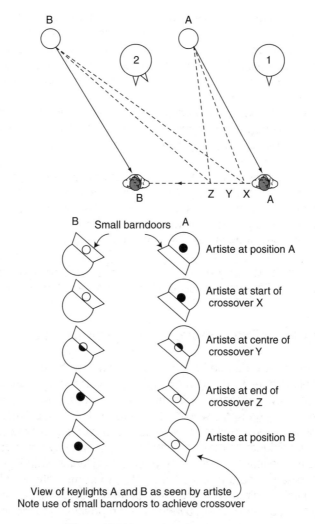

Figure 18.5 The setting of a crossover

To ensure a good crossover, the following points should be observed:

- The artiste should walk towards his keylight, i.e. not turn away from it.
- Both keylights should be identical luminaires and accurately set on position A and position B, respectively.
- The keylights need to be at similar heights, similar angle and similar distances to each area.
- The keylights should be fully flooded.
- The illuminance at area A and area B should be adjusted to be the same.

Ideally, the crossover should be disguised by the action so, in the above case, it is suggested to complete the crossover immediately the artiste starts walking at X. The sequence of operations for setting the crossover would be to adjust the barndoors as indicated in Figure 18.5. This is something of an 'ideal' case. In practice, the barndooring of Key A will be sharper than that of Key B, and Key A will be providing more illuminance than Key B (Key A is closer to the artiste).

Depending on circumstances, half-scrims or veils can be used to control the change in illuminance as Key A is approached. Some practitioners find it easier to simply use scrims/ veils or even half white diffusion on Key A to produce a gradual reduction in illuminance, as Key B is moved into.

The above technique is worth practising on a quiet day to perfect your own technique. It is useful to have a small **analogue** incident light meter to check the evenness of the walk; aim initially at a spread of illuminance within half of one f-stop and see if you feel that this is satisfactory. Start with a 30° angle between keylight and camera, then progress to 0°! When confident with two luminaires, try setting the crossovers for three luminaires, i.e. two crossovers.

Obviously, the backlights can be treated in a similar way for barndooring, but not so critical as the keylights. Fill-lights are used to provide a base light of illuminance.

18.3 Lighting for subject movement – alternatives

- On location there may be a need to cover a long walk without getting lighting stands in shot. The problem here is to maintain lighting level and vertical keying angle. One keylight could satisfy the needs for lighting the start of the walk, but at the end of the action the vertical keying angle would be too steep. This can be resolved, as shown in Figure 18.6, by using two luminaires with a vertical crossover between them.
- Use of bounce techniques to cover artistes' movements provides a very quick and easy way to provide the necessary cover. The principle is illustrated in Figure 18.7 and use is made of the cosine law nature of the light reflected from a diffuse reflector. The centre of the reflected light is directed at the furthest area. For this to be effective, there must be a significant angle difference between the start position and the end position. This is

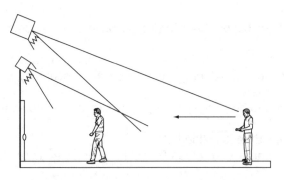

Figure 18.6 Artiste movement coverage in a long walk

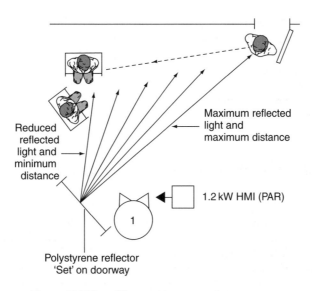

Reduced reflected light and minimum distance

Maximum reflected light and maximum distance

1.2 kW HMI (PAR)

Polystyrene reflector 'Set' on doorway

Figure 18.7 Use of 'bounce' to cover artiste movement

to ensure that as the artiste walks from A to B the 'angle change' to the reflector ensures that, due to the cosine law, he receives less illuminance.

If there are any hot spots on the walk, these can be minimised by placing an appropriate size of veil between the reflector and the artiste. The above technique may also be used to light a stairway in a large foyer (Figure 18.8). At the top of the stairs it is a horizontal key, but the artiste looks down so this is acceptable.
- Fluorescent lights fitted with 60° control screens can be extremely easy to adjust to provide a suitable crossover from one to the other. The soft edge to the light beam means that, with careful adjustment, one can get a smooth transition from one to the other.

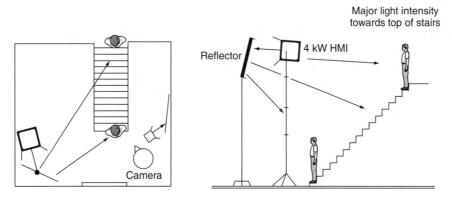

Major light intensity towards top of stairs

Reflector

4 kW HMI

Camera

Figure 18.8 Use of 'bounce' to light subjects descending 'open' stairs

A word of caution on the subject of crossovers/walks. Avoid the situation of a significant increase in lighting level during a walk – this will be most noticeable to the viewer. On the other hand, a slight reduction in illuminance will tend to appear to be more natural and will be accepted by the viewer.

As a rough guide, you should aim to get the coverage on a walk to be within $\frac{1}{2}$ of one f-stop to ensure that any variations in exposure are minimal i.e. $\pm\frac{1}{4}$ of one f-stop.

Fractional f-stops – how much is a half-stop change in illuminance?

Many lightmeters are calibrated in fractional f-stops. The f-number series is a **logarithmic** series with a $\times 2$ increment in **exposure** between each f-stop. So a half-stop increment will result from two identical numbers which multiply to give 2, i.e. $\sqrt{2} = \times 1.4$, or $\times 0.7$ if reducing exposure. Similarly a one-third stop increment results from a change in exposure by $\times \sqrt[3]{2} = \times 1.25$ and a quarter-stop increment requires a change in exposure of $\sqrt[4]{2} = \times 1.19$. Summarising,

$+\frac{1}{2}f$-stop $= \times 1.4$; $-\frac{1}{2}f$-stop $= \times 0.7$

$+\frac{1}{3}f$-stop $= \times 1.25$; $-\frac{1}{3}f$-stop $= \times 0.8$

$+\frac{1}{4}f$-stop $= \times 1.19$; $-\frac{1}{4}f$-stop $= \times 0.84$

18.4   Creating mood – the implicit requirements

Reading the script will reveal the explicit requirements such as day, night, dawn, sunset etc. as straightforward statements. The mood or atmosphere will be indicated as an implicit requirement, often being determined by the interpretation of the reader. It is essential that the lighting is completely in sympathy with this requirement, following effective planning with the director.

Lighting will have a major impact on the created mood or atmosphere in a scene. Costume, scenery and make-up all have a part to play in creating the right mood but they all require lighting to be correct for the scene to work effectively.

Mood can be described as any departure from 'normal', although of course 'normal' itself represents a particular mood. The lighting factors affecting mood are:

Texture
Modelling/contrast
Ambiguity
Clarity
Colour
Exposure

Texture – subjects look more interesting and appear more realistic when texture is revealed to a maximum, i.e. the nature of the surface is revealed by using a large angle between the keylight and the camera. This applies equally to buildings and to people. Dark clothing, for example, is best revealed when lit for texture. Maximum texture will help in the creation of dramatic-looking pictures.

Modelling and contrast – these two factors have a major impact on mood, with more dramatic pictures resulting from lighting which creates maximum modelling (increased shadow areas) and high contrast. Remember to shoot the shadow side of the face, not the lit side, otherwise the modelling will not be revealed to maximum effect.

The term **'key'** is often used to describe mood, namely:

The **distribution** of tones and tonal **contrast**

High key – predominance of light tones within the picture, little shadow (modelling) with low contrast. The pictures have a light cheerful look, almost two-dimensional in appearance. Lighting ratio approx. 1:1 for keylight and fill-lights.

Medium key – 'normal' distribution of tones within the picture. Typical lighting ratio approx. 1:2.

Low key – predominance of dark tones and 'heavy' shadows. Typical lighting ratio approx. 1:4 or greater.

Ambiguity relates to the degree of uncertainty created by lighting. The more ambiguity created, the more mystery created. The lighting of an actor may require just the eyes to be lit or conversely only lighting the lower part of the face, thereby inducing mystery, i.e. who is this person – what is he thinking? Another example would be an exterior moonlit scene. A building lit with a large HMI could be transformed from a 'clear moonlight night' to one which introduced mystery and uncertainty by using a suitable 'cookie' (dapple-plate) or tree-branch gobo in front of the light source.

Clarity in terms of image sharpness and contrast is another factor affecting mood. Camera filters can be used to modify these parameters. The filters are graded in sets of 5, where Filter 1 provides the most subtle effect and Filter 5 results in the most severe effect. This enables the choice of filter to suit each situation, i.e. zoom angle and severity of effect required. On-camera filters are most effective at wide apertures, i.e. $f2.0$–$f2.8$. Some of the filters, e.g. Promist, have more subtle grades, i.e. $^1/_4$ and $^1/_2$. See p. 228.

Before using filters for a particular requirement, it is recommended to experiment with them to determine the most appropriate filters – thus saving time on the shoot day. Use a large, good-quality monitor to assess the filter effects. Camera detail, electronic sharpening of the picture, will also have an effect on the overall picture sharpness.

Colour – the psychological effects of colour has been mentioned elsewhere in this text, namely:

- Red/orange colours are associated with warmth, friendliness.
- Blue colours are associated with cold, night-time, unwelcome feelings.
- Green, as pastel shades can be used to create a cool environment, with deep greens suggesting evil.

Lighting balance – the relative brightness of each part of the picture contribute to the overall effect. A correctly aligned picture monitor or viewfinder can be used for this or a simple 'pan glass'. The latter is a great asset in judging relative brightness – although, of course, the monochrome viewfinder picture also does this!

Exposure – it is so important to get exposure right! Having lit the scene to get the right mood, exposure is the final judgement that ensures that it looks right. Provided the view-finder is correctly set up consistently, a cameraman will make good exposure judgements – based on experience. The Zebra pattern can be used to ensure no overexposure occurs or to make judgements in exposure, i.e. one step down on 'normal' exposure. A waveform monitor is another useful aid.

18.5   On-camera filters

Television camera manufacturers strive to produce cameras which have the highest possible specification in terms of picture sharpness and tonal gradation of the picture. Often, however, there is often a need to move away from the 'technically perfect' picture to create a particular mood or simply for cosmetic reasons, e.g. the 'sharp' camera and hard lighting revealing too much texture on facetones! Camera filters may be used behind the lens (filter wheel) or in front of the lens on a matte box.

The matte box provides the facility for easy rotation of the filter as required and easy change of filters. It is also useful as a lens hood to reduce stray light entering the lens, which helps to maintain contrast and definition of the optical image.

Most filters are available in sets of five, where filter 1 has the most subtle effect and 5 has the greatest effect. Some filters also include $\frac{1}{2}$, $\frac{1}{4}$ and $\frac{1}{8}$ within their range to provide very subtle effects. Usually the filters work best at wide-open apertures. However, the effect will also be affected by lens angle of view.

It is always a good policy to experiment with filters before you use them on a shoot. Observe the effect on:

Facetones
Picture sharpness
Changes to highlights, possible 'halo' around highlights
Changes to black level, reduction in picture contrast

Always use a large good-quality monitor (ideally Grade I or II) to assess the effects of the filter. Some of the more commonly used filters are described below.

Nets – available as black, white or skintone. Black nets soften the 'electronically' sharp television image, reducing the visibility of facial blemishes. White nets perform similarly, but if the filters are backlit the image will be 'sat-up' by the 'flare' introduced by the net. The skintone filter introduces soft diffusion and enhances skintones.

Fog filters – operate by scattering the light, having the greatest effect on highlights, with scattering the highlights into the shadow areas. Resolution is reduced.

Double fog filter – produces a more neutral-looking fog while allowing clearer detail than a standard fog.

Graduated fog filter – used to produce fog at the top of the picture and clear at the bottom. This results in progressively more fog from foreground to background.

Promist – results in removing harsh edges on electronically sharpened pictures, intro-duces a small amount of flare, which reduces picture contrast slightly.

Black Promist – a very popular filter, similar to the Promist but with a more subtle reduction in contrast (less flare into the shadow areas).

Soft/FX – useful for portraiture, it will reduce wrinkles and skin blemishes while retaining overall clarity. Eyes appear sharp.

Warm Promist and **Warm Soft/FX** – combines a warm filter with the effects filter.

Colour Grad filters – these are coloured filters, which are half clear and half coloured with a smooth transition from full colour to clear. Usually used to create coloured skies, taking care to keep the artistes, faces in the 'clear' zone.

ND Grad filter – similar to Colour Grad but in neutral density, useful to help cope with excessively bright skies.

Neutral blended ratio attenuators (NBRA) – similar to an ND Graduated filter except that the graduation is over the whole filter. A one-stop NBRA has a one-stop loss in the centre, two stops at the dark edge and zero loss at the light edge. These filters can be useful to reduce the contrast in a scene, which is part in shadow and part in sunshine. The filter is rotated in the matte box so that the denser part is coincident with the brightly lit area. Opening up one stop to compensate for the filter results in the exposure on the foreground (shadow) being increased by one f-stop and the background (sunlit area) being reduced by one f-stop. A two-stop NBRA would graduate from four stops ND to zero.

Polarisers – reduce 'glare' reflections, resulting in improved colour saturation. They can also be used to darken blue skies to improve contrast with clouds. Remember they have approximately a two-stop loss.

Contrast handling filters – can be used to reduce the contrast ratio between highlights and shadow areas, without loss of sharpness. These are three basic types:

- **Ultra contrast filters** – which introduce ambient light and light from the image area into the shadow areas, but do not result in flare or halation on light sources or hot spots.
- **Low contrast filters** – spread light from the highlights into the shadow areas, they produce a slight halation around the light sources or hot spots.
- **Soft contrast filters** – absorb light, diminishing the highlights while retaining the shadow detail, again giving a slight amount of halation.

18.6 Lighting effects

Often there is a need to create special lighting effects. To ensure that an effect is going to work for a particular venue/requirement it is recommended that a 'test' of the effect be made beforehand. The following are typical effects:

Sunrise/sunset – This obviously requires a warm feeling to the lighting. The light source used needs to be at least $\frac{1}{2}$CTO warmer than the ambient lighting, i.e. a MIRED shift of +109 MIREDs. If the camera white point is at 3200 K (a tungsten-lit scene) the 'sunset' effect can be created with a low elevation tungsten source $+\frac{1}{2}$CTO filter. If the white point is at 5500 K (daylight-lit scene), then use either an HMI/MSR $+\frac{1}{2}$CTO filter or tungsten source with a $\frac{1}{2}$CTB. Depending on the degree of warmth required the filtering could be increased to $\frac{3}{4}$CTO and $\frac{1}{4}$CTB respectively. Hence the value of the test. To ensure that the sunlight effect works, it is important that it is not contaminated with any other source, i.e. seen clearly without any mixing with other sources.

Night-time – this has been covered in detail elsewhere (p. 252).

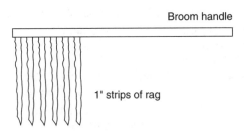

Figure 18.9 Fire-flicker device

Fire-flicker effect – There are several electronic fire-flicker effects available to help in the creation of this effect. Despite these, one of the simplest and most effective ways of achieving this effect is to use strips of rag on a broom handle (Figure 18.9). These are shaken in front of a floor-mounted spotlight. Use full CTO or $^3/_4$CTO filters on the light source to give the appropriate colour (camera white balanced to tungsten). Very dramatic effects can be achieved by using the light source relatively close to the action, which results in large shadows of the artiste on any adjacent walls.

Water-ripple effect – To suggest action near water, use a black water tray 0.6 m × 0.6 m × 0.1 m with broken mirror in the bottom, and half-fill with water. Use a hard light source (Fresnel spotlight) to bounce light off the water and the mirror. The light source should be used close to the tray to collect all of the light beam and the water should be disturbed slightly to obtain the water ripple effect on the set or the artistes (Figure 18.10). An alternative to this would be to use a profile projection with a moving water ripple effect. This would tend to give a more 'regular' effect and not as random as the water tray.

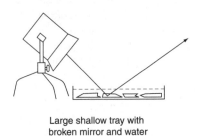

Large shallow tray with
broken mirror and water

Figure 18.10 Water-ripple effect

Candlelight – It is always useful, when working with coloured light on faces, to have the motivation for colour in shot, in this case the candle flame, and the candle. Figure 18.11 illustrates a possible set-up. The important points here are:

● The candle must not be illuminated – use a 'finger' to block any light from the keylight.
● The candlestick must be 'warm'. It is therefore more realistic to 'warm-up' the camera by white balancing through a $^1/_2$CTB or $^3/_4$CTB to ensure that the complete scene is warmed up. This saves time on filtering the light sources. Other variations on this would be to white balance through $^1/_2$CTB and use a $^1/_2$Black Promist, $^1/_2$Warm Promist or $^1/_2$Warm Soft Effect filter on the camera. These will soften the image, and add a glow

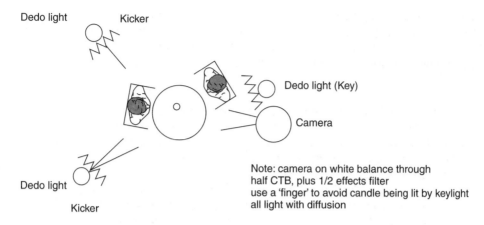

Figure 18.11 Candle-lit scene

to highlights, i.e. the candle. One drawback in this scenario is that the true colour of the candle flame is only seen at about $f16$. This reinforces the argument for moving the white point. Not only does the candle become warmer but also the flame.

Lightning – Best achieved with special 'lightning' units (see p. 134), or a large HMI/MSR fitted with a manual semaphore shutter to enable rapid 'flashing' of the light. Lightning effects should be very intense, best used as side-lights or back-lights. Frontal use of these lights will 'wash-out' the scene.

Light beams – For light to be made visible in the atmosphere it must hit something, e.g. mist, fog, smoke and dust particles. The two essential items for revealing light beams are:

* Strong light sources – sun, HMI PARs, Xenon, large Fresnel spotlight, narrow-angle PAR cans.
* Haze machines/fog machines.

Haze machines are ideal for use in enclosed areas where a general haze can be built up over a period of time and easily maintained. They provide a very even haze. Fog machines are more useful for exterior work, capable of providing large quantities of fog. Some machines have coolers, which cool the fog which then dispenses more slowly. Obviously on a windy day use of an exterior fog machine is going to present problems!

For best results, haze and fog should be backlit, or sidelit to reveal the light beams. Incidentally, water droplets as in fountains should be lit in a similar way for best effect.

18.7 Lighting demonstrations

Examples of demonstration shoots include cooking items, gardening and do-it-yourself repairs and renovations. The simplest demonstration set-up is that of a single artiste to camera, shooting mid-shots and medium close-ups of the artiste supplemented with close-ups of the item being demonstrated. If shooting with two cameras it can be shot very quickly, keeping one camera on the presenter, the second on the close-ups of food etc.

Shooting single camera requires the presenter to be shot and then the close-ups shot as cut-aways. Unless the presenter technique requires everything to be shot on an obvious single-camera, i.e. panning and zooming to follow the action, not a technique which endears itself to viewers! Figure 18.12 illustrates a typical lighting set-up based on the need:

● To provide modelling (form) for the presenter and the item being demonstrated.
● To avoid camera shadows on the demonstration item. Remember, the close-up camera will probably need to crane-up and tilt down to look at the items being demonstrated. Similarly the presenter's camera will need to be on the eyeline, i.e. elevated. Hence the need for an offset keylight as shown.
● To avoid overlighting the front of the table, use of a veil on the keylight is a more precise way of controlling the lighting on the front of the desk than a barndoor.
● To avoid hard shadows of the presenter over the items being demonstrated. Use:

  (a) an offset backlight
  (b) a kicker – this can be barndoored off the table
  (c) two 'soft' backlights

Note: when using soft backlights there is a need for these luminaires to be fitted with egg-crates and tipped down to avoid camera flare. Also be aware of light spill from these lights lighting the background.

The above lighting plot is a basic solution to the problem. Note, however, that there may be a need to reverse the keylight/fill-light position if the item being demonstrated is not clearly defined. Remember, **clarity** of the demonstrated item is paramount!

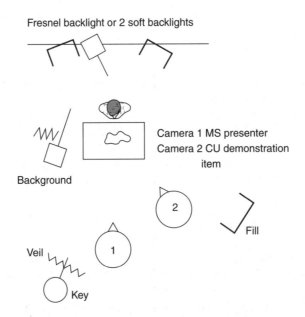

Figure 18.12 Basic demonstration, lighting for a single presenter

This basic set-up may be extended to cater for a two-person presentation, i.e. host plus guest, as shown in Figure 18.13. In this, the guest is placed camera right so that the keylight favours him/her, i.e. the guest turns towards the keylight when talking to the host.

An alternative solution is shown in Figure 18.14 using 'cross-keys'. This set-up is useful when the presenters favour more of an interview discussion rather than working downstage as previous example. Note the use of side half-scrims on the keylights to reduce illuminance on the nearer of the two presenters. One of the keylights needs to be barndoored off the table top to avoid it being overlit.

A by-product of this technique of cross-keying is that the presenter's shadows are less likely to appear in shot than with the more frontal keylight. Where possible avoid in-shot

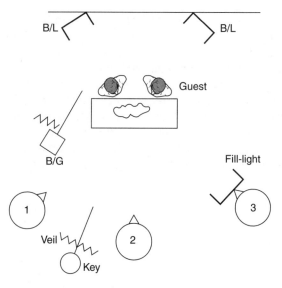

Figure 18.13 Two-handed demonstration, basic plot

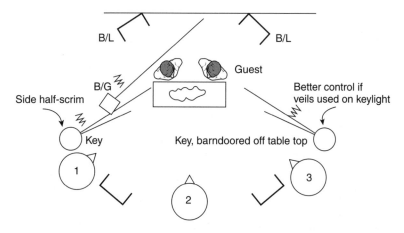

Figure 18.14 Cross-lit demonstration

presenter's shadows, i.e. on backgrounds, unless using large softlights as keys – the soft shadows are less distracting.

To avoid the artistes' shadows on the background, try to gain a good physical separation between the background and the presenter – at least 2 m. If shadows of the presenters on the background are a distraction consider:

(a)   using a frontal keylight – shadows will be behind presenter
(b)   using a side-key plus frontal fill-light.

18.8   Pack shots

Pack shots are shots of 'packages' which exclude a presenter, e.g. a product or a prize, seen in isolation. Many items are straightforward to light, and the general principle is to keep it simple and try to avoid conflicting shadows. Often, effective lighting can be achieved by using a soft keylight from upstage, offset to one side. The keylight also acts as a backlight giving good separation on the items being featured, e.g. a plate of food. A complementary soft fill-light from downstage completes the set-up (Figure 18.15).

Pack shots may give rise to **glare** reflections of the light source. These can be controlled by using a polarising filter on the camera. If **direct** reflections of the source cause problems, these can be controlled by polarising the light source as well as using a polariser on the camera. Glass and metal objects present particular lighting problems and are worth special treatment.

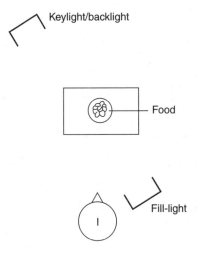

Figure 18.15 Basic lighting of food

Lighting glass

Glass being transparent is difficult to light. Most of the light is transmitted by the glass, and a small amount is absorbed and a small amount is reflected. The light reflected will give rise to a specular reflection that may be a distraction. Two techniques have evolved for lighting glass:

- Bright-field method
- Dark-field method.

The **Bright-field** method relies on placing the glassware in front of an illuminated background with black drapes either side of it. The glass is unlit! The luminaire lighting the white background must be 'flagged' to ensure that no specular reflections are seen in the glass (Figure 18.16).

This reveals the glass as slightly 'smokey', due to less than 100% transmission of the glass with dark edges to the glassware. The dark edges are the black drapes, refracted by the glass. Coloured filters over the background light can be used to great effect. Note, however, that if translucent liquid is introduced into the glass it will turn the glass/liquid into a lens with a consequent reversal of background colour position. If extra shape is required, a reflection of a 'window' can be introduced on the glass by using a white reflector downstage with black tape 'glazing bars' and bouncing a suitable Fresnel spotlight. A similar technique of revealing the shape of, say, a wine bottle can be used, and it also provides illuminance for the label.

The **Dark-field** method, as its name suggests, is the reverse of the Bright-field technique, i.e. the glass object is seen against a black background with out-of-shot white cyclorama either side of it. Figure 18.17 illustrates this technique.

Again, care should be taken to ensure that no specular reflections of the light source are visible on-camera, unless specifically requested. This technique is especially useful for cut-glassware. The image seen on-camera will be that of the glassware against black with the edges showing as highlights – the refracted images of the white drapes. Again, colour can be used to good effect, and downstage soft sources can be used to reveal engravings in the glassware.

Lighting metal, particularly polished metal, usually requires the light source to be revealed (Figure 18.18).

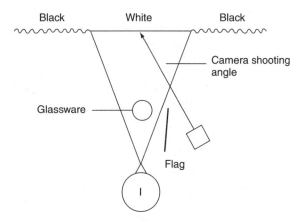

Figure 18.16 Bright-field method

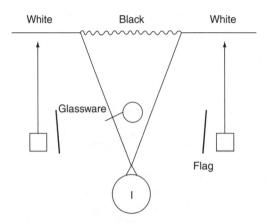

Figure 18.17 Dark-field method

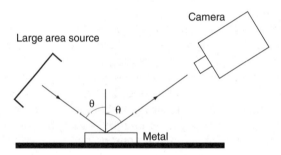

Figure 18.18 Basic technique for lighting metal

Often it is useful to add some 'texture' to the reflection by putting small flags or 'Charlie bars' over the light source. Silver trophies are usually put in a 'tent' of diffusion which is lit from outside. The camera shoots through a small hole in the 'tent'.

This technique is extended for lighting a car. The usual brief is no 'speculars', the car must look sleek and elegant! Observe a car, outdoors, on an overcast day, and the technique for lighting a car will be revealed! The convex curves of the car reflect the sky and at the same time produce a minified image. This results in a car with highlights (the reflected sky) on all the curves, which help to accentuate the 'lines' of the car. At the same time, of course, the car is lit with the skylight. In a studio, this can be realised with the car, against a cyclorama, with a large **butterfly** above. The butterfly fitted with silk or diffusion is lit from above, usually hard sources, but if a perfectly diffused light source (from the butterfly) is required, one could use softlights (Figure 18.19).

The cyclorama can be lit to provide appropriate illuminance of the car sides. If artistes are required to be lit, standing alongside the car, use a Fresnel spotlight, which has been well flagged off the car (to avoid specular reflections).

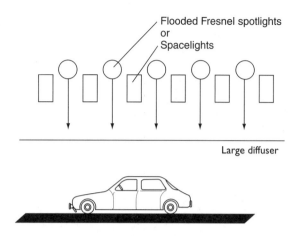

Flooded Fresnel spotlights
or
Spacelights

Large diffuser

Figure 18.19 Lighting a car – basic technique

18.9   Conference lighting

Conferences may take many forms, from a simple single subject to a panel of politicians at a party conference. Points to remember include:

- The subject should be able to see the audience and it is essential that the questioner grilling the speaker should be seen by the speaker. Remember, a vertical keying angle of less than 30° will result in glare for the subject, i.e. well aware of the light source in his eyeline.
- Try to avoid distracting shadows of the speakers on the background. Remember the need to keep the subjects well away from the background – ideally about 2.5 m, or 1.5 m as the absolute minimum.
- If an in-shot shadow on the background cannot be avoided, say, for an end-of-match interview against a background of programme/sports logos, make sure that the subject is lit from **within** the picture so that the shadow falls behind the subject, not in front of them. Using diffusion on the light source will reduce the amount of distraction of an in-shot shadow.
- When multiple subjects are involved avoid mutual shadowing.
- When large halls are involved, try if possible, to gain a camera position at the front of the hall. This will avoid the need for any range extenders and the higher lighting levels subsequently needed.
- Usually large conferences have a lighting truss rigged in front of the conference speaker's table. This gives a good facility to divide the 'table' into sections, lighting each section separately. Always use Fresnel spotlights to have the good control of the beam shape, i.e. provide localised lighting.
- The various options are illustrated in Figure 18.20.
- Presentations against projection screens require good control of light beams to ensure that the projected image is not washed-out with stray light (Figure 18.21).

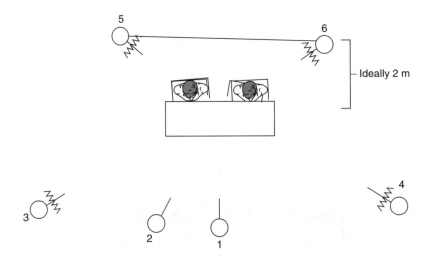

Figure 18.20 Basic alternatives. Lamp 1 used as a frontal keylight if shadow on background is a problem; Lamp 2, better position for keylight if no shadow problem; Lamps 3 and 4 may be used as fill-lights (multi-camera shooting) or as cross-keylights if audience prevents positioning of 1 or 2; Lamps 5 and 6 backlights: 3, 4, 5, 6 with diffusion

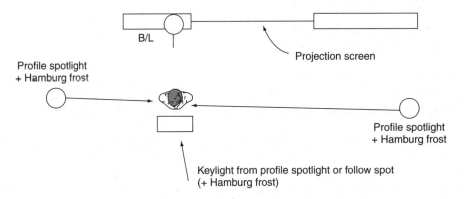

Figure 18.21 Presentation against a projection screen

18.10   Silhouette lighting

Often when subjects do not want to be recognised they need to be seen in silhouette. Basically, this means shooting the unlit subject against a brightly lit background. It is obviously essential that the facetone is at black level. How can the cameraman ensure this?

With all vision control work, the most important aspect is invariably the face. Generally, for normal operations, the face is exposed to be about one stop down on peak white.

Typically, the dynamic range of a colour camera is in excess of 32:1, i.e. equivalent to our five stops. From the discussion on dynamic range, recall that the nine-step grey scale has a contrast ratio of 32:1 between the peak white step and the black step (Figure 18.22). But the black step results in a signal above absolute black level. So if you want the subject

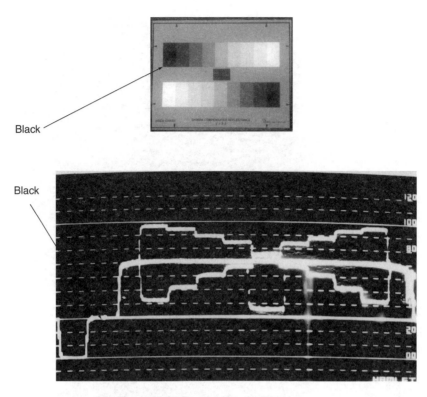

Black

Black

Figure 18.22 The visibility of a 'black' step

to be totally in silhouette, it must be well over five stops down on the lighting level used for the background. The easiest way to achieve this is to shoot the subject against a window. With no light on the subject, expose the sky – the subject will be in total silhouette.

For interiors at night, light only the background to a high lighting level, again removing all light from the subject. Remember, you need at least five stops' difference – a lighting ratio in excess of **32:1, preferably six stops**.

For exteriors, use some form of flag to keep the light off the subject and shoot against the sky or a plain light wall. But again, remember the need for at least a five stop difference in luminance of background and subject.

As a check, open up your camera to exposure the face and note the f-number. Now stop down to correctly expose the background and note the f-number. The difference in f-number should be over five stops and your silhouette will work!

If your camera has DCC or some form of knee, switch it off for the silhouette shot. But do remember that you are not trying to 'burn-out' the background. Opening-up to achieve this will raise the exposure on the subject and may make him visible.

Always frame the subject so that the silhouette has some degree of ambiguity, i.e. not square-on or full profile. If in any doubt about the visibility of the face then shoot the shadow. This will have some degree of distortion. As a further measure, the shadow could be arranged across a radiator or drapes, again giving extra ambiguity to the shape of the silhouette (see Figures 18.23 and 18.24).

Figure 18.23 Basic silhouette, offset to disguise shape

Figure 18.24 Use of shadow on a textured surface to disguise the shape

18.11   Chroma key on location

Often it is required to complete a chroma key **foreground** shot on location for insertion into an appropriate **background** in post-production.

Chroma key principle

Chroma key is an electronic process whereby part of one picture (foreground) is inserted into another (background) (Figure 18.25). The area to be inserted is determined by placing the foreground subject in front of a suitably coloured backing, e.g. blue or green. The RGB signals from the foreground camera are used to devise a suitable **keying** or switching signal which is used to operate a fast-acting switch between foreground and background cameras. Whenever the keying signal is of a high amplitude (when scanning the keying colour) the background picture source is selected.

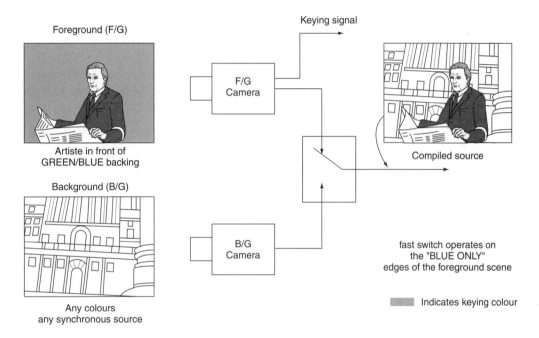

Figure 18.25 Chroma key principle

The keying signal

The keying signal is derived from the RGB signals such that it is a **maximum** for the keying colour. Unfortunately, colours in the foreground subject which have the keying colour in their make-up may give rise to a keying signal, producing erroneous switching. To provide discrimination against unwanted colours operating the switch, the keying signal has to rise above an operational **clipping level**.

Chroma key systems, therefore, use two steps to derive a suitable keying (switching signal):

(i)   a saturated colour backing – hence **chroma key**
(ii) an operation threshold or **clipping** level.

Lighting for chroma key

The lighting of a foreground chroma key set-up requires a few basic principles to be observed to ensure successful chroma key operation in post-production.

- The backing colour should be lit **uniformly** and to a minimum level, consistent with correct switching. **Typically, the backing should be lit to a similar level as the foreground subject**. Collapsible backgrounds in green/blue are available.
- A good depth-of-field is required which 'embraces' all the foreground planes. Any lack of sharp focus on foreground planes will result in a 'mix' between subject edges and the keying colour, i.e. providing uncertainty in setting the clipping level.
- Avoid subject shadows on the keying background, unless 'shadow' chroma key systems are being used. The clipping level would have to be reduced to operate on the darker backing, perhaps allowing unwanted colours to key.
- Use two backlights to provide a good rimlight to the foreground subject. This will wash-out any colour fringing on the foreground subject. A single backlight will not give complete wash-out of the fringe.

To minimise colour fringing of the foreground subject:

- Keep the foreground subject well clear of the background.
- Keep the luminance of the background as low as possible.
- Use two backlights.
- Use minimum area of keying background.

If the background subject is known in advance, the lighting of the foreground subject should relate to it, e.g.

- Keylight from an appropriate angle
- Use hard/soft keylight as appropriate
- Use coloured light as appropriate, i.e. warm/cool
- Shadow density to match background.

For matching purposes record:

1 Camera height
2 Camera lens angle
3 Subject distance
4 Camera tilt angle
5 Lens aperture.

If the inserted background is to be a simple graphic then matching of foreground and background becomes less important.

18.12   Lighting musicians

Musicians and their instruments can provide some of the most interesting subjects to light:

- Remember if the musician is reading music to keep the keylights well away from his eyeline. Bright point sources can give rise to dark 'after-images' and the musicians will complain about too many notes on the music!
- With orchestras it is most important to avoid keylights on the musician's eyeline to the conductor for the same reasons.
- Each musician, if lit individually, needs to be lit to avoid the shadow of the instrument falling on the musicians face, e.g.

  Trombone
  Trumpet
  Harp
  Flute
  Tuba
  French horn
  Violinist's bow.

- Usually stringed instruments require the musician to be lit from the stringed side of the instrument, i.e. from the direction which the musician will tend to look to check fingering etc., e.g.

  Double bass
  Cello
  Guitar.

- Close-ups of the musician's fingers will always be required. Ensure that you have an effective backlight to bring out the shape of the fingers and to separate them from the background.
- Avoid overlighting – a short depth of field is an advantage when shooting musicians and detail shots.
- If using coloured light it is useful to keep a colour theme – appropriate to the music, e.g.

  Black/white plus one colour
  Black/white plus two colours.

- Keep coloured light pure – avoid contamination of colour caused by two colours 'mixing' on stage, i.e. keep coloured light, on one subject, more than 180° apart.
- Choice of colour usually includes the palette of blues, reds, oranges and lavender. Lavender seems to be a colour which will go with any colour. (Colours used should suite the mood of the music and complement or contrast with the musician's costume. Figure 18.26 illustrates the basic colour wheel.)
- Green tends to work well when used in conjunction with instruments featuring wood-work – but use it in moderation!
- When lighting pop groups, using individual keys, light **away from** the centre of the stage, i.e. towards the edge of the stage. This is to avoid the centre-stage being overlit – the meeting point of all the light!

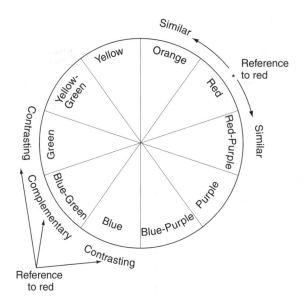

Figure 18.26 Basic colour 'wheel'

- When lighting a choir, keep lighting simple and try to use one keylight. Remember that if your light source is of sufficient beam angle but lacking in intensity, simply doubling the number of lights will obviously double the illuminance – and if using the combination at a long throw it will be most unlikely to see two distinct shadows.
- Conductors of choirs – try to avoid their shadow on the choir. The 'lively' shadow from an arm-waving conductor can be very distracting!
- Finally, lighting a piano is generally regarded as a problem with a unique solution – there really is only one way to light a piano keyboard properly! Figure 18.27 (page 245) illustrates the basic plot where the steep keylight is also the backlight for the piano and the pianist when shot on camera one.

Note: Keyboard light must be steep to avoid long shadows of black notes. Avoid shadow of pianist on keyboard by placing keylight to aim straight along the keyboard. Avoid double keying of keyboard – make sure that the pianist's keylight does not reach any part of the keyboard. Hence use of profile spotlight.

18.13   Lighting in public places (supermarkets/offices/ hospitals)

Supermarkets

The majority of lighting in supermarkets and departmental stores is fluorescent, supplemented with tungsten/CDM lighting to give accents/highlights (Table 18.1). Most modern stores use high-frequency fittings to overcome the annoying flicker problem, which often occurs with mains frequency ballasts. The lighting will of course be 'toppy', although

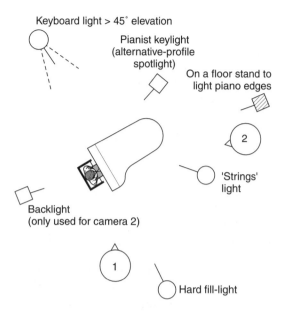

Keyboard light > 45° elevation

Pianist keylight
(alternative-profile
spotlight)

On a floor stand to
light piano edges

2

'Strings'
light

Backlight
(only used for camera 2)

1

Hard fill-light

Figure 18.27 Lighting a piano

Table 18.1 Supermarkets, department stores, offices and hospital lighting

Area	Light source	Illuminance (lux)
Supermarkets	Colour 827	600–700
Department stores	Colour 830	600
Offices	Colour 840	300
Offices (VDU)	Colour 840	500
Drawing offices	Colour 840	500–750
Hospital wards	Colour 840	600–800
Operating theatres	Tungsten halogen	60 000–100 000

generally of sufficient illuminance for modern cameras. Depending on the nature of the shoot there may be a need to remove (flag) lighting to make pictures less 'flat'. The problem with adding light is that of **mixed lighting**. Only when all sources are colour matched will the camera white balance result in a good colour fidelity picture, i.e. the camera will remove any excessive green hues during the white balance. Care should be taken in adding light to ensure that it is coloured matched to fluorescent lighting. Although matched in colour temperature, tungsten and fluorescent sources may have colour errors in the green/magenta axis. Mixed lighting problems need to be solved at the time of the shoot. Only complete colour casts can be corrected in post-production.

Unless shooting under 'controlled' conditions, supermarkets will usually be full of shoppers making it difficult to use lamps on stands. Consequently any lighting will need to be with hand-held, battery-operated sources.

Offices

Offices are usually lit with fluorescent light sources at 4000 K. Offices with VDUs will be lit to about 300 lux and drawing offices will be lit to about 500 lux. Often to avoid problems of mixed lighting it is best to switch off the fluorescent lights and add corrected tungsten lighting to any existing natural lighting.

Hospitals

Generally hospital wards will be lit with fluorescent lighting, usually with localised tungsten angle-poise lamps near the bed-heads. Lighting equipment must **never** be plugged into hospital mains supplies without prior arrangements with the hospital authorities. This is another area where hand-held, battery-operated lighting equipment can be a useful supplement.

Operating theatres have special tungsten lighting over the operating table, supplemented with fluorescent lighting for the remainder of the room. Special arrangements have to be made for shooting in these areas to ensure that no contamination of the area or causing any obstruction to the procedures.

18.14   Stadia lighting – night

Sports stadia, football grounds etc. are generally lit with high intensity discharge sources, which have a correlated colour temperature of 5600 K. This colour temperature was arrived as a 'preferred' colour temperature for these events. Generally, when shooting interviews at these events, there is a need to supplement the stadia lighting; if possible use the stadia lighting as a backlight and add your own keylight. When adding extra light, make sure:

● It is colour matched to the stadia lighting
● It is at the right illuminance to give a similar exposure on the subject as the 'background' of the stadia
● It is diffused to avoid the subject being blinded by the light source

The last point is very important when lighting players against a stadium or cricket pitch in daylight. Often staging of the subject results in the subject having very little natural light on their face, e.g. under stadia roofs or cricket pavilions. You may find subjects objecting to very bright point sources in their eyes just before they go out to bat! Obviously, with sports such as cricket avoid any lights which may accidentally be on the batsman's eyeline!

Lighting levels at stadia depend on the particular role of the stadium, often with three levels of floodlighting to cater for practice, club level and TV coverage. Many early installations were equipped with CSI sources (4000 K), but these are now being replaced with high intensity discharge sources at 5600 K. These match daylight more readily and enable film cameras to be used without any need for on-camera correction filters (Table 18.2).

Table 18.2 High intensity discharge sources (non-TV use)

	Colour temperatures (K)	Colour rendition index (R_a)	Efficacy lumens (W)	Typical uses
High pressure mercury HPL-N	4000	50	63	Street lighting (obsolescent)
High pressure mercury HPL-COMFORT	3500	55–60	60	Street lighting (obsolescent)
Metal halide HPI	4000	68	76	Sports lighting, floodlighting. Area lighting, indoor large areas
Metal halide HPI-T	4500	69	76	Sports lighting, floodlighting. Area lighting, indoor large areas
Metal halide MHD	5600	92	83	Sports lighting, floodlighting
Metal halide MHN-TD	4200	80–85	80	Shops, offices, petrol stations, floodlighting
Metal halide MHN-DA	5600	90	100	Sports lighting, floodlighting

Note: With a wide range of possibilities available for floodlighting, stadia lighting and public area lighting, it is recommended to check the light sources in use so that any possible mixed lighting problems can be evaluated.

The increase in camera sensitivity may be thought a reason to reduce the illuminance. However, the basic needs still need to be satisfied, namely visibility and clarity of players action for:

The players
The referee
The spectators

In many instances, the presence of television coverage has led to lighting levels which have benefited everyone! The increased use of slow-motion cameras has meant that the need for high lighting levels is maintained, and a minimum of 1400 lux is required with typical levels of 1800 lux being the design figure. Some sports require enhanced lighting levels in critical areas, e.g. goalmouth, dartboard, basket ball 'basket' area etc. to ensure a good exposure and adequate depth of field when using high-ratio zoom lenses (zoom ramping).

18.15   Stadia lighting – special events

Often stadia are used to mount special events, concerts etc. where there is a need for long throw follow spotlights and/or xenon beamlights. The xenon light source is excellent for **follow-spotlight** applications:

- it is a very compact source, easy to collect and project the light.
- better efficacy than tungsten.
- excellent colour rendition (R_a 98).
- very stable colour with temperature and with life.
- very easy to match xenon sources.

Table 18.3 Xenon follow spotlights

Name	Candlepower at wide angle (cd)	Wide beam angle	Candlepower at narrow angle (cd)	Narrow beam angle	Throw for 1000 lux at narrow angle (m)
Super Trouper Medium Throw 1 kW	0.5 million	15°	4.3 million	6°	65
Super Trouper Medium Throw 1.6 kW	0.8 million	15°	7 million	6°	83
Super Trouper Long Throw 1.6 kW	2.5 million	8°	10 million	1.9°	100
Super Trouper Long Throw 2 kW	3 million	8°	12 million	1.9°	110
Super Trouper II 2 kW	1.6 million	12.5°	13 million	4°	115
Gladiator II 2.5 kW	2 million	10°	15.6 million	3.2°	125
Gladiator III 3 kW	2.5 million	10°	20 million	3.2°	140

The follow-spotlights have an optical system which incorporates a zoom lens. Consequently the beam angle and intensity can be varied, hence the follow spot data is quoted for both extreme conditions of beam angle. A variable iris is also included which can be used to adjust the size of the projected 'disc' of light (but with no change in illuminance).

Hamburg Frost and Light Hamburg Frost can be used in one of the follow-spot colour frames when requiring a soft-edged beam of light. This is better than defocusing the lens which results in a change in projected image size. Table 18.3 illustrates the performance typical of Xenon follow spotlights.

Xenon beam lights are extremely powerful luminaires, based on using a parabolic mirror system to produce a very narrow, intense beam of light. The optical system has a motorised focus mechanism allowing the beam to be altered from the lamp head, ballast or from a remote location.

One word of caution: the optical system does produce a 'hole' in the centre of the beam. This can be minimised, but avoid using beam lights as a form of follow-spot.

Table 18.4 illustrates the powerful nature of xenon beam lights. The remotely operated pan/tilt, beam focus, colour changer versions of these lights are known as Space Canons, Sky-tracker, Britelights etc.

These luminaires are very powerful, and with the larger units in spot mode, the concentration of heat can crack windows! Nevertheless they can produce spectacular effects, the 16-frame scroller adding an extra dimension to an already impressive light source.

Table 18.4 Xenon beam lights

	Collimated peak intensity (cd)	Candlepower at narrow angle	Candlepower at wide angle
Britelights 1 kW xenon	100 million	10 million cd at 1.7°	2.5 million cd at 3.4°
Britelights 2 kW xenon	200 million	20 million cd at 1.7°	4.4 million cd at 3.4°
Britelights 4 kW xenon	400 million	40 million cd at 2°	10 million cd at 6°
Britelights 7 kW xenon	800 million	75 million cd at 2°	25 million cd at 8.8°
Britelights 10 kW xenon	1000 million	200 million cd at 2.5°	50 million cd at 7°

(*Reminder*: Xenon lamps may explode at room temperature, as the envelope gas pressure is above atmospheric pressure even when cold. Refer to safety handling instructions. All these units require forced air cooling, resulting in noise!)

18.16   Street lighting

Sodium sources predominate in the world of street lighting, mainly for their very high efficacy. There are two basic types:

Low-pressure sodium sources – golden yellow in appearance
High-pressure sodium sources – orange/yellow in appearance

Low-pressure sodium produces light, which is basically monochromatic. Figure 18.28 illustrates the basic problem of shooting with this light source namely that the 'single' yellow wavelength excites the camera green CCD and predominately red CCD, resulting in red/orange pictures! This cannot be improved by any filtering on the camera or light source!

High-pressure sodium sources have been progressively developed to improve the colour rendition, but at the expense of the efficacy (Table 18.5). Their spectral energy distribution is shown in Figure 18.29 and the development in chromaticity is shown in the section of the CIE diagram (Figure 18.30).

When using tungsten lighting and high pressure Sodium street lighting, the effects of the Sodium lighting may be reduced by suitable filtering. These are shown in Table 18.6. Clearly there is a need to test this to determine which street lights are in use. Alternatively, the local council highways department should be able to give the appropriate information on types of street lighting.

For major shoots, the street lights could be fitted with the best appropriate light source or switched off and replaced with especially rigged 'Blondes'.

Remember, when reading data sheets on street lighting, this will refer to **horizontal** illuminance values. Generally we are more interested in vertical illuminance values with vertical subjects!

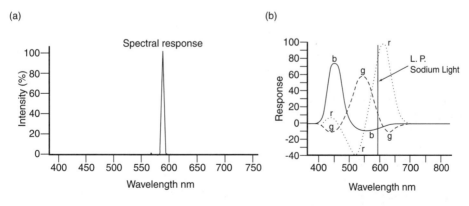

Figure 18.28 (a) Low-pressure sodium (SOX) spectrum; (b) Camera analysis plus SOX source

Table 18.5 Sodium light sources

	Colour temperature (K)	Colour rendition index R_a	Efficacy lumens/(W)
Low pressure Sodium (SOX)	–	–	200
High pressure Sodium (SON)	2000 K	20	120
High pressure Sodium (SON/deluxe)	2000 K	60	92
High pressure Sodium (SON comfort)	2000 K	70	80
High pressure (SDW-t)	2500 K	85	50

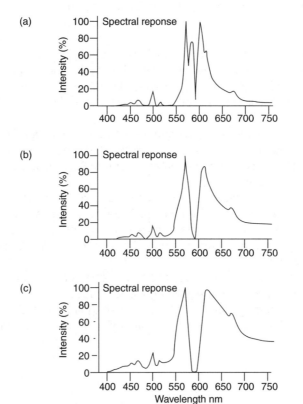

Figure 18.29 (a) High-pressure sodium (SON); (b) high-pressure sodium comfort (SON); (c) high-pressure sodium (SDW)

Floodlighting of buildings is typically about 50–70 lux. Remember, again, that at night buildings need to be visible as lit backgrounds and not have 'daylight' values of luminance.

18.17   Lighting in churches

Lighting churches for a service usually requires a full lighting rig and is normally shot as a live multi-camera outside broadcast. Single-camera operation in churches usually requires

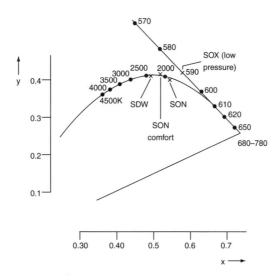

Figure 18.30 Chromaticity of sodium sources (figure shows part of CIE Chromaticity Diagram)

Table 18.6 Minimising the effect of sodium lights

Street light source	Tungsten and filter	Appearance of street lighting
SON	No filter	Pink/orange
SON	$-\frac{1}{2}$green	Orange
SON COMFORT	No filter	Orange
SON COMFORT	Full CTO	White (match)
SON COMFORT	$\frac{3}{4}$CTO	Slightly orange
SON SDW	No filter	Yellow/green
SON SDW	$-\frac{3}{8}$G $+\frac{1}{2}$CTO	White (match)

just part of a church to be lit at any one time. Several aspects should be borne in mind when lighting churches:

- Large old churches and cathedrals are usually quite dark when lit with natural daylight.
- Old churches usually have surfaces which are full of texture, and these should be lit to reveal the texture, i.e. large angle between the camera and the light source.
- Modern churches generally have flatter surfaces, which have a 'lighter' finish. There is a need for good control of light sources to ensure that these surfaces are not overlit, thereby causing a distraction.
- Often in lighting for texture on wood panelling, glare reflections may need to be controlled by using a polarising filter on the camera.
- Stained glass windows absorb a tremendous amount of light! During daylight they are backlit with a large area light source (skylight). Ideally, to reproduce this effect at night the windows needs to be lit with a large HMI (4 kW or larger) and the window lined with white diffusion or a silk. Simply lighting a stained glass window usually does not make it look very brightly lit. An image of the window will be on the ceiling – not in shot (Figure 18.31).

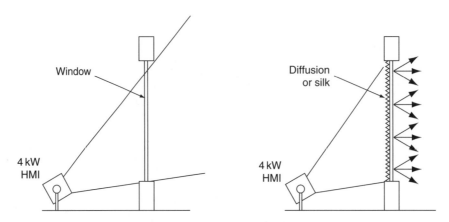

Figure 18.31 Lighting stained glass windows

- Where practical lights appear in shot, e.g. choir stalls, it can be extremely useful to insert a dimmer in their mains feed. This can give valuable control of their 'in-shot' brightness.
- Churches usually contain mixed lighting – candles plus daylight. It can be useful to white balance to $\frac{1}{2}$CTB (4300 K) and use light sources corrected to $\frac{1}{2}$CTB for the artistes. The candles retain a 'warmth' while the windows have a 'cool' look to them.
- For localised night shooting it is useful (and quick) to consider underlighting archways/ building features. This helps to create an atmosphere different from daylight and avoids the need of lighting equipment to be rigged at high level.
- Balloon lights have become popular for lighting large areas of churches/cathedrals (provided ceiling shots are not required).
- Church exteriors, at night, should again be lit for texture. Depending on the size of the building a 4 kW HMI/MSR could be used for one side of a church, provided there is enough clear space for the use of the HMI far enough away to light the complete surface. If this is not possible, devise a lighting plan using several smaller wattage HMIs. Always use a flag to keep the light off the immediate foreground. Where two sides of a church are shot, it can be useful to 'warm-up' one side to give a slight colour difference to the second surface (Figure 18.32). Church windows should appear lit when shooting church exteriors, unless the church is supposed to be empty.
- If there is a need for 'long throw' lighting, the narrow angle PAR cans are particularly useful. They may be used corrected or not. In the latter case if the church/cathedral is very tall the daylight-lit upper parts of the building will be lit 'cooler' and have little effect on the congregation at floor level. Similarly, PAR cans can be useful for lighting church ceilings from the floor, again using narrow angle sources to contain the lighting to the ceilings.

18.18   Night-lighting – principles

The points to be considered for lighting at night on location are similar to those identified for creating mood, i.e. texture, ambiguity, colour, lighting, balance and exposure.

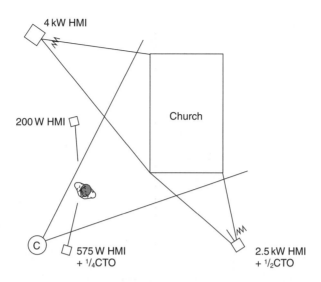

Figure 18.32 Church exterior

Texture is so important when lighting a shot at night. Typically, lighting a location so that it looks like night, i.e. dimly lit, but without texture being revealed results in pictures which will be uninteresting and flat. Clothing, especially dark clothing, is more readily revealed when lit for texture. The same is true for buildings.

Ambiguity, as discussed earlier, is a major parameter in creating an element of mystery. Night-lighting is very much an area for using dapple-plates (cookies) and simple 'dingles' (tree branches) in front of lights to create a shadowed and mysterious look to the location.

The **colour** of light used at night is an area for a major debate, and there are several opinions on what is best. Some Lighting Directors avoid coloured light completely, others use colour according to their own observation and what looks right for them. The correct placing of luminaires is important to create the right effect before considering the use of colour.

The potential light sources at night are:

- moonlight at 4100 K
- domestic tungsten at 2760 K
- street lamps (sodium) at 2000 K (low pressure) – 2400 K (high pressure)
- candles at approximately 1900 K.

So, what about the use of coloured light at night?

The **stylised** film treatment of using a fairly strong blue filter on lights or camera lens originates from the observation that at extremely low levels of illuminance, i.e. moonlight – 0.1 lux – human vision becomes monochromatic and we no longer see any colour, only a black/white landscape. One way to remove the colour from a scene, except of course blue, is to use a blue filter. This leaves the scene very blue.

Another argument for using blue is that when the eye/brain changes from photopic vision (full colour) to scotopic vision (night vision – monochromatic) there is a small shift in the peak response towards the blue end of the spectrum (Figure 18.33). This is sometimes

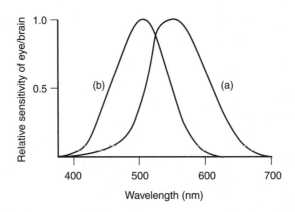

Figure 18.33 Relative spectral sensitivity of the eye/brain. (a) Photopic; (b) scotopic

used as an argument for using blue. However, the eye/brain sees this as a black/white image – not a very convincing argument to use blue!

Probably the best way to tackle the use of colour at night is to look at relative colour differences, say between moonlight and domestic tungsten. Moonlight is reflected sunlight, but without the presence of skylight, so it will be less than average summer sunlight, a colour temperature of 4100 K is usually quoted.

A scene involving absolute reality is shown in Figure 18.34. This lighting plot could be realised with filtering of light sources, e.g.:

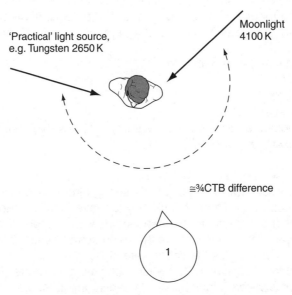

Figure 18.34 Night exterior scene – 'reality'

$$\text{Moonlight} \begin{cases} \text{Tungsten halogen 3200 K} + \frac{1}{2}\text{CTB} \\ \text{or HMI/MSR 5600 K} + \frac{1}{2}\text{CTO} \end{cases} = 4300\,\text{K}$$

Domestic tungsten tungsten halogen $3200\,\text{K} + \frac{1}{4}\text{CTO} = 2650\,\text{K}$

A simpler solution would be to minimise the amount of filtering by just ensuring a **difference** between the sources in the correct colour shift – that is the correct MIRED shift, in this case a $\frac{3}{4}$CTB difference.

18.19 Night-lighting – practice

A practical solution to the 'reality' situation discussed above is shown in Figure 18.35. Another filtering alternative is to use (Full CTB + White Flame Green) in combination to give a cool moonlight, which is not so harsh on facetones. Beware of using tungsten sources on dimmers. The change in colour temperature when dimmed may make the results not look right, i.e. lack of blueness.

Yet another alternative, depending on personal preference, is to reduce the colour temperature difference to half CTB. There will be slight differences in the effect achieved

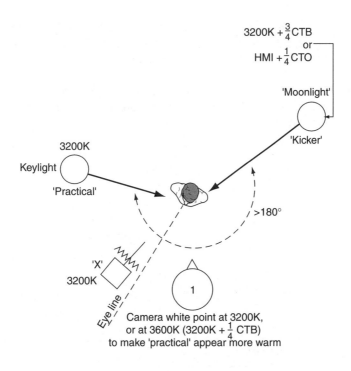

Figure 18.35 Night exterior scene – practical arrangement

from one manufacturer's camera to another. Certainly, the older tube cameras had an enhanced Blue response so half-CTB correction was satisfactory. Generally, aim at subtle use of colour; if it is too strong the effect will look too theatrical. Note the use of a kicker as opposed to an offset elevated backlight. A kicker should be at eye level and aimed at the subject's temple. This reveals more texture on the side of the face and although a 'cheat' on reality, generally produces a better result than the elevated backlight.

Important

- The two main lights must be greater than 180° apart to avoid contamination of coloured light.
- For best results avoid symmetrical lighting on the face from the keylight and kicker.
- The small filler light, plus diffusion, provides a catchlight in the eye, it **must** be positioned to camera left of the eyeline to avoid contamination of coloured light and to maintain good texture on the face. The lighting balance of this light is crucial to the mood created. If only a hint of light around the eyes is required this can best be achieved with a small plastic mirror (e.g. Figure 18.36), or a Dedolight plus projection lens and shutters.

If no diffusion is used, the projected image will have a hard edge. The lit area can be reduced by masking off part of the mirror with gaffer tape. This is a much better way of achieving this effect than trying to barndoor a Fresnel spotlight.

- Remember, moonlight should be less intense than the 'practical' lights.
- Avoid overexposure: generally **exposure** will be approximately one stop down on daylight exposure settings.

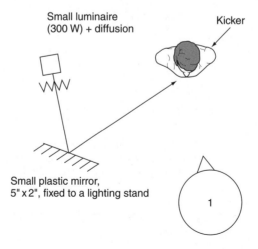

Small luminaire
(300 W) + diffusion

Kicker

Small plastic mirror,
5" x 2", fixed to a lighting stand

1

Figure 18.36 Use of a small mirror for dramatic linking of eyes only

- Remember that the eye/brain will adapt its 'white' point to the prevailing conditions. Consequently, a building lit with an HMI/MSR may not look as blue as you might expect if the eye/brain has adapted to the HMI 'white'. A yellowish building will, of course, look white!
- Buildings do not need to be lit to high lighting levels, they only need to be made visible. Typically, floodlit buildings are lit to 50–70 lux!
- Ideally, use a waveform monitor, e.g. Hamlet Picoscope, to verify levels **or** check relative signal levels by flicking to colour bars to re-establish normal levels on the picture monitor.
- It is recommended to experiment with the above ideas to establish your own preference for use of **colour**, **lighting balance** and **exposure** on night shoots.
- Avoid using unfiltered HMI/MSRs to produce moonlight. It tends to produce a very blue coarse look – not subtle enough.
- Remember that when using minimum lighting levels any ambient light may influence your lighting balance.
- When using a mixture of tungsten and HMI/MSR light sources remember HMI/MSRs have three to four times the efficiency of tungsten sources.

When shooting wide shots, typical techniques are:

- using a large HMI/MSR + correction as a single major backlight
- using smoke upstage, backlit with a suitably corrected HMI/MSR
- using the fire brigade to dampen roads, roofs etc. to help reveal texture
- if long shots are required, try to 'flag' or barndoor all but one of the lights off the ground to avoid conflicting floor shadows.

Remember that at night a moving subject will not necessarily be lit constantly, but could be lit from 'practicals', e.g. street lights, lights from windows, car headlamps, lights on buildings. A technique to cover periods of walking through unlit areas is to ensure that the artiste is always seen in silhouette. Used by itself, this is another way of introducing ambiguity. Another would be to throw the shadow of the subject onto a building and then shoot the shadow only.

Sodium street lights can be simulated by using $\frac{3}{4}$CTO on a tungsten source. Use a similar technique to the moonlight set-up, with a (tungsten + $\frac{3}{4}$CTO) as a kicker to suggest the street light.

Safety at night

- On a large shoot provide a working light to avoid tripping accidents on cables etc.
- Always have a pocket torch handy for checking camera settings.
- Do not use luminaires so that they are a safety hazard for road traffic, seafarers or aircraft.

18.20   Lighting for cars

Daylight – stationary

The major problems in lighting car interiors are:

- Coping with the problems of excessive contrast between the interior of the car and the car exterior (similar to interior subject with back to window).
- Coping with problems of direct sunlight entering the car, again causing excessive contrast problems.
- Lighting the artistes to look right.

Figure 18.37 illustrates one solution to the problem, but how far this lighting plot can be adapted obviously depends on the facilities available. Points to note in the lighting set-up are:

- Except at early morning and late evening the artistes' faces will not be lit with direct sunlight. They will be lit with a softlight.
- Usually the forehead will not be lit as intensely as the lower part of the face, due to the effect of the top of the windscreen. Hence the use of gaffer tape along the top of the windscreen.
- Use of ND filter on the driver's window to the cope with excessive daylight outside the car. If 0.6ND is suitable the use of Rosco Scrim could be substituted (provided depth of field not too large) – this is easy to apply.

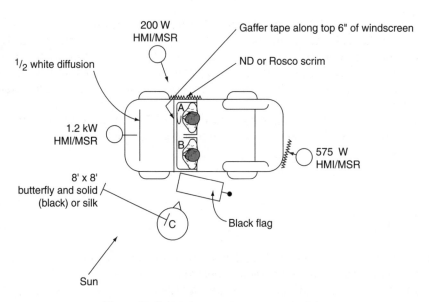

Figure 18.37 Lighting a stationary car – daylight

- Use of an external light to kick the faces from upstage. This helps to preserve the image of being lit from outside, especially if a significant amount of ND filter has been used.
- Use of backlight/kicker. This is especially useful when the upstage artiste looks downstage. It will assist this light if car headrests can be removed.
- Removal of direct sunlight, using an 8 foot × 8 foot butterfly. This may have a silk or black. Black is to be preferred as this will help to keep down the lighting on the downstage artiste. It is imperative that this artiste is not overlit if the total effect is to be believed. An extra black flag may be needed near the open downstage window to help control the lighting on artiste B.
- The correct lighting balance is essential if this is to 'look right'! If artiste A has to get out of the car, then clearly, when the door is opened the problem of excessive exposure returns. Use of a vertical butterfly with a double black net positioned a short distance upstage of the car door can help with this or alternatively the use of a large sheet of acrylic ND held in a suitable frame.
- With stable natural lighting conditions a similar lighting plot can be created using metallic-based reflectors.
- Note the need for **low stands** to ensure the lights are at seated eyeline height!

Daylight – moving

A typical requirement is that of shooting the driver talking to camera, or to the passenger. This has to be achieved without restricting the drivers vision or creating objectionable light sources in the drivers eye-line. A quick solution is shown in Figure 18.38. This uses a battery-operated HMI/MSR 200 W rigged on a magic arm fastened to a vertical 'pole-cat'. Check that the car roof is suitable for this application and remember to include a clean card (beer mat) between the top of the pole-cat and the car roof! The sun visor is used to support a section of Matthews reflector material. The HMI source is aimed at the Matthews reflector to provide a soft fill-light for the subject. ND filter (or Rosco Scrim) is needed on the car window. Frontal shots of the driver and passenger usually requires the use of the car being mounted on a 'low-loader' complete with camera, lighting kit and possibly towing a small generator.

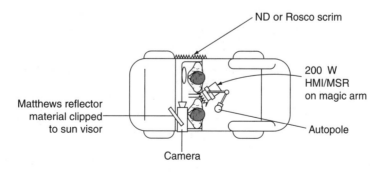

Figure 18.38 Lighting a moving car – daylight

18.21   Cars at night

Stationary

The principles of lighting a car at night are the same as established earlier for night-lighting:

- Texture
- Ambiguity/clarity
- Colour
- Lighting balance
- Exposure.

Again, a typical requirement is for shooting a two-shot of driver plus passenger. The lighting is set up in Figure 18.39 will cater for close-ups, tight two-shots and wider two shots to include some of the car exterior. The principle is to establish a keylight (1) as 3200 K (camera on 3200 K white balance), with the remaining lights suggesting a 'night' feeling by using sources (tungsten + $\frac{1}{2}$CTB) or (tungsten + $\frac{3}{4}$CTB). The lamp marked 2 acts as a kicker to put a blue rim on the driver and passenger. Lamp 3 acts as a backlight but also kicks the downstage side of the driver's face when he/she turns to the passenger.

Lamp 4 is used to backlight smoke to give depth to the shot, or alternatively use an HMI corrected with $\frac{1}{4}$CTO to light buildings/trees and shrubs for maximum texture. When lighting large flat surfaces beware of large specular reflections if the 'angles' are incorrect, i.e. lights reflected directly into the camera lens.

Lamps 5 and 6 are used to provide some lighting for the car exterior and fill-light on the downstage side of the passenger's face. Soft-light is used for this to avoid specular reflections of the light source on the car bodywork.

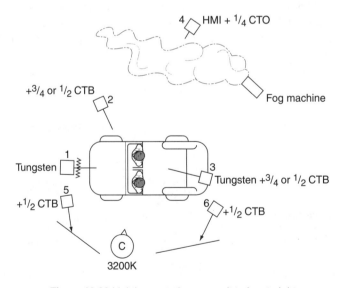

Figure 18.39 Lighting a stationary car interior at night

This is a set-up which can benefit from experimentation to seek out the options available:

- The keylight is suggested as being from street lamp or a light from a building. It is useful to diffuse this, plus add a strip of gaffer tape along the top of the windscreen to reduce the light on the artiste's forehead.
- Choice of colour used is down to personal preference from 'no colour' to $^3/_4$CTB. A useful alternative is white flame green + $^3/_4$CTB or even a pale lavender on tungsten sources, i.e. 3200 K source.
- If possible, remove headrests or use them at the lowest position to avoid a shadow from the kicker (lamp 3).
- Avoid – mutual shadowing of artists
   – shadows of artists on the inside of the car
   – shadow of the rear view mirror on the artistes, or 'in-shot' on the inside of the car.
- Use small wattage lamps, Dedolights or 300 W Fresnel spotlights will work for the main lighting around the car. Lamps 4 will depend on the amount of background to be lit.
- Having established the optimum position of the luminaires and the colour filters to use, the lighting balance and exposure will determine if it 'looks right'. The lighting balance can be judged by eye and checked on a monitor. Exposure is critical, it is important not to overexpose the picture. As a rough guide expose the picture as though it is a 'daylight' scene, note the f-number and then reduce exposure by one f-stop.

Moving car

With the need to preserve the vision of the driver by not obscuring his view and not blinding him with light, the options available tend to be limited. Small fluorescent lighting kits are available which have small sources (≈ 6 inches long). These are battery-operated, very compact and lightweight and may be Velcroed into position on the sun visor, and may be powered from the cigarette lighter.

Lighting from below eye-level, as though from the dashboard lights, results in an 'under-lit' look. Unless specifically requiring this particular look, avoid it! The dashboard light as a light source, with modern cars, is not very convincing!

19
Planning essentials

19.1 Planning

The objective of planning is to gain all necessary information, identify and anticipate possible problems and evolve a strategy to cope with the production requirements. In all but the simplest of location problems a recce or reconnaissance is recommended to identify:

- the requirements of the production actually on-site
- the natural or artificial lighting conditions likely to occur, position of sun etc.
- the power available and its suitability
- problems requiring special lighting units
- problems requiring special rigging facilities
- the need for electricians
- the need for dimmers, plus their location on-site
- the need for a generator or an electrical 'tie-in' to the supply to derive a larger current feed than the available domestic feed
- the dimensions of the location – area and **height**
- any particular safety hazards and problems of access
- features of the location requiring special care, e.g. works of art, listed building, curtains which may be damaged by heat from luminaires too close.

Before making any decisions, there is a need to get as much information as possible:

- 'acting area', subject positions, eyelines, moves in-vision?
- camera positions, in-vision moves?
- shot sizes – dictate the area to be lit
- single-camera or multi-camera shooting?
- do the shots have to match with studio or other locations?
- explicit requirements – day, night, evening etc.

- implicit requirements – required mood – documentary, sit-coms, drama?
- any special lighting effects required?
- any special lighting level problems, i.e. use of range extenders?
- time of day for the shoot – where will the sun be at that time?
- timescale?
- budget for lighting?

The last two factors are interrelated, 'time' means 'money'. There is an adage 'Good, Fast and Cheap' – take any two! You cannot have 'Good, Fast and Cheap' – it is an incompatible statement! When solving any lighting problem the solution will be linked by:

Technology
Technique
Time.

Clearly, any lighting solution will be influenced by the lighting equipment available, and one may have to adapt a particular technique if lighting equipment is limited. The second factor affecting technique is, of course, time (which means money). Again, there may be a need to compromise on technique if time is limited.

When several set-ups are required at the same location, it is an advantage to have enough facilities, equipment and electricians, so that each set-up can be pre-lit. This saves important time for the entire crew, i.e. no calls of 'waiting for lighting'! Don't forget to allow time for the de-rigging of each set-up.

Useful items at the recce include (see also Figure 19.1):

- clipboard, notepad, pencil and eraser
- retractable metal tape measure – to measure height as well as area details
- digital stills camera to record location features for future reference
- exposure meter/spotmeter – to check possible lighting conditions
- small torch – to help in investigating mains supply connections in dark cupboards!
- small compass – useful in establishing position of the sun on overcast recce days.

On a major shoot it is useful to have electricians working in pairs, plus the gaffer to oversee the rigging and troubleshooting any problems as they arise.

19.2 Strategy, lighting kits and timescales

Strategy

Its useful to adopt a strategy, such as below, when tackling lighting problems on location when proper planning/recce have not been possible:

- determine requirements from the director
- set up camera shot, determine shot limits
- review available lighting, at the desired lens aperture

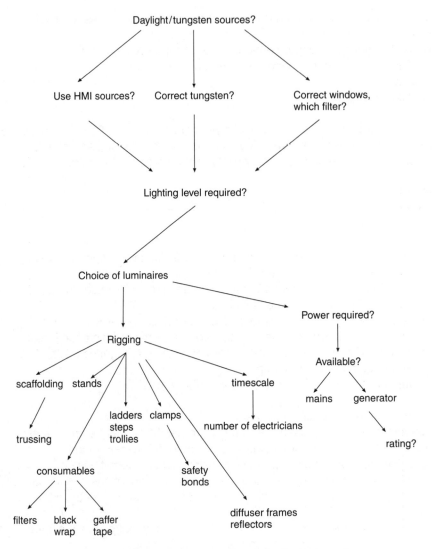

Figure 19.1 Decisions to be made at/following the 'recce'

- decide what to add or take away from existing lighting
- rig luminaires, set luminaires, add coloured filters as required
- determine lighting balance, add ND/scrims as required
- rehearse/record.

Lighting kits

The **technique** adopted for solving any lighting problem will be affected by the **technology** and **time** available. Mention has already been made about a basic lighting kit (p. 166).

However, cameramen will usually expand this basic kit to cope with the needs of more ambitious shoots. The alternative is to hire equipment as required, provided, of course, the budget includes sufficient electricians to cope with the equipment. The latter point is important, especially in areas where the general public have access. **It is essential that each luminaire on a stand is properly supervised to ensure that it cannot be knocked over**. Examples of expanded kits are given below.

Example: Lighting kit favoured by many experienced features cameramen – requiring to cope with many different situations, often with no electrician.

3×650 W ARRI open-faced luminaires
2×300 W ARRI junior Fresnel spotlights
2×650 W ARRI junior Fresnel spotlights
$1 \times$ Rifa light
1×2 kW Blonde
$1 \times$ Dedolight 4 lamphead kit (100 W) and projection lens
$1 \times$ Trace frame and diffusion
Stands, 2 magic arms and flags
Selection of colour temperature correction filters
Selection of assorted colour filters
0.3 ND and 0.6 D plus Rosco Scrim
Matt box with graduated ND and graduated colour filters
Polariser filter
Black nets
Collapsible reflectors with universal bracket
Mains tester
Spare lamps
RCDs and cables
Magic arm and super-clamps
(Hire additional filters as required)
(Hire additional lighting equipment as required, especially Dedolight 400 W MSR)

Another cameraman, using similar accessories operates with a smaller kit, but includes HMI/MSR luminaires, one battery operated, giving very good flexibility to his lighting facilities, i.e.

1×200 W HMI mains-operated light plus Chimera attachment
1×125 W HMI battery-operated light
$1 \times$ Dedolight 4 lamphead kit (100 W) plus projection lens
$1 \times$ Camera headlamp kit tungsten/HMI.

When considering HMI/MSR sources remember their improved efficiency. There is no need to colour correct (only between sources if needed) and up to a 1.2 kW HMI/MSR may be connected to a 13 A power socket (UK). The weight of the 1.2 kW spotlight is such that one electrician can rig it easily.

Timescales

Usually the timescale is not open-ended for a video shoot, consequently there is a need to find out from the director the time available for rigging/setting the lighting equipment. An estimate of time required for lighting can be made based on:

- Tungsten sources on stands requiring minimum time.
- HMI/MSR luminaires rigged from ladders will take the longest time.
  Note: when working with ladders, use electricians in pairs to enable one to 'foot' the ladder, unless it can be 'made fast' at the top of the ladder.
- If dimmer packs are to be used, extra time will be required to make the mains connection – useful to get this done in advance so that no time is wasted waiting for the local electricity board to connect your circuit breaker plus tails to the supply.
- Cable runs, long or short? Will there be a need for cable ramps?
- Number of electricians available.

The lighting gaffer will be able to give a good indication of what might be possible within the available timescale using the resources of the lighting budget. Depending on the nature of the shoot and budget available, the option for extra electricians will help to achieve a short timescale.

Alternatively there may be a need to simplify the lighting set-up to meet budget constraints! On shoots using multi-set-ups at one location, pre-lighting of sets can save time where the electricians can be rigging the lighting of the next set-up whilst one set-up is being used. This will, of course, require extra equipment and probably more electricians.

20
Lighting and sound pick-up

Team work is an essential part of television programme making, and often compromises need to be made in order that a colleague is able to cope with problems created by lighting. Sound pick-up is an activity which can create some mutual problems. Unfortunately we cannot operate in isolation and we must be aware of the problems which lighting may create for colleagues.

With one-man operation, the lighting and sound pick-up is covered by the same person, so there shouldn't be too much of a conflict. However when involved with larger crewing there is a need to be aware of the basic techniques of sound pick-up and how they may affect lighting.

The sound pick-up technique will be influenced by:

- The situation, e.g. single person, two persons, multi-person group etc.
- The action, e.g. static, walking or mobile (car)
- The environment, e.g. interior/exterior, crowded street/open country
- The sound facilities, including staff, available.

The basic options available are:

- Hand-held microphone, with wind gag, held out of shot by subject
- Miniature personal microphone – may be visible or hidden. It is sometimes practical to rig these microphones in the hair of the subject!
- Hand-held microphone, with wind gag, held out of shot by Sound Assistant
- Fish-pole used either below lens height, or above lens height
- Microphone boom usually used above eyeline but may be used from below eyeline. Usually, the first two options use an omni-directional microphone and the other options use directional microphones.

Directional microphones enable the Sound Assistant to concentrate the sound pick-up on the subject and exclude unwanted sounds, e.g. traffic noise, footsteps etc. The basic lighting problem in sound pick-up is to avoid creating in-shot shadows of the microphone and fish-pole/microphone and boom. This is where the use of a fish-pole from below the eyeline is particularly useful. Shadows will generally fall out of shot onto the floor (unless lighting from below the eye-line!) (Usually, the fish-pole/boom is placed on the opposite of the camera to the keylight position.)

Figure 20.1 illustrates the basic technique in avoiding boom shadows by ensuring the angle between the keylight and the camera is proportioned to the camera lens angle.

Note: If the subject moves upstage, the microphone shadow will move towards the subject (Figure 20.2). Also, be aware of the change in shadow which happens as an object, such as a microphone boom, moves towards a wall. If lit with soft light the shadow will be soft-edged but as the microphone is moved towards a wall, the shadow becomes progressively harder!

If shooting a two-handed interview, with single-camera operation it is relatively easy to use a hand-held microphone below the eyeline and use an upstage keylight to avoid microphone shadows. When shooting this multi-camera it is desirable to use upstage keylights or keylights 180° apart, to avoid potential microphone shadows.

If there are microphone shadow problems, check:

● Is the microphone in the right place for the lighting angles?
● Is the camera in the right position and shooting on correct lens angle?
● Is the subject too close to the background?

If shadow still persists, ask can:

● Camera shot size/camera position be changed?
● Microphone position be changed?
● Alternative sound pick-up be used?

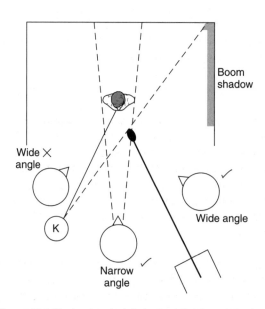

Figure 20.1 The basic principle for avoiding boom shadows

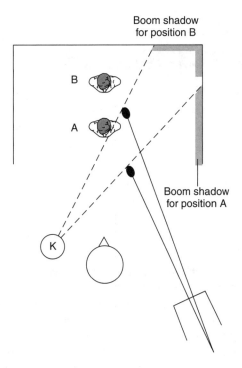

Figure 20.2 The shadow problem when subject and microphone move upstage

If nothing can be done, then check:

- Barndooring on keylight
- Increase horizontal keying angle?
- Increase vertical keying angle?
- Use a cutter or flag to get more localised lighting of subject
- If lighting subject and background with same light – localise lighting on subject and use a second light on the background.
- Can shadow be 'lit out'? A technique sometimes used to obscure 'muddy' shadows (as a last resort!).
- If shadow can be disguised by putting a suitable plant in the shadow area.

21
Lighting standards

'Compromise' is one of the most overworked words in television. However, despite having to make compromises there is still a need to maintain good lighting standards. The aim is to achieve the lighting required by the Director within budget and within the given timescale. Good lighting or 'when it looks right' will be when you see on camera the picture which you visualised at the planning stage.

One of the difficult decisions is knowing when to stop making lighting adjustments (lighting 'tweaks') – a point will be reached where further tweaks will be to the detriment of the lighting. Rather like water colour painting – many a painting has been spoilt through not stopping when it looks right!

There are a number of factors to consider when it doesn't look right, namely:

● incorrect lighting balance
● overexposure of part of the picture, worse case would be facetones!
● colour temperature problems – incorrect white balance on the camera
                                    – mixed lighting
● mutual shadowing of artistes
● 'in-shot' camera shadows
● 'in-shot' microphone/fish-pole shadows
● distracting shadows of subject on the background
● double keying of artiste – strive to maintain a single-shadow philosophy
● overlighting of the foreground – picture will look 'lit'
● incorrect exposure of facetone for the particular situation
● excessive keylight/camera angle both vertical and horizontal
● lack of tonal separation of subject's face and background
● background tone much brighter than facetone – facetones subjectively will look darker
● background lit in conflict to key lighting of foreground subject
● lack of texture
● too little contrast
● too much contrast
● lighting direction not as motivated
● on-camera 'flare' from light sources

- reflection of hard sources from shiny objects – direct or glare reflection
- lighting effect on background – overstated/understated? Beware of 'overstating' a lighting effect you particularly like!
- quality of light incorrect for the situation, i.e. hard/soft
- excessive highlight towards picture frame edges – eye will be drawn out of the picture
- excessive use of colour in creating a particular mood – too theatrical
- generation of 'illegal' colours when adding coloured light to a background
- lack of lighting continuity between shots
- inappropriate gobo used
- wrong focus for gobo
- gobo effect too weak or to dramatic
- 'flat' illumination – the ultimate 'brickbat'!

Avoiding camera flares

1 Use barndoor/flag on offending light.
2 Use an on-camera flag.

Spectacles

For subjects wearing spectacles:

- Avoid placing the subject facing a window, as this will result in annoying window reflections in the spectacles.
- A regular presenter should be encouraged to use spectacles with an anti-reflection coating.
- To minimise a reflection try tipping down the spectacles a few degrees. Remember, the reflection moves twice the tipped-down angle. It may be necessary to fix the end of the frames with a discreet piece of tape to keep the spectacles in place.
- Avoid a shadow of the spectacle frame on the eyes. With 'heavy' frames it is often useful to use a keylight from over the camera to ensure that light reaches the eyes clearly.

With an interview subject:

- A keylight offset from the camera may result in an annoying reflection of the light source. If this cannot be removed by any of the above means try moving the keylight towards the camera.

Avoiding highlights off glossy paintwork

Where there are curved surfaces there will always be a noticeable specular reflection when using hard sources. This can be minimised by using 'Dulling Spray' or soap. When the soap has dried it will leave a matt surface.

Glare reflectors can be controlled using a polarising filter provided the angles of incidence are greater than about 45°. When a complete background has a glossy finish the reflection of lights can be minimised by placing camera/lighting as in Figure 21.1.

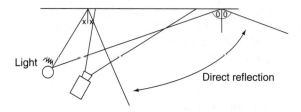

Figure 21.1 Overcoming reflections from a shiny wall

Bibliography

Lighting

Alton, J. (1995). *Painting with Light*, University of California Press.

Bermingham, A. (1989). *Colour Temperature: Colour Temperature Correction and Neutral Density Filters in TV Lighting*, Society of TV Lighting Directors.

Blair, D. (1993). *The Portrait: Professional Techniques and Practices in Portrait Photography* (Kodak Publication No. O-24), Sterling Publications.

Box, H. C. (edited by Fitt, B.) (1998). *The Gaffers' Handbook*, Focal Press.

Brown, B. (1995). *Motion Picture and Video Lighting*, Focal Press.

Carlson, V. and Carlson, S. E. (1991). *Professional Lighting Handbook*, second edition, Focal Press.

Doeffinger, D. (1998). *The Art of Seeing: A Creative Approach to Photography* (Kodak Workshop Series), fourth edition, Sterling Publications.

Fitt, B. (1999). *A–Z of Lighting Terms*, Focal Press.

Freeman, M. (1988). *Light* (Collin's Photography Workshop), Collins.

Gregory, R. L. (1997). *Eye and the Brain*, Princeton University Press.

Hunter, F. and Fuqua, P. (1997). *Light – Science and Magic: An Introduction to Photographic Lighting*, Focal Press.

Lowell, R. (1999). *Matters of Light and Depth: Creating Memorable Images for Video, Film, and Stills Through Lighting*, Lowel-Light Manufacturing, Inc.

Malkiewicz, K. (1992). *Film Lighting*, Simon & Schuster.

Mathias, H. and Patterson, R. (1985). *Electronic Cinematography: Achieving Photographic Control over the Video Image*, Wadsworth Pub Co.

Millerson, G. (1999). *Lighting for TV and Film*, third edition, Focal Press.

Schaefer, D. and Salvato, L. (1986). *Masters of Light: Conversations With Contemporary Cinematographers*, University of California Press.

Schwarz, T., Stoppee, B. and O'Connor, T. (1986). *The Photographer's Guide to Using Light*, Watson-Guptill Publications.

Taub, E. (1995). *Gaffers, Grips and Best Boys*, St. Martins Press.

Uren, M. (2001). *BKSTS Illustrated Dictionary of Moving Image Technology*, fourth edition, Focal Press.

Viera, D. (1992). *Lighting for Film and Electronic Cinematography*, Wadsworth Publishing Co.

Ward, P., Bermingham, A. and Wherry, C. (2000). *Multiskilling for Television Production*, Focal Press.

Engineering

Bermingham, A., Boyce, E., Angold-Stephens, K. and Talbot-Smith, M. (1994). *The Video Studio*, Focal Press.

Hodges, P. (1994). *The Video Camera Operator's Handbook*, Focal Press.

Hodges, P. (2001). *An Introduction to Video Measurement*, second edition, Focal Press.

Park, R. (ed.) (2002). *The Digital Fact Book*, eleventh edition, Quantel.

Steinberg, V. (1997). *Video Standards*, Snell & Wilcox.

Tancock, M. (out of print). *Broadcast Television Fundamentals*, Pentech Press.

Watkinson, J. (1995). *Your Essential Guide to Digital*, Snell & Wilcox.

Watkinson, J. (1996). *The Engineer's Guide to Compression*, Snell & Wilcox.

Watkinson, J. (1996). *Television Fundamentals*, Focal Press.

Watkinson, J. (2002). *An Introduction of Digital Video*, second edition, Focal Press.

Safety

HSC (1998). *Safe Use of Lifting Equipment. Lifting Operations and Lifting Equipment Regulations 1998*, L 113, HSE Books.

HSE (1994). *Maintaining Portable and Transportable Electrical Equipment*, HSG 107, HSE Books.

HSE, Broadcasting and Performing Arts Joint Advisory Committee (1997). *Camera Operations on Location: Guidance for managers and camera crews for work in news gathering, current affairs and factual programming*. HSG 169, HSE Books.

Glossary

ASA (1) American Standards Association (now the ANSI). (2) Method of rating the speed of film. Replaced by International Standard Organisation (ISO) or Exposure Index (EI).

Best boy The assistant chief electrician, the gaffer's chief assistant.
Black wrap Black anodised aluminium foil. Used to control spill light or shaping a light beam.
Brightness Term often incorrectly used to mean luminaire. Brightness is a subjective effect, it is how bright we see an object.
Butterfly Large frame to hold nets, silks or blacks (6 ft × 6 ft, 12 ft × 12 ft, 20 ft × 20 ft).

Chroma Another name for saturation, control usually found on monitors.
Chroma key An electronic process for inserting an artiste (foreground) into a background picture; also known as colour separation overlay (CSO) in the BBC.
Colour bars Special test signal used in colour television.
Colour Temperature A convenient way to describe the colour of a light source by relating it to a black-body radiator (e.g. heated poker). Measured in Kelvins (K) after Lord Kelvin (physicist).
Cookie or Cucoloris A perforated plate used in front of a luminaire to break up the light beam, producing a dapple effect.
Cosine law The illuminance on a surface is proportional to the *cosine* of the angle of incidence, i.e. maximum when angle of incidence is zero.
CSO Colour separation overlay – (see *Chroma key*).
Cue A particular lighting condition or indication for action to start (e.g. actor to start performing or lighting change to start).
Cutter As *Flag* but long and narrow, usually used to darken off the top of a set.
Cyclorama General-purpose background curtains, usually off-white and stretched.

Density A measure of the light transmitted by a film or filter:

$$\text{Density} = \log_{10} \frac{1}{\text{Transmission}} = \log_{10} \text{Opacity}$$

Depth of field Range of object distances within acceptable focus.
Depth of focus Range of image plane movement possible while keeping the image within acceptable focus.

Dichroic filter   A filter typically made of multi-layers of titanium dioxide, magnesium fluoride or zinc sulphide to produce characteristics which reflect or transmit a band of wavelengths. Used in light-splitting blocks, colour temperature correction filters and luminaire reflectors.

Diffuser   Material which scatters the light to create a softer light source.

Dimmer   An electronic device for controlling the light output from a light source. Usually a thyristor or silicon-controlled rectifier (SCR) but recent developments have seen the transistor dimmer and sine wave dimmer.

Dingle   Branches placed in front of a luminaire to create a dapple effect (also the name given to branches placed in the top of frame to give foreground interest).

DMX 512   Digital multiplex system for sending dimmer/moving light information down one pair of wires for 512 channels in a digital system.

Facetone   Signal level derived from facetones, typically about 0.5 V.

Fill-light   Light source used to make shadows transparent, i.e. reduce the contrast.

Flag   A rectangular black board or black serge on a wire frame, used to mask unwanted light.

Foot-candle   Unit of illuminance in imperial units: 1 lumen/ft^2 = 1 foot-candle.

Fresnel   Stepped lens used in the Fresnel spotlight.

Gaffer   Chief lighting electrician.

Gamma   The 'index' which describes the law of the transfer characteristic of a system, i.e. relationship between input and output signals.

Gobo   Stainless steel stencil used in profile projectors to create effects, e.g. windows, abstract, moon etc.

Golden Hour   The period immediately after sunrise and the period immediately before sunset. Not an hour long!

Grip   Supporting equipment for lighting on camera equipment. Also the name of the technicians responsible for handling grip equipment.

Hertz   Unit of frequency, 1 Hertz = 1 cycle/second.

High key   Picture with predominance of light tones and thin shadows.

Hot head   Remotely controlled camera head – usually on the end of a jib arm.

Hue   The dominant wavelength, colour describing what we see, e.g. red.

Illuminance   Unit of incident light measured in lux (lumens/m^2) or foot-candles (lumens/ft^2). Formally known as illumination.

Inverse square law   Fundamental law in lighting and sound where the intensity of light and sound falls off as the inverse of the distance squared.

Iris   Variable circular aperture in the camera used to control exposure. Calibrated in f-stops. Also found in profile projectors and following spotlights.

Kicker   Light used at eye-level from upstage to 'kick' the side of an artiste's head.

Limbo   Term usually used to describe action against a peak white floor/background with no horizon line. In some countries it means the reverse, i.e. artiste against black.

Low key   Picture with a predominance of dark tones and strong shadows.

Lumen   Unit of quantity of light flow per second, '**weighted**' by the photopic curve.

Luminaire   Name given for a complete lighting unit, i.e. light source or lamp plus its casing.

Luminance   (L) a measure of the light **reflected** from a surface. A total flux reflected of 1 lumen/m^2 has a luminance of 1 **Apostilb**. (Imperial measurement 1 lumen/ft^2 = 1 foot-lambert.)

Magic Hour   The period of dawn immediately before sunrise and also the period of dusk immediately after sunset (it is not an hour!).

Opacity   The reciprocal of transmission of light through a film or filter.
Oscilloscope   Cathode ray oscilloscope used to provide a visual display of electrical signals.

Pan glass   A 1% transmission neutral density filter (ND 2.0) used to evaluate scene contrast. Also useful when setting luminaires accurately or observing sun/cloud movement.
PAT   Portable appliance test, the annual safety test for portable mains-operated equipment.
Peak white   Either 100% video signal level or a 60% reflectance neutral grey surface.
Picture monitor   Good-quality viewing monitor, similar to a receiver but without radio frequency (RF) and sound sections.
PLUGE   (Picture line-up generating equipment). Test signal used for alignment of monitor contrast and brightness.
Polecat   Adjustable spring-loaded aluminium tube with rubber feet. Can be used vertically or horizontally to support lightweight luminaires.
Pole-operation   System for remotely adjusting pan/tilt, spot/flood etc. from the floor, using an operating pole.
Practical   An in-shot light source (e.g. wall light, table lamp).
Progressive scan   A system of scanning the television lines in sequence, not interlaced. Referred to as 24P, equivalent to film frame rate; 25P, for countries using 25 pictures/second; and 30P for countries using 30 pictures/second. Interlaced scanning systems are indicated as 50i and 60i.

Quantise   In a digital system, allocation of 'sample' level prior to coding to a digital number.

Robotic camera   Camera with a remotely controlled camera head, i.e. pan/tilt, zoom and focus. May also include camera position and height.

Saturation   A measure of the purity of a colour (e.g. pale red or deep red).
Signal to noise ratio   The ratio of maximum video signal to video noise expressed as a logarithmic ratio in decibels (dB).
Solar location diagram   Chart used to calculate the altitude and azimuth of the sun from sunrise to sunset at a given latitude (e.g. London) for a series of dates throughout the year.

Termination $75\,\Omega$ resistor included across the video cable at the end of a transmission chain. Inclusion of $75\,\Omega$ termination ensures no reflection of energy, and ensures that the signal level is correct. With DMX systems this is $120\,\Omega$.
Translucent   Semi-transparent; usually some form of light diffuser.
Turtle   Very low lighting stand for rigging luminaires at floor level.
Tweak   Term used for small adjustments to lighting rig or operational settings (e.g. black level or iris setting).

Vectorscope   Special oscilloscope designed to display the chrominance information in an easily recognisable way, i.e. hue and saturation.
Virtual reality   System of chroma key where the background is computer generated. The size and positioning of the background is controlled by the foreground camera movements.

Waveform monitor   Oscilloscope with appropriate time-base for displaying the television waveform. Usually includes a face-plate graticule to indicate sync level, black level and peak white.

Basic conversion table

1 metre	=	3.28 feet
1 square metre	=	10.76 square feet
1 inch	=	2.54 cm
1 foot	=	30.48 cm = 0.3048 metres
10 feet	=	3.05 metres
1 square foot	=	0.0929 square metres

Index

 **Focal Press**

www.focalpress.com

Join Focal Press on-line
As a member you will enjoy the following benefits:

- an email bulletin with **information on new books**

- a regular **Focal Press Newsletter**:

    - featuring a selection of new titles

    - keeps you informed of **special offers, discounts and freebies**

    - alerts you to **Focal Press news and events** such as author signings and
      seminars

- complete access to **free content** and reference material on the focalpress site, such as
  the focalXtra articles and commentary from our authors

- a **Sneak Preview** of selected titles (sample chapters) *before* they publish

- a chance to have your say on our **discussion boards** and **review books** for other Focal
  readers

Focal Club Members are invited to give us feedback on our products and services.
Email: worldmarketing@focalpress.com – we want to hear your views!

Membership is **FREE**. To join, visit our website and register. If you require any further information
regarding the on-line club please contact:

> Lucy Lomas-Walker
> Email: l.lomas@elsevier.com
> Tel: +44 (0) 1865 314438
> Fax: +44 (0)1865 314572
> Address: Focal Press, Linacre House,
> Jordan Hill, Oxford, UK, OX2 8DP

Catalogue

For information on all Focal Press titles, our full catalogue is available online at www.focalpress.com
and all titles can be purchased here via secure online ordering, or contact us for a free printed
version:

USA
Email: christine.degon@bhusa.com
Tel: +1 781 904 2607 T

Europe and rest of world
Email: j.blackford@elsevier.com
Tel: +44 (0)1865 314220

Potential authors

If you have an idea for a book, please get in touch:

USA
editors@focalpress.com

Europe and rest of world
focal.press@elsevier.com

Guildford College
Learning Resource Centre

Please return on or before the last date shown.
No further issues or renewals if any items are overdue.
"7 Day" loans are **NOT** renewable.

2 9 NOV 2005